STUDY GUIDE SERIES

THE NEW TESTAMENT
LUKE-ACTS

Freshly translated by Nicholas King

For Richard and Sue,
with love

First published in 2006 by
KEVIN MAYHEW LTD
Buxhall, Stowmarket, Suffolk, IP14 3BW
E-mail: info@kevinmayhewltd.com
www.kevinmayhew.com

The text for *Luke-Acts* first appeared in Nicholas King's translation of *The New Testament*.

9 8 7 6 5 4 3 2 1 0

ISBN 1 84417 529 4
Catalogue No. 1500887

Cover Design: Jonathan Stroulger
Editors: Peter Dainty, Marian Reid
Typesetting: Richard Weaver

Set in Simoncini Garamond and *Abadi MT Lt It*

Nihil Obstat: This translation has been examined by the Theology Committee of the Bishops' Conference of England and Wales and is declared free from doctrinal error. It is not authorised for use in the Liturgy of the Church and is approved for publication, in accord with Canon 825§1.

Mgr Andrew Summersgill, General Secretary, 8 June 2004

Printed and bound in Great Britain

Introduction

The publisher's welcome decision to reissue this translation of the New Testament in separate volumes has enabled me to do something I have always wanted to do, which is really to persuade people to read as a single unit the two parts of Luke's great work which our Bibles (for perfectly understandable reasons) have separated. It has also allowed me to read the two of them again, just as Luke wrote them, and for that privilege I am grateful.

As you read through these two sets of stories, you will find that they are really a single story, covering the life of Jesus and the life of the early Church; that story is the story of the Holy Spirit. And I should like you to look out for some features of the way Luke tells his story. They have struck me with renewed force in preparing this volume for the press.

Luke is, of all the Gospel-writers, the most artistic; he tells the best stories (it is a fair bet that your favourite New Testament tale will turn out to have come from his pen – check it and see), and it is surely no accident that so many artists have attempted to paint so many scenes from his Gospel and from Acts. A part of this gift of his is what I have called 'Lucan summaries', and I should like you to look out for them. They reveal his extraordinary ability to create atmosphere with a few deft brush-strokes.

If he is the most artistic, Luke is also the most charming of the evangelists, and you feel that there is no one whom he regards as an enemy. Don't be too misled by this, however, for there is also an underlying toughness about Luke, and his attitude to the affluent verges on the hostile. At various points in the commentary I suggest that this may be because the community that he was writing for may have been a wealthy one, and the evangelist needed to remind them of the dangers of having too much.

There are one or two points in particular that I should like you to look out for (and don't take my word for it – check them against the text and see if you agree).

- Luke has a habit of giving us a glimpse of what lies ahead. For example, the first two chapters of his Gospel can, I think, be regarded as 'Rules for the Reading of the Gospel', Luke offering a kind of overture to the work as a whole. He does something of this sort in that extraordinary scene in the synagogue at Nazareth (Luke 4:16-30), where he presents us with what you might call Jesus' 'mission-statement'.

- The whole of Luke-Acts is a journey, from Jerusalem to Rome. As a matter of fact, as you are about to see, it is a great deal more complex than that; the first two chapters alone have something like nine moves between Galilee and Judaea; then the Gospel proper is a one-way journey from Galilee, through Samaria into Jerusalem, where Jesus meets his death. In Acts the journey moves outwards, in obedience to Jesus' command to be his 'witnesses, in Jerusalem, and in all Judaea and Samaria, and right to the ends of the earth'. And because the Spirit is now driving it, the word of God is sent further than we should ever have expected; it keeps coming back to Jerusalem, however, until that last, solemn moment at Acts 21:30 when the Temple doors are finally closed. Luke has many ways of signalling this 'journey';

but as you read, watch out for what I have called Luke's favourite 'journeying word', and for the 'ripple effect', whereby Jesus' reputation spreads way beyond the territory covered by his own journeying.

- Luke is often called 'the Gospel of the poor', and this is perfectly correct. This may be connected with what I suggested above, with the relatively affluent status of his congregation. But his interests are wider than simply the poor, and embrace all kinds of minorities: women, lepers, Samaritans and widows, for example, all attract his gentle gaze. As you read, you might ask where the Spirit is directing our attention today.
- You must look out for this on your own, but Luke is unmistakably the evangelist of prayer.
- This is the Gospel of repentance and forgiveness (and if you want somewhere to start on that, try the fifteenth chapter of the Gospel).
- Finally, there are two other patterns that you can explore as you read, involving both parts of this work. One is the theme that Luke detects, whereby the Gospel goes first to the synagogue, where it is rejected (look at chapters 4 and 6 of the Gospel, and almost anywhere in Acts), and then in consequence going out to the Gentiles. The second is the link that Luke keeps sketching between Luke and Acts. See how many episodes you can see in Part 2 that parallel events previously related in Part 1.

Both of these patterns have to do with how the Spirit operates. I hope that you will become increasingly aware of that Spirit as you read.

According to Luke

According to Luke

The Prologue

1 1-4 Seeing that a good many people have set their hand to compile a narrative of the things that have been fulfilled amongst us, just as those who from the beginning were eyewitnesses and ministers of the word have handed down to us, I also have decided, having investigated everything from the outset, to write it down for you, most excellent Theophilus, carefully and in order. My intention is that you should have a complete knowledge of the truth of the things which you have been taught.

Luke's is the only Gospel to start with a statement of what he is about (unless you count the rather brief heading which Mark offers); and it may be helpful for our reading of the Gospel if we start by looking at what he says. First, it is addressed to 'most excellent Theophilus', who might be a real person, of high social standing, perhaps one of the Equites, who formed the second rank of Roman society. Or, given that the name Theophilus means 'Lover of God' or 'Beloved by God', it might be addressed to any interested Christian.

Second, Luke's language shows that he is aiming at some kind of historical accuracy: he even suggests that his predecessors (Mark?) have not succeeded in this aim. And we notice his insistence on careful investigation, and his stated intention of writing 'carefully and in order', and his stress on the importance of 'eyewitnesses'.

Third, however, Luke is not just trying to write history. The alert reader will have noticed one or two words that belong rather in the area of religious education: 'hand down', 'fulfilled', 'ministers', 'truth' (or 'infallibility') of the things which you have been taught (or 'catechised'). So there is a religious aim here also.

Finally, notice that Jesus is not mentioned here, nor anywhere in Chapter 1 until we reach the encounter between the angel Gabriel and Mary; so presumably this work is intended for circulation only among Christians, who already know what it is about.

What is Luke's Gospel about?

THE ANNUNCIATION OF JOHN THE BAPTIST (5-25)

Setting the scene

5-7 There was in the days of Herod, King of Judaea, a certain priest, Zachariah by name, of the division of Abijah; and his wife was of the daughters of Aaron, and her name was Elisabeth. They were both upright before God, walking blameless in all the commandments and precepts of the Lord. And they had no child, because Elisabeth was barren, and they were both advanced in their days.

Luke is the most artistic of all the Gospels, and probably more of Luke's stories have been painted than those in any other Gospel. We see his artistry here, deft touches that set the scene; and we need to stand back and admire the entire composition. He starts with the story of John the Baptist, who is in turn going to point to the more important reality of Jesus. Neither figure has been mentioned so far, and yet the reader is following without difficulty. Such is Luke's skill.

Now look at the details. First of all, the air we are breathing here is that of the Old Testament. Even Luke's language makes that point (though it is hard to put it into English without sounding contrived). We notice this charming couple, both of priestly ancestry (she is 'of the daughters of Aaron'); so John the Baptist's parentage is similar to that of the prophet Jeremiah. They are observant Jews, 'walking blameless in all the commandments and precepts of the Lord'. And they have no child – so readers familiar with the Hebrew Bible know that, according to the rules of the game, a child is on its way. Even the names signal that something important is going ahead. Zachariah means 'the Lord has remembered', Abijah, 'My Father is the Lord', and Elisabeth, 'My God has sworn an oath'.

Finally, look at the first name we meet: 'in the days of Herod, King of Judaea'. Here we see another instance of Luke's artistry. For there is a clear echo here of the Books of Kings, where events are frequently dated by the reigns of one or other of the Kings of Judah or Israel (see, for example, 1 Kings 15:1, 9); and so the reader is immediately transported into the world of the Old Testament. The name of Herod, however, strikes a jarring note; any member of that family is liable to mean trouble, and this particular one was 'Herod the Great', the most remarkable fact about whom is that he succeeded in dying in his bed (albeit very unpleasantly, according to the Jewish historian Josephus). The readers of Luke's Gospel will have been well aware that it was his son who would appear in Luke's account of Jesus' last days (Luke 23:7ff.).

Who is the most important character here?

First appearance of the angel Gabriel

8-25 It came to pass, as [Zachariah] was doing his priestly duty, in the appointed order of his division, before God; according to the custom of the priesthood it fell to his lot to enter the Temple of the Lord and burn incense. And the whole crowd of the populace was praying outside at the hour of the incense offering. And the angel of the Lord appeared to him, standing on the right of the altar of incense. And Zachariah was disturbed when he saw it; and fear fell upon him. And the angel said to him,

'Do not be afraid, Zachariah, because your supplication has been heard, and your wife Elisabeth will bear a son for you, and you will call his name John. And there shall be joy and exultation and many will rejoice at his birth, for he shall be great before the Lord. "And he shall not drink wine and strong drink" and he shall be filled with the Holy Spirit right from his mother's womb. And he shall turn many of the children of Israel to the Lord their God. And he shall go before him in the spirit and power of

Elijah, to turn the hearts of fathers to their children and the disobedient [so as to walk] in the understanding of justice, to prepare for the Lord a people that has been made ready.'

And Zachariah said to the angel, 'How shall I know this? For I am old, and my wife is advanced in her years.'

And the angel replied and said to him, 'I am Gabriel, who stands before God. And I was sent to speak to you, and to give you these good tidings. And look! you will be silent and unable to speak until the day when these things came to pass, because you did not believe these words of mine, which ***will*** be fulfilled at their right time.'

And the populace [was] waiting for Zachariah, and they were astonished that he took so long in the Temple. When he came out, he could not speak to them, and they realised that he had seen a vision in the Temple. And he kept nodding to them, and he remained dumb. And it came to pass that when the days of his service were fulfilled, he went back to his home.

After these days, Elisabeth his wife conceived, and she hid herself for six months, saying, 'Thus the Lord has done for me in the days when he looked with favour on me, to take away my shame in the eyes of human beings.'

Luke the artist is very much in evidence here. The biblical tone of his Greek continues, and I have tried to hint at it in the translation. The scene is painted with great skill: the Temple setting is depicted in a couple of effortless strokes of the brush. And then there is 'the populace'. Luke has them there from the beginning, 'praying outside'. This has two effects: first, they act as the background of the dialogue between Zachariah and the angel. Second, Luke is going to employ them later in the scene, to emphasise the startling nature of what has occurred.

Another name appears (still no Jesus!), that of John ('God has acted graciously'). We learn of him first, looking back, that 'he shall not drink wine and strong drink', which is a direct quotation of Leviticus 10:9 and Numbers 6:3; and we recall 1 Samuel 1:11, where Hannah, another childless wife, is praying for a boy. Her prayer will be granted, and she will produce the prophet Samuel (be careful what you pray for!). Second, looking forward, 'he shall be filled with the Holy Spirit'. The two-volume work Luke-Acts is the story of what happens when people allow themselves to be 'filled with the Holy Spirit'. Others to whom it will happen are: Elisabeth, Mary, Jesus, Peter, Stephen, and, of course, Paul.

Zachariah's question may strike us as a perfectly reasonable one, and not all that different from what Mary says a few verses later ('How will this be?'); but Zachariah is punished for his question, and Mary is not. Why this unequal distribution of sanctions? First, Mary's question accepts what is going to happen, and simply indicates a perfectly sensible difficulty. Second, it is artistically necessary for Luke to make Zachariah a bit (but not too much) inferior to Mary – because her child, who has still not been mentioned, is going to be much more important than his.

Lastly, the perceptive populace realises that Zachariah has seen a vision. Later on we shall meet 24:23 where the same word is used to refer, disparagingly, to the evidence of the women who found Jesus' tomb empty. And they, of course, were right to believe what the angels had told them . . .

What does it mean to be 'filled with the Holy Spirit'?

Second appearance of Gabriel

26-38 In the sixth month the angel Gabriel was sent to a city of Galilee whose name is Nazareth, to a virgin engaged to a man whose name was Joseph, of the house of David; and the name of the virgin was Mary.

And going in to her he said, 'Rejoice, you who have received favour: the Lord is with you.'

She was deeply disturbed at the remark, and wondered what kind of thing this greeting might be.

And the angel said to her, 'Do not be afraid, Mary. For you have found favour with God. And look! you will conceive in the womb, and bear a son. And you shall call his name Jesus. This one will be great, and will be called Son of the Most High. And the Lord will give him the throne of his ancestor David. And he shall rule over the house of David for ever and of his reign there shall be no end.'

And Mary said to the angel, 'How will this be, since I do not know a man?'

And the angel answered and said to her, '[The] Holy Spirit will come upon you, and the power of the Most High will overshadow you. Therefore that which is conceived is holy and will be called Son of God. And look, Elisabeth, your kinswoman, she too has conceived a son in her old age, and this is the sixth month for her who was called "Barren"; because there is no such thing as an impossibility to God.'

Mary said, 'Look, the Lord's slave-woman. Let it happen to me in accordance with your word.' And the angel went from her.

This lovely picture, which a thousand artists have tried to paint, needs to be seen together with its companion-piece, the announcement to Zachariah. Like him, Mary is told 'do not be afraid'; like him, she notes the difficulty of it. The difference is that this is not depicted as an answer to Mary's prayer (how could it be?), and that Mary is more straightforwardly ready to go along with the divine invitation. We may also notice (as something that we shall see in Luke's Gospel) that Mary, the girl of no status from an utterly insignificant village, turns out to be the person in whom Luke is most interested in the opening two chapters.

Or rather, not quite; for one character is not mentioned, and yet underlies every line of the text, namely God. Consider what Luke is saying when he says at the beginning of this section, 'the angel Gabriel was sent': by whom? By, clearly, God, who is in sole charge of all the events that Luke narrates. That is something for us to remember in our reading of the whole of the rest of the Gospel.

What differences do you notice between the announcement to Zachariah and the announcement to Mary?

Two mothers are brought together

39-56 Mary arose in those days and journeyed in a hurry to the hill-country, to a city of Judah, and she entered the house of Zachariah and greeted Elisabeth. And it happened when Elisabeth heard Mary's greeting, the unborn child leapt in her womb, and Elisabeth was filled with the Holy Spirit, and she cried out in a loud voice and said, 'Blessed are you among women, and blessed is the fruit of your womb. And how does this happen to me, that the Mother of my Lord should come to me? For look! as the sound of your greeting came to my ears, the unborn child leapt with exultation in my womb. And happy is she who believed that there would be a fulfilment of the things spoken to her from the Lord.'

And Mary said,

'My soul extols the Lord
and my spirit has exulted in God my Saviour
because he has looked [favourably] on the humble state of his slave girl.
For look! From now on, all generations will congratulate me
because the Powerful One has done great things for me,
and holy is his name.
And his mercy is for generation after generation on those who fear him.
He has done a mighty deed with his arm.
He has scattered those who are haughty in the thoughts of their heart.
He has deposed rulers from their thrones
and raised up the humble.
The hungry he has filled with good things
and the wealthy he has sent away empty.
He has helped his servant Israel, remembering his mercy.
As he spoke to our ancestors,
to Abraham and his descendants for ever.'

Mary remained with her about three months, and she returned to her home.

In this episode, with consummate artistry, Luke brings two stories, those of John the Baptist and Jesus, effortlessly together. Notice two themes that are becoming familiar: those of 'journeying', and being 'filled with the Holy Spirit'. Luke also delicately indicates that although John the Baptist comes first, he is actually inferior to Mary's child.

Another theme that is of importance to Luke's Gospel underlies the Magnificat. Possibly because his church was from the more well-to-do section of society (you must decide as you read the Gospel whether or not you agree with this possibility), Luke emphasises more than the other Gospels God's preference for those at the bottom of society's priorities: Mary is a 'slave girl' and 'humble', and God exalts the 'hungry'. The 'great things' that God is praised for having done to Mary are etymologically connected with the word that we have translated 'extols'; sometimes it is rendered 'magnifies'.

Do you think that God prefers the poor?

First birth and its attendant circumstances

57-80 Meanwhile, for Elisabeth her time was fulfilled to bring forth her child – and she bore a son. And her neighbours and relatives heard that the Lord had multiplied his mercy in regard to her; and they rejoiced with her. And it happened on the eighth day that they came to circumcise the child; and they were trying to call him by the name of his father Zachariah. And his mother responded and said, 'No – on the contrary; he shall be called John.'

And they said to her, 'There's no one from [among] your kinsfolk who's called by this name.' And they started nodding to his father, [to know] what he wanted him to be called. And he asked for a little writing-tablet and wrote, 'John is his name.' And they were all amazed. And his mouth was opened immediately, and he spoke, blessing God. And there came fear upon all their neighbours; and in the whole hill-country of Judaea all these events were discussed; and all those who heard [them] placed [them] in their hearts, saying 'so what is this child going to be?' For indeed the hand of the Lord was with him.

And Zachariah his father was filled with the Holy Spirit, and prophesied, saying,

'Blessed is the Lord, the God of Israel,
for he has looked at his people, and brought about their release
and raised up a horn of salvation for us
in the house of David his servant,
as he spoke through the mouth of the holy ones of old, his prophets,
salvation from our enemies, and from the hands of all those who hate us,
to work mercy with our ancestors
and to remember his holy covenant,
an oath which he swore to Abraham our ancestor
to grant to us, once we had been fearlessly delivered from enemy hands,
to worship him in holiness and righteousness
before him all our days.
And you, little child, you shall be called a prophet of the Most High;
for you shall go before the Lord, to prepare his ways,
to give knowledge of salvation to his people, through forgiveness of their sins
through the compassionate heart of our God,
by which he will visit us, the risen sun from on high,
to appear to those who sit in darkness and in the shadow of death,
to straighten our feet into the way of peace.'

And the little child grew and was strengthened in the spirit; and he was in the desert until the day of his revelation to Israel.

John the Baptist's birth is splendidly told: Elisabeth's independence of spirit, as she insists that the boy is not to be called Zachariah, and the comic touch of the relatives frantically 'nodding' to Zachariah, pardonably forgetting that his problem is not deafness, but an inability to speak. He recovers the power of speech when he supports his wife's assertion that the boy is to be called 'God has acted graciously'.

Zachariah is, like his wife and Mary before him, 'filled with the Holy Spirit', and utters another song like Mary's, which the Church still sings to itself in the morning, just as it sings Mary's song in the evening.

Notice, finally, how artistically Luke places John the Baptist in the desert, from where he will be reintroduced at the beginning of Chapter 3.

What does God do in this episode?

Second birth and its attendant circumstances

2 1-7 It came to pass in those days that a decree went out from Caesar Augustus that the whole world [or: empire] should be registered. This, the first registration, took place when Quirinius was governor of Syria. And everyone journeyed to be registered, each to their own city. Joseph also went up from Galilee, from the city of Nazareth, to Judaea, to the city of David which is called Bethlehem, because he was of the house and family of David, to be registered along with Mary, his betrothed – who was pregnant. It came to pass while they were there that the days were fulfilled for her to give birth and she brought forth her son, the first-born; and she wrapped him round with swathing-bands, and laid him down in a feeding-trough, because there was no room for them in the lodging house.

This all-too-familiar passage is in certain respects a shocking one. It is far from the birth that we should expect of one who 'will be called great, and Son of the Most High', who will 'sit on the throne of his ancestor David', and 'will reign over the house of Jacob for ever, and of his reign there shall be no end'. The references to Caesar Augustus, the most powerful man in the world, and to Quirinius, his local representative, flatter only to deceive. These two potentates know nothing of Jesus, and their actions have the unforeseen consequence (unforeseen by them at any rate) that Jesus is born in Bethlehem. Not only that, but he is born in less than ideal circumstances: there is no room in the town's single lodging house, so the child is born like one of the poor and put in a 'feeding-trough'.

As a matter of fact, Luke has got his dates a bit muddled, since Quirinius was governor of Syria about ten years after Jesus was born, and we know nothing of the 'registration' of which Luke speaks. That, however, is not important. What matters to Luke is the contrast between the 'great ones' of the earth and the child that has been born.

Lastly, notice the shock of the reference to Mary's pregnancy. It is true that we already know the circumstances; nevertheless, the way Luke expresses it brings us up short, and I have tried to reflect this in the translation.

Luke's Greek retains its biblical flavour here, and I have made some attempts to represent the sound in English.

Do you think that Luke's Gospel might be rather shocking?

Third appearance of the angel

8-20 And there were shepherds in the same region, who were living in the fields, and keeping careful watch by night over their flock. And the Angel of the Lord stood near them; and the glory of the Lord shone about them; and they feared with a great fear.

And the angel said to them, 'Do not be afraid. For look – I bring you good news, great joy which will be for all the people, that there has been born for you today a Saviour, who is Christ the Lord in the city of David; and this is the sign for you: you will find the baby wrapped in swathing-bands and lying in a feeding-trough.'

And suddenly there was with the angel a crowd of the heavenly army praising God and saying,

'Glory in the highest to God
and on earth peace among human beings who are pleasing to God.'

And it came to pass, when the angels went from them into heaven, the shepherds started saying to each other, 'Let us go to Bethlehem, and see this thing that has happened, which the Lord has made known to us.'

And they went in a hurry, and they searched for Mary and Joseph, and the baby, which lay in the feeding-trough. When they saw [them], they revealed about the word that had been spoken to them about this little child. And all those who heard were astonished about the things spoken to them by the shepherds.

But Mary kept all these words, pondering them in her heart.

And the shepherds went back, glorifying and praising God for all that they had heard and seen, as it had been spoken to them.

This third angelic appearance confirms all that has gone before, including the superiority of Jesus over John the Baptist. There is also at least one shock, however; for the recipients of the vision are not, like Zachariah, Temple priests going about their business, nor, like Mary, quietly ready to do God's bidding; they are, frankly, cowboys, people living on the margins of society, and making up their rules as they go along, perhaps the very people that Luke's well-to-do Christians would have had least in common with. They live out of doors, and are not even respectable enough to sleep at nights.

Nevertheless, it is to these 'cowboys' that the Lord's revelation comes; and, remarkably, they do not hesitate to believe, especially after the 'heavenly army' has sung a chorus for them. This is of a piece with the (repeated) shock that the 'Saviour, Christ the Lord' is currently lying in a feeding-trough. Another repetition or echo is that, like Mary earlier, the shepherds respond 'in a hurry'.

Lastly, notice how Luke enables us to reflect on the episode by offering three separate reactions to it: 'those who heard' are astonished by it; Mary is quietly reflective about it; the shepherds go home glorifying God for it. There is a kind of completeness about this.

For discussion: The reader may want to ask what Luke means by 'Lord'; clearly at many points in this episode it is God himself. What does it mean when applied to Christ?

Jesus' circumcision and presentation

21-40 And when the eight days were fulfilled for him to be circumcised, his name was called Jesus, which [he] had been called by the angel before he had been conceived in the womb.

And when the days of their purification were fulfilled according to the Law of Moses, they took him up to Jerusalem, to offer him to the Lord, as it is written in the Law of the Lord that 'every male that opens his mother's womb shall be called holy to the Lord', and to give sacrifice according to what is written in the Law of the Lord, 'a pair of turtle-doves, or two young doves'.

And look! There was a man in Jerusalem, whose name was Simeon, and this man was righteous and pious, and waiting for Israel's comfort; and the Holy Spirit was on him. And it had been revealed to him by the Holy Spirit [that he would not] see death before he saw the Christ of the Lord. And he came in the Spirit into the Temple; and as the parents brought in the child Jesus, for them to act in accordance with the Law about him, he himself took him into his arms and blessed God and said,

'Now you are letting your slave go, Master,
according to your word in peace;
because my eyes have seen your salvation
which you have prepared before the face of all the peoples,
a light for the revelation of the gentiles
and the glory of your people Israel.'

And the child's father and mother were in a state of astonishment at the things being said about him; and Simeon blessed them, and said to Mary his mother: 'Look! This one is destined for the fall and rising of many in Israel, and as a sign of contradiction (and your own soul will be pierced by a sword) so that the thoughts of many hearts may be revealed.'

And there was Hanna, a prophetess, a daughter of Phanuel, of the tribe of Asher; she was advanced, with many days, having lived with her husband for seven years from her virginity, she was now a widow of as many as eighty-four years; she did not leave the Temple, worshipping with fasting and prayer, day and night. And at that hour, she stood and praised God and spoke of him to all those who were waiting for the redemption of Israel.

And when they had completed everything in accordance with the Law of the Lord, they returned to Galilee, to their own city of Nazareth.

And the child grew and gained strength, filled with wisdom, and God's favour was on him.

In this combination of episodes, Luke shows his skill at creating atmosphere. Five times it is emphasised that Jesus' parents observe the Law, and Simeon and Hanna, another couple straight from the pages of the Old Testament, reinforce this picture. However, the reader will know that by the end of the two-volume work of Luke-Acts, the group of Jesus' followers will have clearly separated from their Jewish matrix; and for Luke it is the Holy Spirit that directs that separation, so the Spirit is mentioned no less than three times in this passage. Likewise Simeon's song, which has been for a millennium and a half part of the Church's night prayer, refers implicitly to the separation, with its reference to 'revelation of Gentiles', along with 'glory of Israel'. Simeon sides with the lowly, classing himself as a slave, just as Mary does.

Above all, though, it is a central theme of Luke-Acts that God is in charge; and this is indicated quite emphatically in the account of Jesus' circumcision, which is performed in accordance with God's Law, but also (and more specifically) in accordance with the instruction of the angel Gabriel to Mary. As before, we are invited to contemplate the meaning of the child, through the lens of his parents' 'astonishment', Simeon's song of farewell, and Hanna's praise of God.

One last point to notice is the theme, once more, of journeying. Count carefully in these first two chapters, and you will find that the scene shifts no less than nine times, between Judaea and Galilee. The rest of the Gospel can be seen as a steady journey towards Jerusalem; then Acts is a journey outwards, concluding in Rome, but with occasional returns to Jerusalem, until the Gospel definitively turns its back on that city.

Is it helpful to think of the Gospel as a 'journey'?

Passover in Jerusalem

41-52 And his parents used to journey each year to Jerusalem for the Passover festival. And when he was twelve years old, when they went up according to the custom of the feast, and when they had completed the days, as they returned, the boy Jesus stayed behind in Jerusalem; and his parents did not know. Thinking that he was in the caravan, they went a day's journey, and then started to hunt for him everywhere among their relatives and acquaintances; and when they couldn't find him, they returned to Jerusalem in their hunt for him; and so it was that after three days they found him sitting in the Temple in the middle of the teachers, and [he was] listening to them and asking them questions; and all those who heard him were astonished at his intellect and at his responses. And when they saw him they were overwhelmed; and his mother said to him, 'Child, why did you do this to us? Look – your father and I have been looking for you in agony.'

And he said to them, 'Why were you looking for me? Didn't you know that I had to be on my Father's business [or: 'in my Father's house']?' And they did not understand the word that he had spoken to them.

And he went down with them to Nazareth, and put himself under their authority. And his mother kept all these events [or: words] in her heart.

And Jesus advanced in wisdom and stature and favour before God and human beings.

Luke ends his account of Jesus' early years with a characteristically dramatic vignette. Once again the parents are presented as observant Jews, going up to Jerusalem on pilgrimage; but a note of suspense is injected into the story when they discover that they have actually lost this child that has been so carefully entrusted to them.

The drama is not just for its own sake, however, but for what it hints about Jesus' future. The Jesus of Luke's Gospel is not about to be easily pinned down; and the child who reacts harshly to 'your father and I' by deliberately redefining his parentage ('my Father'), is the one who is going to 'cause division' (Luke 12:49-53; and see also 8:19-21).

Yet again the evangelist encourages us to reflect on Jesus through the lens of Mary, who 'kept all these things in her heart'; and household order is restored, with Jesus submitting to parental authority and then growing up in the normal way.

'She kept all these things in her heart': does Luke see Mary as a model for us?

John the Baptist begins his mission

3 1, 2 In the fifteenth year of the Imperium of Tiberius Caesar, when Pontius Pilate was governor of Judaea, and Herod was tetrarch of Galilee, and Philip his brother was tetrarch of Iturea and the district of Trachonitis, and Lysanias was tetrarch of Abilene, under the High Priesthood of Annas and Caiaphas, the word of God came to John, the son of Zachariah, in the desert.

This very elaborate introduction to John the Baptist's mission contains the only date in the whole of the New Testament (AD 28–29) It is quite a good example of Luke's 'sleight of hand', whereby he feints in one direction, when his intention is to go somewhere else altogether. He lists, in descending order of priority, the most important people as far as the history and geography of the region are concerned: Tiberius, the unpleasant emperor of Rome (successor to Augustus, who was mentioned in the last chapter), his local representative Pontius Pilate (the literary if not political successor to Quirinius); then Herod, son of the King Herod of Chapter 1, and his brothers, who share, under moderately strict Roman conditions, their father's empire; then come the local religious figures, Annas and Caiaphas. Finally, while we ponder this list, as unwholesome a collection of brigands as you could wish to meet on a dark night, Luke brings us to the person he is really interested in, our old friend 'John son of Zachariah'. And he is in the desert, where Luke had conveniently placed him, a chapter ago.

John's mission

3-9 And he came to the whole country around the Jordan, proclaiming a baptism of repentance for the forgiveness of sins, as it is written in the scroll of words of Isaiah the prophet:

'A voice of one shouting in the desert:
"Prepare the way of the Lord,
make straight his paths."
Every valley shall be filled in,
and every mountain and hill made low,
and the crooked places shall turn straight
and the rough places turn into smooth roads.
And all flesh shall see the saving power of God.'

So he would tell the crowds who journeyed out to be baptised by him, 'Offspring of vipers, who taught you to flee from the anger that is coming? So produce fruits worthy of repentance; and don't start saying to yourselves, "We have Abraham as our father". Because I tell you that God can raise up children for Abraham from these stones. Already the axe is laid to the root of the trees. So every tree that does not give fruit is cut down and cast into the fire.'

John the Baptist here introduces a theme that will be very important in the Gospel of Luke, that of 'repentance for the forgiveness of sins', though here the phrase is taken over directly from Mark 1:4, and the 'fruits worthy of repentance' is almost identically found in Matthew 3:8. The quotation is from Isaiah 40:3-5.

You might have expected the crowds to drift away, seeing John the Baptist's rather aggressive speech to them; but it doesn't seem to have put them off. Why is this, do you think? Would it have put **you** *off?*

John and the crowds

10-18 And the crowds asked him, saying, 'What are we to do, then?'

In answer he said to them, 'Let the one who has two tunics share with the one who has none; and let the one who has food to eat do the same.'

Tax collectors also came and said to him, 'Teacher, what are we to do?'

He said to them, 'Exact nothing beyond what is commanded you.'

There were also some who were serving in the army; they asked him, 'What about us? What are ***we**** to do?'

And he said to them, 'No extortion; no false accusations; be satisfied with your wages.'

The populace was agog; everyone was arguing about John [wondering] whether perhaps he might be the Messiah. So John responded to them all, 'I'm baptising you in water – but the one who is stronger than me is on his way, and I am not fit to untie the thong of his sandals. He will baptise you with the Holy Spirit and with fire. His winnowing-shovel is in his hand to clean the threshing-floor thoroughly – and the chaff he will burn with a fire that cannot be extinguished.'

With many other consoling remarks he spread the good news among the people.

Luke is a very gentle evangelist; but that should not blind us to the starkness of his message. John the Baptist's message will have struck Luke's Christians as chillingly severe, especially if, as I suspect, they were relatively comfortably off: sharing tunics and food comes less easily to the rich. Tax collectors and soldiers will have wondered how they could possibly make a living under this dispensation; and am I alone in hearing a touch of irony in Luke's concluding remark about 'consoling' and 'good news'?

The alert reader will have noticed yet another reference here to the 'Holy Spirit', but in connection with Jesus' mission, now, not John's.

Is John the Baptist's message **really** *good news?*

---

* Words in bold throughout the text are my emphasis

John the Baptist and Herod

19, 20 Now Herod the tetrarch, having been rebuked [by John] in respect of Herodias his brother's wife, and in respect of all the evil things that Herod had done, added this also to everything else, and locked John up in prison.

The starkness continues; if this is John the Baptist's fate, what is going to happen to Jesus? This is, we observe, now the third reference in the Gospel to this unpleasant family.

The baptism of Jesus

21, 22 It happened when the whole populace had been baptised, and as Jesus had been baptised and was praying, heaven was opened and the Holy Spirit came down in bodily form, like a dove, upon him, and a voice came from heaven, 'You are my Son, the Beloved – in you I am well pleased.'

Luke's is very much the Gospel of prayer; at several keypoints, as we shall see, Luke shows us Jesus at prayer, and this is the first such occasion.

All the way through the Gospel, we need to be asking, 'Who is Jesus for Luke?' The first two chapters gave us a number of implicit and explicit clues. Here, Luke makes the contrast between Jesus and John the Baptist; he does not explicitly mention, we notice, that Jesus was baptised by John, but hurries on to assert that Jesus is Son of God. This assertion is now supported in a rather different way in the genealogy.

Who is Jesus for Luke?

Jesus' genealogy

23-38 And Jesus himself was, when he started, about thirty years old. He was the son, so it was supposed, of Joseph, son of Heli, son of Matthat, son of Levi, son of Melchi, son of Jannai, son of Joseph, son of Mattathias, son of Amos, son of Nahum, son of Esli, son of Naggai, son of Maath, son of Mattathias, son of Semein, son of Josech, son of Joda, son of Ioanan, son of Rhesa, son of Zerubbabel, son of Shealtiel, son of Neri, son of Melchi, son of Addi, son of Kosam, son of Elmadam, son of Er, son of Joshua, son of Eliezer, son of Jorim, son of Matthat, son of Levi, son of Symeon, son of Judah, son of Joseph, son of Jonam, son of Eliakim, son of Melea, son of Menna, son of Mattatha, son of Nathan, son of David, son of Jesse, son of Obed, son of Boaz, son of Sala, son of Nahshon, son of Aminadab, son of Admin, son of Arni, son of Hezron, son of Perez, son of Judah, son of Jacob, son of Isaac, son of Abraham, son of Terah, son of Nahor, son of Serug, son of Ragai, son of Peleg, son of Eber, son of Shela, son of Cainan, son of Arphaxad, son of Shem, son of Noah, son of Lamech, son of Methusaleh, son of Enoch, son of Jared, son of Mahaleel, son of Kainan, son of Enos, son of Seth, son of Adam, son of God.

Luke puts in a genealogy at this point, after Jesus' baptism and as he starts his ministry. Matthew, by contrast, **begins** *with Jesus' genealogy. For Matthew, Jesus' family tree sums up the whole of Israel's history. Luke, on the other hand, traces the story back to 'Adam, son of God', so embracing the whole human race; by the end of this two-volume work, the Gospel will have reached all humanity. Beyond this observation, there is no great need to worry too much about the genealogy. Gallant attempts have been made to reconcile this one with what we find in Matthew; generally they have not carried conviction. The alert reader will notice here several repetitions, which may suggest that Luke was short of information on the matter.*

The temptation of Jesus in the desert

4 1-13 Jesus, full of the Holy Spirit, returned from the Jordan, and was led by the Spirit in the desert, being tempted by the devil for forty days. And he ate nothing in those days; and when they were completed, he was hungry.

The devil said to him, 'If you ***are*** the Son of God, tell this stone to become a loaf of bread.'

And Jesus answered him; 'It is written, "Human beings shall not live by bread alone."'

And leading him up, he showed him all the kingdoms of the world in an instant of time, and the devil said to him, 'I shall give you all this authority, and the glory of them, because it has been handed over to me, and I give it to whomsoever I want. So, as for you, if you bow down before me, it will all be yours.'

And Jesus answered and said to him, 'It is written, "The Lord your God shall you worship – and him alone shall you adore."'

He led him up to Jerusalem, and set him on the summit of the Temple, and said to him, 'If you ***are*** the Son of God, throw yourself down from here. For it is written, "He will command his angels about you, to protect you," and "On their hands they will bear you up, lest you strike your foot on a stone."'

And Jesus in reply said to him, 'It is said, "You shall not tempt the Lord your God."'

And having completed the whole temptation, the devil withdrew from him until a suitable occasion.

This episode starts, possibly for our comfort, with a double reference to the Holy Spirit (Mark at this point has a rather violent-sounding reference to the Spirit 'expelling' Jesus into the desert; Luke, characteristically, is more gentle). Luke and Matthew have a threefold pattern of temptation from the devil, trying to persuade Jesus to gratify some immediate need, and also, more importantly, to take his eyes off the mission that he has been given by God. Each time Jesus effortlessly repels the temptation by quoting Deuteronomy. The three temptations are in a slightly different order in Matthew and Luke. Some scholars think that Luke deliberately made the 'Temple' temptation the climax: Luke's Gospel begins and ends in the Temple, and the Temple is clearly of importance to him.

The final line ('until a suitable occasion') sounds like a threat, whose implication only becomes clear as we approach the end of the Gospel story.

What does this episode teach us about Jesus?

The ministry begins in Nazareth

14-30 And Jesus returned to Galilee in the power of the Spirit. And a report about him went out through the whole district; and he was teaching in their synagogues, being glorified by everybody.

And he came to Nazareth, where he had been brought up, and, as was his custom, he went in on the Sabbath-day to the synagogue, and rose up to read. And there was given to him the scroll of the prophet Isaiah, and unrolling the scroll he found the place where it was written,

'The Spirit of the Lord is upon me,
therefore he has anointed me
to give good news to the destitute.
He has sent me
to proclaim freedom to prisoners
and recovery-of-sight to the blind,
to set the oppressed free,
to proclaim an acceptable year of the Lord.'

And rolling up the scroll he gave it back to the assistant and sat down. And all eyes in the synagogue were gazing at him. He began to speak to them, 'Today this Scripture is fulfilled as you listen.'

And they all bore witness to him, and they wondered at the graceful words that came out of his mouth; and they started saying, 'Isn't this Joseph's son?'

And he said to them, 'Certainly you'll tell me this proverb, "Doctor, heal yourself. Do also here in your home territory the things that we have heard of occurring in Caphernaum." Amen I tell you, no prophet is acceptable in his home territory. In truth I tell you, there were many widows in Israel in Elijah's day, when heaven was shut for three years and six months, when a great famine hit the whole earth; and Elijah was sent to none of them, but to Sarepta of Sidon, to a widow-woman [there]. And there were many lepers in Israel in the time of Elisha the prophet; and none of them was cleansed but Naaman the Syrian.'

And they were all filled with rage in the synagogue as they heard this; and they arose and started throwing him out of the city; and they led him to the brow of the hill on which their city was built, so as to throw him down. But he passed through the middle of them and travelled on.

Luke has placed this Nazareth episode (which takes place at a later stage in both Matthew and Mark) right at the beginning of Jesus' ministry, apparently because he wants various themes to surface from the very start. I may mention the following:

- *the 'ripple' effect conveyed by the phrase 'a report went out through the whole district' – an oral extension of the journeying motif that we have already encountered;*
- *the reader will have to get used to the idea of the 'Lucan summary': the opening lines of this passage, which do not refer to any particular episode, but create atmosphere, give an impression of what it was like. This is something that we shall see again. Luke uses it very effectively in Acts;*
- *the text of Jesus' sermon. Luke is the Gospel of the poor and oppressed, as the author signals once more by the text that Jesus is given to read (Isaiah 61:1, 2a). This message is hammered home by Jesus' sermon, the shortest on record. He claims, 'today this Scripture is fulfilled';*
- *and the word 'today', one of great importance in Luke: it is used in the annunciation to the shepherds, in the Zacchaeus story, and will be used in the story of the thief who recognised Jesus on the Cross. Each of these stories is important in the unfolding of the Gospel narrative;*
- *Finally, another important theme of this Gospel is the spread of the gospel to the Gentiles, symbolised here by the widow of Sarepta, and by Naaman the Syrian.*

Does the episode at Nazareth sharpen up your picture of Jesus?

The first day of the apostolate

31-44 And he went down to Caphernaum, a city of Galilee, and he used to teach them on the Sabbath-day; and they would be amazed at his teaching, because his speech was marked with authority.

And in the synagogue there was a man who had the spirit of an unclean demon; and it cried out in a loud voice, 'Leave us alone – what have we got to do with you, Jesus the Nazarene? Have you come to destroy us? I know who you are – the Holy One of God!'

And Jesus rebuked it, 'Be silent, and come out of him.'

And the demon threw him into the middle and came out of him, causing him no harm! And astonishment came upon them all, and they spoke to each other saying, 'What is this word? Because he commands the unclean spirits with authority and with power – and they come out!' And the rumour about him started to go out to every place in the area round about.

He arose out of the synagogue and went into the house of Simon. Simon's mother-in-law was in the grip of a great fever, and they asked him about her. And he stood over her and rebuked the fever; and it left her. Straightaway she arose and ministered to them.

When the sun set, all those who had people sick with different kinds of diseases brought them to him. He laid his hands on every single one of them, and healed them. Demons came out from many people, shouting and saying, 'You are the Son of God.' He rebuked them, and did not allow them to speak – because they knew that he was the Messiah.

When day came, he went out and journeyed to a desert place; and the crowds went looking for him, and they came up to him and restrained him from journeying away from them. He told them, 'It is necessary for me to proclaim the good news of the kingdom of God in the other cities also, because this is my mission.'

And he was preaching in the synagogues of Judaea.

We can see here signs of Luke's careful planning of his material, to give a sense of what Jesus' mission was like, and what it was about, from the very beginning. This passage begins and ends with a 'Lucan summary', setting the mood, but with the important difference that whereas the first summary is set in Galilee, the second is in Judaea, thereby stressing the 'journeying' theme.

Second, the demons correctly identify Jesus as 'Holy One of God' and 'Son of God' – but this has to be kept quiet.

Third, we see once more the 'ripple effect' in the 'rumour' that went out about him.

Fourth, feminists sometimes get irritated when Simon Peter's mother-in-law is cured, only to start waiting on the males; but notice that, like Mary (1:39) and Jesus (4:16) before her, she 'arose'. We are meant to applaud and imitate her.

Fifth, Luke once more underlines respect for Jewish traditions – it is only when the sun sets, and therefore the Sabbath ends, that the sick are brought to Jesus.

Finally, one of the oddest features of Luke as the Gospel of prayer is that when Jesus goes out to the desert place (where in Mark and Matthew he prays), prayer is not mentioned. And in this Gospel it is the crowds, and not Simon Peter, who come and try to stop his 'journeying'.

What do you think is the most important aspect of Jesus' first day at work?

The calling of Simon

5 1-11 It happened when the crowd was pressing upon him and listening to the word of God, and he was standing by the Lake Gennesaret; and he saw two boats standing by the lake. The fishermen had come ashore and were washing the nets. He went on board one of the boats, which was Simon's, and asked him to put out a little bit from the land. He then sat down and taught the crowds from the boat.

When he stopped speaking, he said to Simon, 'Put out into the deep, and let down your nets to catch something.'

In response, Simon said, 'Master, the whole night we have been labouring and caught nothing – but at your word I shall let down the nets.' They did this – and they enclosed an enormous number of fish – and their nets were starting to break; and they signalled, nodding to their colleagues in the other boat to come and assist them. They came, and they filled both boats, to a point where they were sinking!

When Simon Peter saw this, he fell at Jesus' knees and said, 'Go away from me, because I am a sinful human being, Lord.' For astonishment had seized him, and all those with him, at the catch of fish which they had taken, and similarly James and John the sons of Zebedee, who were colleagues of Simon.

And Jesus said to Simon, 'Do not be afraid. From now on, you will be catching human beings.' And drawing up their boats on to the shore, they abandoned everything and followed him.

This is an extraordinary story, different from and similar to the version told by Mark (1:16-20). The reader must decide whether there are two different stories here, or whether Luke has adapted Mark's story for his own purposes. Certainly some scholars have found echoes here of Mark 4:1, 2 and John 21:1-19.

However you answer this question, you will notice some familiar touches that are typical of Luke. In the first place, Jesus breaks into Simon's life, without a by-your-leave, as Gabriel did into the lives of Zachariah and Mary.

Second, like Mary to Gabriel, Simon (no doubt a very sceptical professional fisherman), expressly acquiesces in Jesus' 'word'.

Third, he becomes 'Peter' as well as Simon, as soon as he gives his consent.

Fourth, he discovers in the light of the miracle of the fish that he is a 'sinful human being', and he learns to call Jesus 'Lord'. He is mistaken, however, in thinking that this means that Jesus must go away from him. Sinners have to repent, not send the Lord away.

Finally, and this is something we shall see frequently in Luke, discipleship is a matter of 'abandoning everything'. This may count as evidence in favour of the view that Luke is writing for a well-to-do church, a group that needed to be reminded that their possessions could be an obstacle to the work of the Holy Spirit in them.

Do you think that Simon's reaction is common among people who meet Jesus?

A leper asks to be healed

12-16 And it happened, when he was in one of the cities, and look! A man full of leprosy, seeing Jesus, fell on his face and implored him, 'Lord, if you want, you can cleanse me.' And stretching out his hand he touched him, saying, 'I want – be cleansed.' And immediately the leprosy went away from him.

And he commanded him, 'Tell nobody. Instead, go and show yourself to the priest and offer [the offering] as prescribed by Moses for your cleansing, as evidence to them.' The report about him spread even further; and great crowds started gathering to hear and to be cured of their sicknesses; but he was [ever] withdrawing in[to] desert places and praying.

This passage feels a bit like one of those 'Lucan summaries', a story that serves to set the mood, a typical incident in the life of Jesus. Certainly it ends with what is unmistakably such a summary.

Once again there are some typical Lucan touches. The theme of the 'Gospel of prayer' is twice touched upon, first in the prayer of the leper (he 'implored him'), and then at the end, when we learn of Jesus' regular habit of prayer.

Like his own parents, and like Zachariah and Elisabeth, Jesus is presented to us as very observant of the Jewish Law ('as prescribed by Moses', he orders the cured leper).

And we see once more our familiar 'ripple effect': 'the report about him spread even further . . . ' which is a variation on the 'journeying theme'.

What do we learn about Jesus here?

The cure of a paralysed man – and the first signs of official opposition

17-26 And it happened on one of the days that he was teaching, and Pharisees and teachers of the Law were sitting; they had come from every village of Galilee and Judaea and Jerusalem. And the power of the Lord was that he should heal. And look! Men carrying someone on a bed, who was paralysed. And they were looking for a way to bring him in and to put him before him. When they did not find any way of bringing him in, because of the crowd, they went up to the roof, and let him down through the tiles, with [his] little bed, in the middle, in front of Jesus. And seeing their faith, he said, 'Man, your sins are forgiven you.' And the scribes and the Pharisees began to argue, saying, 'Who is this who is talking blasphemies? Who can forgive sins, except only God?'

Jesus, knowing their arguments, said to them in response, 'Why are you arguing in your hearts? What is easier – to say, "Your sins are forgiven you" or to say "Arise and walk"? But in order that you people may know that the Son of Man has authority on earth to forgive sins' – he said to the paralytic – 'I tell you, arise, take up your little bed, and go to your house.'

And straightaway he arose before them, taking up that on which he had been lying, and went off to his house, glorifying God. And amazement seized all of them, and they glorified God, and were filled with fear, saying, 'We have seen glorious things today.'

Luke found this story in Mark's Gospel, though he has added one or two touches of his own. The first thing we notice is a heavy overload of Pharisees and teachers of the Law; at first blush it seems as though there is no room for anyone else, especially since they come from every single village in the land. We shall probably be correct in detecting here our 'journeying' theme in the reference to Galilee, Judaea and Jerusalem.

If you look carefully at Mark's version, you will notice that where Mark speaks of 'unroofing the roof', Luke speaks of going through the tiles. It may well be that they have in view two different styles of building: Mark the rougher Palestinian construction, and Luke thinking of the roofs of Greek-style villas. This could be another indication that he has a more affluent audience in view.

The references at the end to 'glorifying God' are very Lucan: we have already seen shepherds (2:20) and crowds (4:15) doing the same; and there will be other examples.

When Jesus is accused of 'talking blasphemies', the reader must ask whether the accusation is true, in Luke's view. If not, what does this say about Jesus?

The call of Levi: the first 'disastrous dinner party'

27-32 And after this he went out, and he saw a tax collector named Levi sitting at the tax-collecting place, and he said to him, 'Follow me.' And abandoning everything he rose up and followed him. And Levi gave a great reception in his house, and there was a great crowd of tax collectors and others who were with him, lying down to eat. And the Pharisees and their scribes complained to his disciples, 'Why do you people eat and drink with tax collectors and sinners?'

Jesus in reply said to them, 'The healthy have no need of a doctor – no, it's those who are ill. I did not come to call the just, but sinners, to repentance.'

Levi's call, like that of Peter and his colleagues, clearly involves 'abandoning everything'; and like Mary and Jesus before him, we learn that he 'arose' or 'rose up'. At the end of the episode we notice the characteristic Lucan theme of repentance for sin. We learn, too, that for Luke the 'Pharisees and their scribes' stand for those who do not see the possibility (or the need?) of repentance.

This is the first of a series of what I call 'disastrous dinner parties' in Luke's Gospel. Not all of them are really dinner parties, and not all of them are utterly disastrous; but it is one of the ways he has of organising his material, and perhaps such a setting would have sent a message to his affluent Christian community.

What kind of people does Jesus prefer?

Is Jesus a serious religious figure? No – he's something new

33-39 They said to him, 'John's disciples fast frequently, and make intercessions, just like those of the Pharisees, but yours [just] eat and drink.'

Jesus said to them, 'Surely you can't compel the wedding guests [or: bridegroom's attendants] to fast while the bridegroom is with them? But days will come, and when the bridegroom is taken from them, then they will fast in those days.'

He also spoke a parable to them: 'No one tears a patch from a new garment and patches it on to an old one. Otherwise the new one will tear, and the patch from the new one won't match with the old one. Likewise no one puts new wine into old flasks. Otherwise the new wine will burst the flasks; then it will spill out, and the flasks will be destroyed. No – new wine must be put into new flasks. No one who has drunk old wine wants new wine, for they say, "The old is good."'

Luke has slightly tidied up Mark's version here, to make it a bit clearer how the parables about new cloth and new wine fit the controversy with the Pharisees. There is a slight puzzle at the end: the reader feels that the new wine stands for Jesus, but it is the old wine that is 'good'. Perhaps Luke's well-to-do audience were accustomed to vintage wine. Or perhaps it is the attitude of the Pharisees that Jesus is trying to describe here: people who prefer the 'old wine' of the Law to the 'new wine' of the gospel. Or perhaps he's just keeping us on our toes.

What is so 'new' about Jesus?

Can you pluck grain and heal on the Sabbath? Two examples

6 1-11 It happened on a Sabbath-day that he was going through the grain fields; and his disciples started plucking and eating the ears of grain, rubbing them in their hands. Some of the Pharisees said, 'Why are you doing what is not allowed on the Sabbath?'

And Jesus responded to them, 'Haven't you even read what David did when he and those with him were hungry? How he went into the house of God, and took the Loaves of Presentation and ate them and gave them to those with him? But no one is allowed to eat those loaves, except the priests alone.' And he said to them, 'The Son of Man is Lord of the Sabbath.'

On another Sabbath-day, it happened that he went into the synagogue and taught. And a man was there, and his right hand was paralysed [or: withered]. And they were watching him, the scribes and the Pharisees, to see if he cured on the Sabbath, in order that they might find something to accuse him of. He however knew their thoughts, and said to the man with the paralysed hand, 'Up you get, and stand out into the middle.' And he arose and stood.

Jesus said to them, 'I ask you: is it allowed on the Sabbath-day to do good, or to do evil? To save life or to destroy it?' And he looked round at all of them and told the man, 'Stretch out your hand.' He did so – and his hand was restored! They were mad with rage, and they discussed with each other what they might do to Jesus.

This passage with its two controversies confirms our impression of the way things are going: there's trouble ahead, symbolised by the readiness of Jesus' opponents to criticise, and by the fact that 'they were watching him'. Evidently he is already regarded as a menace; and being right is not going to make it any easier for him. But Luke's version of the story is less stark than Mark's account (Mark 2:23–3:6).

What is the battle between Jesus and his opponents really about?

Jesus prays and then chooses the Twelve

12-16 It happened in these days that he went out on to the mountain to pray. And he was spending the whole night in prayer to God. And when day dawned, he called his disciples, and chose twelve from among them, whom he named 'apostles': Simon, whom he named 'Rock', and Andrew his brother, and James and John, and Philip and Bartholomew, and Matthew and Thomas, and James of Alphaeus, and Simon, nicknamed 'Zealot', and Judas of James; and Judas Iscariot, who became a traitor.

Luke typically inserts the reference to prayer. Some readers may feel that after a night spent in meditation, the Lord might have selected a more satisfactory team than this particular group of cowards and traitors. But there is consolation for us here: we do not have to be out of the top drawer in order to be close to Jesus.

Does the list of names give you some reassurance?

THE 'SERMON ON THE PLAIN' (17-49)

Introduction

17-19 And he came down with them, and stood on a level place, he and a crowd of his disciples, and a great throng of the populace from all of Judaea and Jerusalem and the sea-coast of Tyre and Sidon, who came to listen to him, and to be healed from their diseases; and those who were troubled by unclean spirits were getting cured, and the whole crowd tried to find ways of touching him, because power was coming from him, and was healing everybody.

Luke places this 'sermon' on a 'plain' or a 'level place'. Matthew's equivalent, which in some ways is like Luke's and contains almost all of Luke's material, is placed on a 'mountain', and is altogether a much more organised affair. Luke introduces the sermon with these various healings, as a kind of 'Lucan summary'.

Congratulations and woes

20-26 And he raised his eyes up to his disciples and said,

'Congratulations to the poor – for yours is the kingdom of heaven.
Congratulations to those who are hungry now – for you will be sated.
Congratulations to you who weep now – because you will laugh.
Congratulations when people hate you, and when they ostracise you and heap insults on you, and spurn your name as evil, for the sake of the Son of Man.
Rejoice in that day, and leap about.
For look! Your reward is great in heaven;
for in just the same way their ancestors used to treat the prophets.
BUT woe to you who are rich – for you have your comfort in full.
Woe to you who are filled now – for you will be hungry.
Woe to you who laugh now – for you will mourn and weep.
Woe to you whenever all people speak well of you.
For in just the same way their ancestors used to treat the false prophets.'

Again the reader must decide whether Luke is speaking to an audience that is largely affluent. Certainly he does not, as Matthew does, speak of the 'poor in spirit'; and although he has fewer 'congratulations' than Matthew in the

Sermon on the Mount, he sharpens the effect by throwing in four 'woes' to match the 'congratulations'. These two sections, the woes and the congratulations, are nicely balanced; some scholars see here the original version of the beatitudes.

Do the 'congratulations' and 'woes' make you feel uncomfortable? If so, why?

On being children of the Father

27-49 'But I am speaking to you who are listening:

Love your enemies.
Do good to those who hate you.
Bless those who persecute you.
Pray for those who threaten you.
To the one who strikes you on the cheek, turn the other also.
And from the one who takes away your cloak, do not refuse your tunic.
To everyone who begs from you, give.
And to those who take what is yours, do not demand it back.

'And as you want people to do to you, do likewise to them. If you only love those who love you, what credit is that to you? For even sinners love those who love them. And if you do good to those who do good to you, what credit is that to you? Even sinners do that same thing. And if you lend money to people from whom you expect to get it back, what credit is that to you? Even sinners lend money to sinners in order to get the same amount back. No – love your enemies, and do good and lend without any expectation of return, and your reward will be great, and you will be children of the Most High, for he is kind even to the ungrateful and the wicked.

'Learn to be compassionate, just as your Father is compassionate. And don't judge, and you won't be judged. Don't condemn, and you won't be condemned. Let people off, and you will be let off. Give, and it will be given to you; they will give a generous measure, pressed down, shaken up and overflowing into your lap. For in the measure that you measure out, it will be measured to you in return.'

He also told them a parable: 'Can a blind person guide a[nother] blind person? Will they not both fall into a pit? The pupil does not have a higher status than the teacher; if they are fully trained, they will be just like their teacher.

'Why do you look at the [tiny] speck that is in your fellow's eye, but do not perceive the [huge] beam that is in your own eye? How can you say to your brother or sister, "Brother/sister: let me get rid of the speck that is in your eye", and all the while you yourself do not see the beam that is in your eye? Hypocrite [literally, 'actor'], first get the beam out of your eye, and then you will see the speck that is in the eye of your brother or sister.

'You see, there is no such thing as a good tree that produces rotten fruit. Nor is there such a thing as a rotten tree that produces good fruit. For each tree is recognised by its own fruit. They don't, you see, gather figs off thorn bushes; nor do they pick a bunch of grapes off brambles. A good person produces good things from the good treasure chest of their heart; the wicked person produces wickedness from what is wicked. You see, their mouth speaks out of the fullness of the heart.

'Why do you call me "Lord, Lord", and not do what I say? Everyone who comes to me and hears my words and does them – I'll show you what they are like. They are like a person building a house, who dug deep, and laid a foundation on the rock; and when the flood came, the river burst against that house, and it could not shake [the house], because it was well-built.

'However the one who hears and does not perform is like a person who built a house on soil, with no foundation; the river burst on it, and immediately it fell in, and the collapse of that house was enormous.'

Read one way, this can sound like very stark teaching indeed. Try seeing it, however, as springing from Jesus' central insight that we are all children of the one Father, and it all falls into place: all of us are equal, no one is better than anyone else, and the affluent (to whom alone, surely, the instructions about lending are directed) should be delighted to be generously at the service of other human beings.

Notice the difference, in the parable of the house which comes at the end of the discourse, between house-building techniques in Luke and in Matthew. The houses at the end of Matthew's Sermon on the Mount (Matthew 7:24-27) are built either on rock or on sand; whereas the Lucan houses, perhaps in Greek cities rather than the Palestinian countryside, either have or do not have proper foundations.

How do you feel about the teaching of this 'sermon'?

A centurion's slave is healed

7 1-10 When he had completed all his words in the ears of the populace, he went into Caphernaum.

Now a certain centurion had a slave who was in a bad way and on the point of death. The slave was valuable to him; and hearing about Jesus, he sent elders of the Jews to him, asking him to come and save his slave. They came to Jesus, and begged him earnestly, saying, 'He deserves that you should grant him this. For he loves our people, and has himself built a synagogue for us.'

Jesus journeyed with them. When he was now not far off from the house, the centurion sent friends, saying, 'Lord, do not trouble yourself, for I am not good enough for you to enter under my roof. Therefore I didn't even think that I deserved to come to you. Just say the word, and let my servant be healed. For I am also a man placed under authority, with soldiers under me. And I say to this one, "Quick march," and he marches, and to another, "Come here," and he comes, and to my slave, "Do this," and he does it.'

When Jesus heard this, he was astonished at him; and he turned to the crowd that followed him and said, 'I tell you – not even in Israel have I found so much faith.' And those who had been sent returned and found the slave in good health.

This remarkable story is also in Matthew 8:5-13 and John 4:46-54, though it is far more detailed here, and the centurion is very sympathetically treated by Luke. He is perhaps a symbol for Luke of Gentile openness to the Gospel. Luke alone offers the detail about the centurion building the synagogue, and his friendly relationship with the Jews of Caphernaum; and Luke omits Matthew's severe judgement on Israel.

What is this story about?

The widow's son at Nain

11-17 The next thing that happened was that he journeyed to a city called Nain, and his disciples and a large crowd were journeying with him. When he drew near to the gate of the city, look! There was being carried out one who had died, the only son of his mother – and she was a widow. And there was a good crowd of the city with her. And when he saw her, the Lord had pity on her and said to her, 'Do not weep.' He approached and touched the coffin; the bearers halted, and he said, 'Young man, I say to you, arise.'

And the young man sat up and began to talk. And he gave him to his mother. Fear seized all of them, and they glorified God, saying, 'A great prophet has been raised up among us, and God has visited his people.' And this report went out about him in the whole of Judaea, and the whole area round about.

This is a charming story, characteristic of Luke, not least in the fact that it concerns a widow; widows, like lepers, are among Luke's favourite class of people, for they are marginalised in such a society. We notice, with no real surprise, that Jesus is unafraid to contract ritual impurity by touching the corpse. Once again we hear the people glorify God, and they even quote the Benedictus (1:68): 'God has visited his people.' Once again we have an instance of the 'ripple effect': ('the report went out about him . . . ').

When Luke says 'the Lord had pity', it is the first time that as narrator he has explicitly named Jesus with the awesome title of 'the Lord'. This title is used in the Greek translation of the Old Testament for the sacred and unpronounceable name of God, and in the language of the Roman Empire it was being increasingly used for the Emperor, often in connection with his divination. So Christian use of it for Jesus is subversive in two directions at once.

Who takes the initiative in this episode?

Comparing Jesus (once more) with John the Baptist

18-35 And his disciples repeated to John about all these things. And John summoned two of his disciples and sent them to the Lord, saying, 'Are you the Coming One, or are we to expect another?' And when they reached him, the men said, 'John the Baptist sent us to you. He said, "Are you the Coming One, or are we to expect another?".'

At that moment he cured many from diseases and afflictions and evil spirits, and gave many blind people the free gift of sight. He replied to them, 'On your way, and tell John what you saw and heard: "The blind see again; the lame walk; lepers are cleansed and the deaf hear; the dead are raised; the poor have the good news preached to them." And happy is anyone who is not affronted by me.'

As John's messengers went off, he began to talk to the crowds about John: 'What did you go out into the desert to see? A reed shaken by the wind? No? What ***did*** you go out to see? A man dressed in gorgeous clothes? Look – people who wear splendid clothing and live in luxury are in palaces. No? What ***did*** you go out to see? A prophet? Yes, I tell you, and far better than a prophet. This is the one of whom it is written, 'Look – I am sending my messenger before my face, who will prepare your way before you.' I tell you: no one is greater among the sons of women than John – but the most insignificant in the kingdom of God is greater than he.'

And the whole populace who heard, and the tax collectors, justified God by being baptised with John's baptism. But the Pharisees and lawyers set aside God's will, refusing to be baptised by him.

'So to what shall I compare the people of this generation, what are they like? They are like children who sit in the market place and call out to each other and say,

"We piped for you – and you didn't dance.
We mourned – and you didn't weep."

'For John the Baptist came, not eating bread, nor drinking wine, and you say, "He's got a demon!" The Son of Man came, eating and drinking, and you say, "Look! A glutton and a wine drinker! A friend of tax collectors and sinners!" And Wisdom is justified by ***all*** her children.'

This is a slightly enigmatic passage. Clearly Luke wants us to accept that Jesus is John the Baptist's superior; we have already seen as much in the opening chapters of the Gospel. In this passage, moreover, John is uncertain enough to have to send a deputation, to check whether Jesus really **is** *the expected one. Jesus shows no doubts whatever. John is said to be inferior to 'the most insignificant in the kingdom of God'; and Jesus reminds us of his 'mission statement' at Nazareth in Chapter 4: 'the poor have the gospel (good news) preached to them', and John is criticised for being 'affronted' by Jesus.*

At the same time, John is praised for being an austere and serious religious figure, and Jesus indicates that John's mission was foretold in Scripture. John's baptism gives glory to God. The accusation that Jesus' opponents are like children, at the end of the passage, implicitly affirms the mission of both Jesus and John: the one more austere, the other less so, 'and wisdom is justified by **all** *her children', both John and Jesus, and anyone else who listens to God.*

The ones who are on the outside are those who see no need to listen to God, here classed as 'Pharisees and lawyers'. We have already seen the former as opponents of Jesus; the latter appear here for the first time. We shall see them a few times more in Luke's Gospel, nearly always behaving badly, or at least in opposition to Jesus. It is one of the former who behaves badly in the story that immediately follows.

What is the significance of John the Baptist's question to Jesus?

The second 'disastrous dinner party'

36-50 One of the Pharisees invited him to eat with him; and he went into the house of the Pharisee and lay down.

And look! A woman who was a sinner in the city, and who had found out that he was lying down in the house of the Pharisee, bringing an alabaster jar of myrrh, and standing behind, weeping beside his feet, began to wet his feet with her tears, and with the hair of her head began wiping [them] and kissing his feet and anointing them with myrrh.

When the Pharisee who had invited him saw [this], he said to himself, 'If this fellow were a prophet, he would know who this woman is who is touching him, and what sort of person – she's a sinner!'

Jesus responded to him, 'Simon, I have something to tell you.'

He said, 'Speak, teacher.'

'A moneylender had two people in debt to him. One owed fifty denarii, and the other five hundred. Because they had no way of repaying, he let them both off. Which of them, then, will love him more?'

Simon replied, 'I suppose the one whom he let off the most.'

He said to him, 'Right verdict.' And he turned to the woman and said to Simon, 'Do you see this woman? I came into your house – you didn't give me water for my feet. She by contrast wet my feet with her tears and wiped them with her hair. You gave me no kiss – she by contrast, ever since I entered, has not stopped kissing my feet. You did not anoint my head with oil – she, by contrast, anointed my feet with myrrh. Therefore, I tell you, they are forgiven, her many sins, because she loved much. A person who is forgiven [only] a little loves [only] a little.'

He said to her, 'Your sins are forgiven.' And those who were lying down with him began saying to themselves, 'Who is this, who can forgive sins?'

He said to the woman, 'Your faith has saved you – on your way in peace.'

This is the second of several 'disastrous dinner parties' in Luke's Gospel. Jesus cannot have been altogether an easy guest to have for a meal, and we may imagine the host or hostess rolling their eyes in despair at the flickering tensions that Jesus engendered; Luke's affluent readers may also have felt the unease. This story is in some ways very similar to that which the other three evangelists place at the beginning of the Passion story (Matthew 26:6-13; Mark 14:3-9; John 12:1-8), but not all scholars agree that it is the same story.

Certainly the point of the story is different. As we have seen several times already in this Gospel, and will see again, Jesus shocks his contemporaries by having some thoroughly disreputable friends, sinners who repent (we have already seen that repentance and forgiveness is a major theme of this Gospel). The woman is a good example, and she is singled out for praise, in contrast to Jesus' rather negligent (but religiously observant) host. The Pharisee (why on earth did he invite Jesus?) is watching Jesus like a hawk, and notices that Jesus allows this impure woman to touch him. The reader, however, has already seen Jesus voluntarily touch a coffin, a few verses earlier, so we already know that he is indifferent to ritual taboos.

Luke's Jesus is not afraid to shock, and not afraid, either, to attack his host. The beautiful and gentle ending to the story should not blind us to the fact that he is an uncomfortable guest at a party.

Do you find Jesus uncomfortable?

Jesus' men and women companions

8 1-3 And the next thing was that he made his way through town and village proclaiming, and preaching the good news of the kingdom of God; and the Twelve [were] with him, and certain women, who had been cured from evil spirits and sickness, Mary called Magdalene, from whom seven demons had come out, and Joanna the wife of Chuza, Herod's steward, and Susanna, and many other women, who ministered to them from their resources.

This is something of a 'Lucan summary', describing Jesus' itinerant group, and the 'support group' of women, apparently from the upper end of the social scale, whose relative wealth made the ministry possible. This may count as further evidence that Luke is writing for fairly affluent Christians.

Parables told and explained

4-18 A large crowd accompanied him, consisting of those who journeyed to him, town by town; and he spoke in a parable:

'The sower went out to sow his seed. And as he sowed, some fell by the way and was trampled underfoot, and the birds of the air gobbled it up. And another fell on the rock, and it grew up and withered, because it had no moisture. And another fell in the middle of thorns, and the thorns grew up with it and choked it. And another fell on good soil, and when it grew up it produced fruit, a hundredfold.' When he said this, he called out, 'Let those who have ears listen.'

His disciples asked him what this parable might mean.

He said, 'To you it is given to know the mysteries of the kingdom of God, but to the rest – in parables, that "seeing they may not see and hearing they may not understand". This is the parable: the seed is the word of God. Those who are "by the way" are those who hear, [but] then the devil comes and takes the word from their hearts; otherwise they might believe and be saved. Those who are "on the rock" are the ones who, when they hear the word, receive it with joy, and they have no root – they believe for a time, and in the time of temptation they withdraw. That which falls into the thorns, they are the ones who hear, and as they journey they are suffocated by the cares and affluence and pleasures of life; and they do not bring it to maturity. The seed in the "good soil" are those who hear with a noble and right heart; they hold on to the word and bear fruit patiently.

'No one who lights a lamp hides it in a pot or puts it under a bed. No – they put it on a lamp-stand, so that all who come [or: 'journey'] in may see the light. For there is nothing hidden which will not become visible; and there is nothing secret which will not become known, and come into the open.

'So watch out how you listen. For whoever has, it will be given to them, and whoever does not have, even what they think they have will be taken from them.'

Luke makes less of the parable section than either Mark or Matthew (though, as we shall see, he has plenty of very memorable parables of his own). As befits his gentler temperament, Luke is more lenient than Mark in his verdict on the uncomprehending disciples, and on those who do not grasp Jesus' message (see Mark 4:11-13).

The interpretation of the 'seed that fell among thorns' sounds a warning against the dangers of affluence, rather different from Mark's version (4:19); this may be further evidence for the view that Luke's church was a wealthy one.

In what ways is affluence 'dangerous'?

Jesus' mother and brothers

19-21 His mother and his brothers came to him, and they could not meet up with him, because of the crowd. It was reported to him, 'Your mother and your brothers are standing outside wanting to see you.' He replied to them, 'A mother to me, and brothers to me, are those who hear God's word and perform it.'

In comparison with the rather stark version of this at Mark 3:31-35, this is quite gentle, as befits the gentlest of the evangelists.

Jesus calms a storm on the Lake

22-25 It happened on one of the days that he went on board a boat, along with his disciples; and he said to them, 'Let us go to the other side of the Lake'; and they put out to sea. As they were sailing, he fell asleep. And a fierce gust of wind came down on to the Lake; and they were being swamped, and were in danger. They came and woke him up, saying 'Master, master, we're dying!' He woke up and rebuked the gale and the roughness of the waves. And they stopped; and there was a great calm. He said to them, 'Where's your faith?' They were awestruck, and they said to each other in astonishment, 'So who ***is*** this? Because he even gives order[s] to the winds and the water – and they obey him!'

Luke more or less reproduces here what he found in Mark (4:35-41). He has tidied it up, softened its rough edges, and omitted unnecessary material. One example of Lucan 'softening' is the way he has the disciples repeat their title for Jesus: 'Master, master'. And we shall see a similar repetition later, at 10:41: 'Martha, Martha'.

So who **is** *this?*

A demoniac in the land of the Gerasenes

26-39 And they sailed away to the land of the Gerasenes, which is opposite Galilee. As he disembarked on to land, a man from the city met him, who had demons; and for a good long time he had not worn a cloak, and would not stay in a house, but among tombs. Seeing Jesus, he cried out and fell down before him, and said in a loud voice, 'What do you want with me, Jesus, Son of God Most High? I implore you, don't torment me.' For he was directing the unclean spirit to come out of the man. For on many occasions it had seized him; and so he was bound in chains and kept secure with fetters; and he would break the shackles, and be driven by the demon into the desert places.

Jesus asked him, 'What is your name?' He said, 'Legion', because many demons had entered into him. And they begged him not to direct them to go off into the Abyss. Now there was there a sizable herd of pigs, grazing on the mountain. And they begged him to allow them to enter them; and he allowed them. The demons went out of the person, and entered the pigs; and the herd rushed down the cliff into the lake and was drowned.

When the herdsmen saw what had happened, they ran away and reported it in the city and in the countryside. They came out to see the phenomenon; and they approached Jesus and found the person from whom the demons had come out, sitting, wearing clothes, and in his right mind, at Jesus' feet. And they were awestruck.

Those who had seen [it] reported to them how the one who had been possessed by demons had been saved. And the whole throng of the area of the Gerasenes asked him to leave them, because they were seized with great awe. He went on board ship and returned. The man from whom the demons had come out begged to be with him; but he let him go, saying, 'Back to your house, and recount what great things God has done for you.'

And he went off through the whole city proclaiming what great things Jesus had done for him.

This is a powerful and dramatic story, revealing a good deal about how Luke sees Jesus. The demoniac moves from living naked among graves (an exceedingly bad sign) to sitting quietly at Jesus' feet (a very good sign). Not only is he 'saved', which is altogether a more powerful thing than being healed; but Jesus was up against immense odds: the demons were numerous, powerful enough to break chains, and sufficient in numbers to send a herd of pigs to a watery grave in Galilee (and thereby cease to be a threat). Jesus' mastery of them is effortless, and as we ask Luke who Jesus is we may notice that the man, who has been told to recount what great things **God** *has done for him, ends up by proclaiming the great things that* **Jesus** *has done for him. There is no hint here that Luke thinks that the man has disobeyed Jesus, or got him wrong.*

What does this story tell us about the relationship between Jesus and God?

Jairus's only daughter, and a woman with a haemorrhage

40-56 As Jesus returned, the crowd welcomed him. For they were all waiting for him. And look! A man came, whose name was Jairus; and he was ruler of the synagogue, and falling at Jesus' feet he begged him to come into his house, because his only daughter was about twelve – and she was dying.

As he went, the crowds were crushing him. And a woman who had had a flow of blood for twelve years, who had spent all her livelihood on doctors, couldn't be cured by anybody, approached from behind and touched the hem of his garment. And straightaway the flow of her blood stopped!

And Jesus said, 'Who is the one who touched me?' They all denied it, and Peter said, 'Master, the crowds are pressing hard on you and jostling you . . . '

But Jesus said, 'Someone touched me, because I felt power going out of me.' The woman realised that she had not got away with it. Trembling, she came and fell before him, and, before all the populace, recounted the reason why she had touched him, and how she had been healed straightaway.

He said to her, 'Daughter, your faith has saved you – go in peace.'

While he was still speaking, someone comes from the president of the synagogue's house saying, 'Your daughter is dead. Don't bother the teacher any more.'

Jesus heard [this] and answered him, 'Don't be afraid – just believe, and she will be saved.' When he came into the house, he allowed no one to come with him except Peter and John and James, and the father and mother of the child. They were all weeping and mourning for her; but he said, 'Don't weep; she hasn't died, but is asleep.'

And they laughed at him – they knew that she was dead.

And he took her hand and spoke to her, saying, 'Girl, arise.' And her spirit returned, and she arose straightaway; and he gave instructions that something [should] be given her to eat. And her parents were amazed; but he directed them to tell no one what had happened.

Luke found this story ready-made in Mark's Gospel, two tales, one wrapped round the other. He has made some changes, but mainly in the direction of tidying up Mark's roughnesses and smoothing his angularities. Mark portrays Peter's response as harsh and sarcastic, for example, where Luke has made it gentler. They remain two very charming stories, and demonstrate Jesus' ease with women and his indifference to ritual impurity (a woman with a haemorrhage and a woman who might be a corpse were serious snares for those who worried about such things).

Why do these two stories come together, do you think?

The Twelve are sent out (and there is an interlude)

9 1-10 Summoning the Twelve, he gave them power and authority over all demons, and to cure diseases, and he sent them to proclaim the kingdom of God and to heal the sick; and he said to them, 'Do not take anything for the way, neither a staff nor a bag, nor bread nor silver – and not even to have two tunics. And whatever house you enter, remain there and come out from there. And whoever fails to give you hospitality, when you come out from that city, shake the dust off your feet as a sign against them.'

They went out and went through one village after another, preaching the gospel, and healing everywhere.

INTERLUDE

Herod the tetrarch heard the things that were happening; and he was quite perplexed, because it was being said by some people that John the Baptist had been raised from the dead, by some that Elijah had appeared, and by others again that one of the prophets of the ancients had arisen. But Herod said, 'John? I beheaded him; but who is this about whom I hear such things?'

And he was wanting to see him.

And when they returned, the apostles explained to him what great things they had done. And he took them and retreated in privacy to a city called Bethsaida.

Luke is more or less following Mark here, though he emphasises the healing of the sick slightly more. One change that he has apparently made concerns the 'interlude'. While the apostles were out on the mission, Mark inserted the story of the death of John, partly, no doubt, to fill the gap, but also partly to remind the reader of what discipleship might involve. Luke has done something slightly different. He has placed the imprisonment of John the Baptist, and its reason (accusations about Herodias) back in Chapter 3, where it brings John's ministry to an end. Then in our present passage, he adds that 'he was wanting to see him', which will be picked up at the time of Jesus' passion, when Luke alone reports a meeting between Jesus and this same Herod (Luke 23:6-12, especially verse 8).

The apostles report having done 'great things'. Are you called to do the same?

The feeding of the five thousand men

11-17 But the crowds found out and followed him. And he welcomed them and started speaking to them about the kingdom of God; and those who had need of healing he cured. The day began to wane, and the Twelve approached and said to him, 'Let the crowd go, so that they may journey to the villages and farms round about, and rest and find provisions, because here we're in a desert place.'

He said to them, 'Give them something to eat yourselves.'

But they said, 'We have no more than five loaves and two fish. Unless we are to go [journey] and buy foodstuffs for the whole of this crowd?' (For they were about five thousand men.)

He said to his disciples, 'Make them lie down to eat in groups of about fifty.' And they did so, and made them all lie down.

And taking the five loaves and the two fish, he looked up to heaven and blessed them and broke them and gave them to the disciples to set before the crowd. And they all ate and were satisfied, and their surplus was taken up, twelve baskets of fragments.

This is a powerful story; Luke tells it more or less as Mark has told it, except that Luke and John have only one story of feeding the multitudes, where Mark and Matthew have two. Luke characteristically adds the action of Jesus' 'hospitality' ('he welcomed them') and the healing of diseases. We are taken back to the story of God's feeding the People of Israel in the desert (see, for example, Exodus 16:13-18).

The idea of 'hospitality' is very important in Luke's Gospel. Why do you think this is?

Peter's identification of Jesus, and the teaching it provokes

18-27 And it happened when he was praying on his own, his disciples were with him, and he asked them, 'Who do the crowds say I am?' They answered and said, 'John the Baptist; and others Elijah; and others that one of the prophets of old has arisen.'

He said to them, 'But you people, who do ***you*** say I am?'

Peter replied and said, 'The Messiah of God.' He scolded them, and instructed them to say this to nobody, saying, 'The Son of Man must suffer many things and be rejected by the elders and high priests and scribes and be killed – and on the third day be raised up.'

He said to everyone, 'If anyone wants to come after me, let them deny themselves, and take up their cross every day and follow me. For whoever wants to preserve their life will lose it, and whoever loses their life for my sake, that person will preserve it. For how is a person helped, if they gain the whole world and lose or forfeit their very self? For whoever is ashamed of me and of my words, the Son of Man will be ashamed of that person, when he comes in his splendour, and in the splendour of his Father and of the holy angels. I tell you truly, there are some of those standing here who will not taste death until they see the kingdom of God.'

Luke, we have said, is the Gospel of prayer, and it is characteristic that he presents Jesus as praying at this important moment of Peter's accurate recognition of him. Much less is made by Luke than by Mark and Matthew of Peter's subsequent failure to grasp what **kind** *of Messiah he is.*

You may puzzle about how Jesus can be both 'on his own' and with his disciples. Perhaps we should not ask Luke this question. Another puzzle concerns Jesus' statement that 'there are some of those standing here who will not taste death until they see the kingdom of God'. Jesus and the early Church certainly seem to have expected the Second Coming fairly soon after the Resurrection. We have learnt not to expect it to be coming so soon.

Notice that the range of answers to the question who Jesus is coincides, almost exactly, with the suggestions earlier in the chapter. Luke is perhaps here tidying up what he found in Mark; but he is also making this recognition moment far less central than it was in Mark's Gospel; he even removes the reference to Caesarea Philippi. At the same time, the reference to the 'splendour of the Son of Man', in the context of the Father and the angels, indicates that Luke has a very 'high' view of who Jesus is; he is God, or the nearest thing to God. And, in the same vein, notice the references to 'splendour' in the story that now follows.

Are we a bit complacent about Jesus' Second Coming?

The glory of Jesus with Moses and Elijah

28-36 It happened about eight days after these words [or: 'events'] that taking Peter and John and James he went up onto the mountain to pray. And it happened as he prayed that the appearance of his face was different; and his clothing was white, gleaming like lightning. And look! Two men were speaking with him, who were Moses and Elijah. They appeared in splendour, and were speaking of his departure [or: exodus] which he was to accomplish in Jerusalem.

Now Peter and those with him were overcome with sleep; and when they were fully awake, they saw his splendour, and the two men standing with him. And when they were separated from him, Peter said to Jesus, 'Master, it is right for us to be here – and let's make three tents, one for you and one for Moses and one for Elijah (having no idea what he was saying)'. As he was saying this, there was a cloud, and it overshadowed them. They were afraid when they entered the cloud; and a voice came from the cloud, saying, 'This is my Son, the Chosen One – listen to him.' And when the voice had come, Jesus alone was there. And they were silent; and in those days they reported to nobody any of the things which they had seen.

Luke makes some small changes (and we may notice that he has omitted much of Mark's Chapters 6 to 8). Once again, he has Jesus at prayer; the transfiguration itself is in a slightly lower key (unlike Mark, he does not even use the word). Luke alone has Moses and Elijah speaking of Jesus' 'exodus' or 'departure'. This could also refer to his death, of course, and it looks ahead, as this Gospel has always done, to Jerusalem. The 'overshadowing' is also in Mark, but it reminds Luke's reader of what happened to Mary when Jesus was conceived (1:35). Luke alone has the disciples weighed down by sleep. Finally, Luke has softened Mark's abrupt command to silence at the end of the story.

'Listen to him.' Is this a command to us?

The spirit the disciples couldn't expel

37-43a It happened on the next day, as they went down from the mountain, that a great crowd met them. And look! A man shouted from the crowd, 'Teacher, I implore you to look kindly on my son, because he is my only one, and look! A spirit takes him, and he suddenly cries out, and it convulses him and he foams; and it hardly leaves him, and it wears him out. And I asked your disciples to expel it – and they couldn't!'

Jesus responded, 'O faithless and perverted generation – how long shall I be with you and put up with you? Bring your son here.'

As he was still approaching, the demon threw him down and convulsed him. Jesus rebuked the unclean spirit, and healed the boy, and restored him to his father. They were all struck by the greatness of God.

This is a much briefer version than Mark's account of the incident (Mark 9:14-29), and Luke is gentler with the disciples. There are at least three characteristic Lucan touches: 'the next day' (see 7:11); 'look kindly' (1:48), and 'the greatness of God' (see, for example 1:46, 49, 58; 9:43, each of which uses the same Greek root). There is less detail in Luke's version, but he has introduced a typical reference to 'healing'.

'They were all struck by the greatness of God.' Is there something for us here?

The suffering of the Son of Man; the unresponsive disciples

43b-50 While everyone wondered at everything that he was doing, he said to his disciples, 'Put these words into your ears: you see, the Son of Man is about to be handed over into the power of human beings.'

But they had no idea of this matter, and it was concealed from them, so that they should [not] understand it – and they were afraid to ask him about this matter.

An argument arose among them – 'Who was likely to be the Most Important?' Jesus knew about the argument of their heart; and he took hold of a little boy, and stood him next to him, and said to them, 'Whoever welcomes this little boy in my name welcomes me. And whoever welcomes me welcomes the one who sent me. For the least significant among you, that is Mr Big.'

John responded, 'Master, we saw someone casting out demons in your name – and we tried to prevent him, because he is not a disciple with us.'

Jesus said, 'Don't prevent him – for whoever is not against you is on your side.'

The three elements that make up this section are all in Mark 9:30-41, but Luke is gentler, less harshly mysterious than Mark, and includes less detail.

What is the picture of Jesus that emerges from these scenes?

THE JOURNEY TO JERUSALEM (9:51-19:40)

The journey begins

51-62 It happened when the days of his taking-up were fulfilled, he also set his face to journey to Jerusalem. And he sent messengers before his face. And as they journeyed, they went into a village of the Samaritans, to prepare for him. And they did not offer him hospitality, because his face was journeying to Jerusalem. When they saw it, disciples James and John said, 'Lord, do you want us to tell fire to come down from heaven and annihilate them?'

But he turned and rebuked them – and they journeyed to another village.

And as they journeyed on the way, someone said to him, 'I'll follow you wherever you go.'

And Jesus said to him, 'Foxes have lairs, and birds of the sky have places to live, but the Son of Man has nowhere to recline his head.'

He said to another, 'Follow me.' But he said, 'Lord, let me first go and bury my father.'

But he said to him, 'Let the corpses bury their own corpses – as for you, off you go and proclaim the kingdom of God far and wide.'

And another said, 'I'll follow you, Lord – but first allow me to say farewell to those at my house.'

Jesus said to him, 'No one who puts his hand to the plough and looks back is suitable for the kingdom of God.'

At this point, Luke turns his Gospel very firmly in the direction of Jerusalem. The use of the word 'fulfilled' takes us back to 1:1, where we have the same idea, if not precisely the same Greek word. He uses the word 'taking-up' here. The verb is the one used in Acts for Jesus' Ascension; but in the light of the recent conversation that we have overheard between Moses, Elijah and Jesus, we also know that it refers to Jesus' Death and Resurrection.

Luke uses his 'journeying' word five times in these few lines, to underline that something is starting here, which only ends with his arrival in Jerusalem at the end of Chapter 19. There are other aspects to the journey:

- *it includes Samaria (important in the journey, and also in the reverse journey that is Acts, at least at its beginning; we should note that Samaritans generally get a good press in Luke – see 10:33, 17:16. They were highly unpopular with the inhabitants of Judah, for they were thought to be of mixed race and doubtful orthodoxy);*
- *the quotation about 'messengers before his face' is used by Mark (1:2) and Matthew (11:10) for John the Baptist;*
- *note the three (rather discouraging) remarks to would-be disciples. Luke has collected them here as a preface to the journey, just as he made the episode in the synagogue at Nazareth a preface to Jesus' ministry as a whole. The third episode is not paralleled in Matthew, but echoes the call of Elisha in 1 Kings 19:20;*
- *the fiery desires of James and John may explain why (according to Mark) they were nicknamed 'Sons of Thunder'. It may be significant that they echo Elijah (2 Kings 1:10, 12);*
- *notice that Jesus 'turns' to these would-be terrorists. In Luke this word denotes careful attention. See 7:9, 44; 10:29; 14:25, and especially perhaps 22:61 (Peter) and 23:28 (the women of Jerusalem).*

What kind of a journey are we on here?

The mission of the seventy-two, and their joyful return

10 1-24 After this, the Lord appointed another seventy-two, and sent them in pairs before his face to every town and place where he was intending to go. He said to them, 'The harvest is great, but the labourers are few; therefore implore the Lord of the harvest to send out labourers into his harvest.

'Go. Look! I am sending you as lambs in the midst of wolves. Do not carry a money bag or a knapsack, or sandals, and greet no one on the way. Whatever house you enter, first say, "Peace upon this house!" and if there is a peace-person [literally: 'son of peace'] there, your peace will rest upon that person. Otherwise it will return to you. Stay in that house, eating and drinking their food and drink; for the labourer is worthy of his hire. Do not transfer from house to house. And whatever city you enter, and they give you hospitality, eat what is put before you, and cure the sick who are in the city, and tell them, "The kingdom of God has drawn near upon you." Whatever city you enter, and they fail to give you hospitality, go out into its streets and say, "Because of you [or: 'for you'] we shall even wipe off the dust that clings to us from your city. But be aware that the kingdom of God has drawn near." I am telling you: it will be more bearable for Sodom on that day than for that city.

'Woe to you, Chorazin; woe to you, Bethsaida. Because if the miracles that took place in you had happened in Tyre and Sidon, they would long since have sat down and repented. But for Tyre and Sidon it will be more bearable at the Judgement than it will be for you.

'And you Caphernaum – do you want to be exalted up to heaven? You will go down to Hades!

'The one who listens to you people, listens to me; the one who rejects you rejects me; and the one who rejects me rejects the one who sent me.'

The seventy-two returned joyfully; they said, 'Lord – even the demons do what we tell them [literally: 'are subordinated to us'] in your name!'

He told them, 'I saw Satan falling from heaven like lightning. Look! I have given you authority to tread on snakes and scorpions, and on all the Enemy's power – and no way will anything hurt you. But don't rejoice because the spirits do what you tell them; instead, rejoice that your names are written in heaven.'

At that moment, he rejoiced in the Holy Spirit and said, 'I give thanks to you, Father, Lord of heaven and earth, because you have hidden these things from clever and intelligent people, and revealed them to infants. Yes, Father, because that was the way you wanted it to be. Everything is handed over to me by my Father; and no one knows who the Son is except the Father, nor who the Father is except the Son, and whoever the Son wishes to reveal it to.'

And turning privately to the disciples he said, 'Happy are the eyes who see what you see. For I tell you that many prophets and kings wanted to see what you see, and didn't see it, and to hear what you hear and didn't hear it.'

These instructions before the seventy-two go out, and the comments on their return, are really a version of the 'ripple effect', and so part of the journeying theme. Matthew (9:37, 38; 10:7-15) has a good deal of the material, but only Luke makes it a preliminary to Jesus' mission. Luke has some slightly daunting touches, such as the instruction to 'greet nobody on the way'. Luke alone has the tail-wagging return of the emissaries, to which he joins Jesus' thanksgiving to the Father, which is also in Matthew, but not part of this episode. The same is true of the congratulations to the disciples. Luke has made a coherent unit out of it, perhaps an indication of the importance he gives to the 'ripple effect'.

Are the instructions to the seventy-two aimed also at us?

The lawyer's question, and a *good* Samaritan!

25-37 And look! A certain lawyer stood up, putting him to the test, and said, 'Teacher, what shall I do to inherit eternal life?'

He said, 'In the Torah what is written? How do you read [it]?'

He answered, '"You will love the Lord your God with all your heart and with all your soul and with all your strength and with all your understanding, and your neighbour as yourself." '

He said to him, 'You have given the correct answer. Do this, and you will live.'

But he wanted to put himself in the right, and said to Jesus, 'And who ***is*** my neighbour?'

Jesus took up the thread and said, 'A man was going down from Jerusalem to Jericho, and he fell into the hands of muggers. They took his clothes off, rained blows on him, and went off leaving him half dead. By coincidence, a priest was going down on that road, and, seeing him, passed by on the opposite side. A Levite also went down by that spot, and when he saw him, similarly passed by on the opposite side. Then a travelling Samaritan came upon him, and when he saw [him] he had compassion! He approached and bound up his wounds, pouring olive oil and wine on them; and he put him on his own animal, and took him to an inn, and looked after him. And the next day he took out two denarii and gave them to the innkeeper, and said, "Look after him, and whatever extra you spend, I'll repay you when I return."

'Which of these three, in your view, acted as neighbour to the one who had fallen into the muggers' hands?'

He said, 'The one who did the mercy on him.'

Jesus said to him, 'Journey on, and [make sure] you do the same.'

This is the first of many lovely Lucan parables. A version of this episode is in both Mark (12:28-31) and Matthew (22:35-40), each with their own differences. Lawyers on the whole do not do well in Luke's Gospel, whereas Samaritans generally get a good press from him.

The alert reader will notice that the story is set in the context of some rather dangerous journeying, and that at the end the lawyer is told to 'journey'.

The road on which the story is set will doubtless have been familiar to Jesus' hearers, as will the perils of it, for it runs through the desert, with hills on either side, ideal for setting an ambush.

The best stories are told in threes ('an Englishman, an Irishman and a Scotsman', for example), and the third member contains the key. We may imagine Jesus' audience chuckling at the behaviour of the clergy, expecting No. 3 to be 'an ordinary layman' perhaps, and then getting a dreadful shock when he turned out to be a hated Samaritan.

What class of person would you use when telling this story in ***your*** *situation?*

The third 'disastrous dinner party': Martha and Mary

38-42 As they journeyed, ***he*** went into a village. Now a woman called Martha gave him hospitality; and she had a sister called Mary, who, when she had sat down by the Lord's feet, kept listening to what he said. Now Martha was distracted with much service, and she came up and said, 'Lord – don't you care that my sister has abandoned me to serve all alone? So tell her to come and help me.'

The Lord said to her in reply, 'Martha, Martha: you're over-anxious and disturbed about many things; there is need only of one thing. You see, Mary has chosen the better portion, and it won't be taken away from her.'

This is another lovely story; the companions of the journey suddenly disappear, and we find Jesus alone with two women, which must have seemed odd for a religious teacher. The women, however, are presented as people in their own right: Martha is the hostess (no man in sight), and Mary a disciple. Martha is not given the help that she asks for, but the gentle repetition of her name softens any lurking rebuke, though we may observe that, just as the lawyer in the previous story could not sully his lips with the word 'Samaritan', so here Martha cannot bring herself to mention her sister's name.

Mary is like that other woman (7:38), sitting at Jesus' feet; Martha's plight is neatly expressed in the notion of 'much service' and 'serving all alone': 'service' is a value in Luke's Gospel, but when it is experienced as heavy, and as lonely, then it has turned into something else, and Martha finds herself giving orders to her eminent guest, which puts her mildly in the wrong, although Luke does not tell us how the remainder of the dinner party goes.

Do you sympathise with Martha or with Mary? What does that tell you about yourself?

Teaching about prayer

11 1-13 And it happened when he was in a certain place praying. When he ceased, one of his disciples said to him, 'Lord, teach us to pray, as John also taught his disciples.'

He said to them, 'When you pray, say:

Father – may your name be sanctified.
May your kingdom come.
Each day, give us our bread for the coming day.
And forgive us our sins,
for we ourselves also forgive everyone who is in debt to us.
And do not put us to the test.'

And he said to them, 'Suppose one of you has a friend come to him in the middle of the night and say to him, "My friend, lend me three loaves, because my friend has appeared at my house after a journey, and I have nothing to put before him" – would any of you reply from inside, "Don't bother me: the door is already locked, and my children and I are in bed. I can't get up and give you [anything]"? I tell you – even if he won't get up and give him something because he's a friend, his friend's persistence will make him arise and give him all he needs.

'And ***I*** am telling ***you***: ask, and it will be given you; seek, and you will find; knock [at the door], and it will be opened to you. For everyone who asks receives; the one who seeks, finds; and to the one who knocks [on the door] it is opened.

'Suppose that one of you is a father, and his son asks for a fish – is he going to give him a snake instead of a fish? Or suppose he asks for an egg – is he going to give him a scorpion?

'So – if you people (who are wicked) are competent to give appropriate gifts to your children, will not your Heavenly Father all the more give the Holy Spirit to those who ask him?'

Luke, as we have already said, is the Gospel of prayer; this passage is the first place where the evangelist has put together any explicit teaching on prayer. The beginning and the end are in Matthew's Sermon on the Mount (6:9-13 and 7:7-11), while the middle section, the quietly humorous tale of the friend who arrives at midnight, is only in Luke. The first section is Luke's version of the Lord's Prayer, different in many respects from Matthew's (which Christians know better), but still recognisably the same. Luke's version is shorter, and many scholars think it may be more original.

What is the teaching about prayer? First, the disciples regard it as a bit puzzling, but something that they ought to do, and that Jesus ought to teach them to do, if only to keep up with the spiritual Jones's ('the disciples of John the Baptist'). Second the parable of the friend at midnight with gentle humour (imagining God as someone who would rather stay in bed!) teaches what prayer is like: it is a relationship between friends, who will cheerfully give other friends what they need. There are three 'friends' in the parable, the one in bed, the one who wants bread, and the one who has been on a journey, and the repetition of the word may seem a bit clumsy, until we realise what Luke is doing: the key to prayer is friendship. God is not, therefore, a drinks dispenser, which discharges the appropriate substance when the appropriate coin is inserted and the right button pressed. That is the explanation of the otherwise very difficult passage, 'ask and it will be given you . . . '; and when Luke uses the 'divine passives', such as 'it will be given', he is reminding us that we are speaking of God. We can be confident of God's unfailing generosity; but it is not for us to lay down the rules. And we are positively encouraged to be persistent, to the point of shamelessness. Third, though, we should notice that Jesus uses quite powerful, active verbs for talking about prayer: 'ask', 'seek', and 'find' suggest that we are supposed to take an initiative in prayer, and present our needs: Luke's version of the Lord's Prayer is all requests, although of course we may always have to recognise that God may know better than we do what we need.

How should we pray?

Is Jesus working *with* the demons or *against* them?

14-26 And he was expelling a demon; and it was dumb. It turned out that when the demon left, the dumb man spoke – and the crowds were astonished. Some of them, however, said, 'It is by Beelzeboul, the ruler of the demons, that he casts out demons,' while others put him to the test by asking him for a sign from heaven. But he knew their thoughts, and told them, 'Every kingdom that is divided against itself is laid waste, and house falls on house. Now – if Satan is divided against himself, how is his kingdom going to stand, since you say that it is by Beelzeboul that I am expelling demons? You see, if it is by Beelzeboul that I am expelling demons, by whom do your people expel them? So it is they who will be your judges. If, on the other hand, it is by the finger of God that I expel demons – then the kingdom of God has come upon you!

'When the strong man, fully armed, is guarding his own palace, then his possessions are at peace. However whenever someone who is stronger than he is comes and defeats him, he takes away the full armour that he had relied on; and he shares out his booty.

'The one who is not with me is against me; and the one who does not gather with me scatters.

'When the unclean spirit leaves the person, he goes through waterless places, looking for rest, and not finding it. Then it says, "I'll go back to the home I came from." And it comes and finds it swept and decorated. Then it goes on a journey and finds seven other [demons] wickeder than it is – and they go in and dwell there. And that person's final state is worse than their first.'

Like Jesus' contemporaries, Luke's readers have to decide who Jesus is: clearly he meets with demons as a worthy opponent. So is he on their side or on God's side? Jesus here makes one or two sensible observations to help answer the question – and we cannot evade the conclusion, that 'the kingdom of God has come upon you', nor the challenge: are we for him or against him? And we are warned to take the demons seriously.

Are you for Jesus or against him?

A woman's intervention is capped

27, 28 It happened as he was saying this that a woman from the crowd raised her voice and said to him, 'Happy the womb that bore you, and the breasts which you sucked.' But he said, 'On the contrary – happy are those who hear the word of God and keep it.'

Luke is the Gospel of women; but that does not mean that women always get it right. Here, a woman's attempt to congratulate Jesus' mother turns into a congratulation of all disciples 'who hear the word of God and keep it'. We remember Mary, of course, in the previous chapter, who did just that, not to mention that other Mary, Jesus' mother, who 'kept all these words, pondering them in her heart' and 'kept all these events in her heart'.

Teaching: repentance and visibility

29-36 When the crowds had gathered even more, he began to say, 'This generation is a wicked generation: it looks for a sign, and it won't be given a sign, except for Jonah's sign; for just as Jonah was a sign for the people of Nineveh, that's how the Son of Man will be for this generation. The Queen of the South will rise up at the Judgement with the men of this generation, and condemn them – because she came from the ends of the earth to hear the wisdom of Solomon; and look! There's [something] more than Solomon here. The men of Nineveh will rise up with this generation at the Judgement and condemn it – because they repented at Jonah's proclamation. And look! There's [something] more than Jonah here.

'No one lights a lamp and puts it in a cellar, but on the lamp-stand, so that those who journey into [the house] may see the light.

'The light of the body is your eye. When your eye is healthy [or: simple, clear], then the whole of your body is illuminated. But if it is bad, then your body is darkened. Watch out: [you don't want] the light that is in you to become darkness. So if your whole body is illuminated, not having even a little bit [of it] darkened, it will be entirely illuminated, as when the lamp illuminates you with its beam.'

These bits of teaching are found also in Matthew, though in different places (Matthew 12:38-42; 5:15; 6:34), so perhaps it is Luke who has brought them together, except that they do not obviously belong together. We may notice, though, that the 'sign of Jonah' in Matthew 12:40 had to do with the Resurrection, whereas in Luke, the 'Gospel of repentance', it is about repentance. The alert reader will have noticed that Luke has already used a different version of the saying about 'lighting a lamp' back in 8:16. We may also observe that it is men, and not women, who are going to be judged, and that the Queen of Sheba, not only a woman, but also a foreigner, will be doing the judgement. Luke is the Gospel of the marginalised.

Could we be accused of 'looking for signs' instead of repenting?

The fourth 'disastrous dinner party'

37-54 As he was speaking, a Pharisee invited him to have breakfast with him at his house. He went in and lay down. When the Pharisee saw [it], he was surprised that he didn't have a ritual washing first, before breakfast. The Lord said to him, 'Now you Pharisees, you clean the outside of cup and dish; but your inside is full of robbery and wickedness. Fools! Did not the One who made the outside also make the inside? So – give alms on what is within, and see, everything will be clean for you.

'No – woe to you Pharisees: you pay tithes of mint and rue, and every kind of vegetable, and you overlook God's judgement and love; ***that***'s what you should have performed, without overlooking the other things.

'Woe to you, Pharisees: you love the chief seats in the synagogues and being greeted in the market place.

'Woe to you: you are like graves which are not seen, and people walk on top without knowing.'

One of the lawyers answered, 'Teacher, when you say this, it's us also whom you are insulting.' And he said, 'And to you lawyers also, woe! Because you put hard-to-bear burdens on to people; but you yourselves do not touch the burdens with [even] a single finger!

'Woe to you, because you build the prophets' tombs. Your ancestors killed them: you are witnesses, and you approve of your ancestors' deeds, because they killed them and you build [their tombs]. For this reason, the Wisdom of God said, "I shall send them prophets and apostles, and some of them they will kill and persecute," in order that vengeance may be exacted for the blood of all the prophets which has been shed since the foundation of the world, from Abel's blood to the blood of Zechariah, who was killed between altar and Temple. And, I tell you, it will be exacted from this generation.

'Woe to you lawyers, because you took away the key of knowledge: you yourselves didn't enter, and you managed to thwart those who were trying to enter.'

And when he went out of there, the scribes and the Pharisees started to be very resentful and to watch closely what he said on a wider range of topics, and to plot to catch him out in something he might say.

This fourth 'disastrous dinner party' ends with the battlelines clearly drawn. Jesus has deliberately annoyed Pharisees, lawyers and scribes, admittedly after his host had thought disapproving thoughts about his lack of ritual observance (the word translated as 'surprised', with more than a hint of disapproval, elsewhere in Luke means, positively, 'marvel'), and now they are out to get him. Some of what Jesus says to the lawyers is very obscure, especially the utterance by the 'Wisdom of God' and the talk about 'building' – but there is nothing obscure about our sense that conflict is brewing.

When the conflict comes, whose side are you on?

Teaching the disciples

12 1-12 In the middle of this, as vast numbers of the crowd had gathered, [so many] that they were trampling each other, he began to speak to his disciples: 'First and foremost, steer clear of the leaven (which is hypocrisy) of the Pharisees.

'Nothing is hidden which will not be revealed; and nothing concealed which will not be made known. Therefore whatever you say in the darkness will be heard in the light, and whatever you speak confidentially [literally: 'into the ear'] in the innermost rooms will be proclaimed on the rooftops.

'I am telling you who are my friends: don't be fearful of those who kill the body, and after that have nothing further [that they can] do; I'll show you whom to fear: be afraid of the one who, after he has killed you, has authority to throw you into Gehenna. Yes, I tell you: be afraid of that one.

'Are not five sparrows sold for two assaria? And not one of these is forgotten by [literally: 'before'] God. No – the hairs of your head are all numbered. Don't be afraid; you are worth more than many sparrows.

'I tell you, everyone who speaks up for me before human beings, the Son of Man will speak up for that person before God's angels. And the person who denies me before human beings will be denied before the angels of God.

'And whoever says a word against the Son of Man, it will be forgiven him; whereas the one who blasphemes against the Holy Spirit will not be forgiven.

'When they bring you in before synagogues and authorities and magistrates, don't get anxious about how to make your defence or what to say. For the Holy Spirit at that moment will give you what you must say.'

The connections between the various parts of this speech are not easy to see, unless the link is the idea of unfailing faithfulness even when persecution comes. Jesus' disciples must expect the same treatment as he received. This passage starts with a reference back to the Pharisees of the previous episode ('beware of their leaven'), continues with some general warnings: don't presume confidentiality; don't fear the wrong people; be confident of your worth before God; don't be ashamed of the Son of Man; (above all) don't blaspheme the Holy Spirit, who will tell you what to say when you are arraigned.

Assarion: one-sixteenth of a denarius. Just think of the smallest coin that you can imagine. The word Gehenna means (or nearly means) 'Valley of the Brothers Hinnom', a valley in Jerusalem where waste was burnt and corpses buried, so a symbol of decay and pollution.

In what ways do we deny Christ?

Teaching about riches

13-21 Someone spoke to him from the crowd, 'Teacher, tell my brother to divide the inheritance with me.'

But he said to him, 'Man! Who appointed me a referee or arbitrator over you people?'

He said to them, 'Look out and guard yourselves from all greed; because a person's life does not consist in having enough-and-to-spare in the way of possessions.'

He told them a parable: 'A certain wealthy person had an estate that had done well. And he debated with himself: "What then am I to do? I have nowhere to put my produce." He said, "This is what I shall do: I'll pull down all my storehouses and build bigger ones; and I'll bring all my grain and all my goods together in them. And I'll tell my soul, 'Soul – you have many good things stored up for many years. Take it easy – eat and drink and have a good time.'" But God said to him, "Fool! This very night your life [or: soul] is being asked back from you. The stuff that you prepared – whose will it be?" That's how it is with people who save up for themselves and are not wealthy in regard to God.'

This passage is only in Luke, the request and Jesus' response. It is characteristic of Luke's rather negative attitude to wealth, which may have sent a shiver down the spine of his affluent church (assuming that is what they were). The parable is a bit starker than Luke generally goes in for, and the characterisation rather more two-dimensional (though see also the story of Lazarus and the rich man – Luke 16:19-31), but that may simply reflect the urgency he gives to the principle of detachment from possessions in the Christian life.

Jesus' response 'Man' may sound like modern American slang, but a) it is a literal translation and b) it probably catches the tone of the original. The phrase translated as 'is being asked back' literally means 'they are asking back'. Like 'these things will be added to you' in the next section (12:31), this is Luke's discreet way of indicating that God is at work.

In what way is life 'more than food and the body more than clothing'?

No material worries: God will look after you

22-34 He said to his disciples, 'For this reason, I'm telling you: Don't worry about your life [or: soul], what you are to eat, nor about your body, what you're to wear. For life is more than food, and the body is more than clothing. Think of the ravens: they don't sow or reap; they have no cellars or storehouses, and God feeds them! How much more important are you than [mere] birds? Which of you, by worrying, can add an hour to the length of your life? So if you can't even do the tiniest thing, why are you worrying about the rest? Look at how lilies grow: they don't work [for a living]; nor do they weave [cloth]. But I'm telling you, not even Solomon in all his glory was dressed like one of them! Now – if God dresses up hay like this, which is in the field today, and tomorrow thrown into an oven, won't [he do] all the more for you, people of little faith? So don't you start looking for something to eat or something to drink; and don't be anxious. You see this is what the nations of the world are looking for; but your Father knows that you need these things. Just look for his kingdom, and God will supply you with these things in addition. Don't be afraid, little flock – because your Father in heaven has been pleased to give you the kingdom.

'Sell your possessions and give alms. Manufacture moneybags for yourselves that never grow old, inexhaustible treasure in heaven, where no burglar approaches, and no moths gobble [it] up. For where your treasure is, that is where your heart will be.'

This passage fits well enough with the previous passage and Luke's emphasis on the danger of possessions, although it is a text that Luke largely shares with Matthew, with the order slightly altered.

'Don't worry,' he tells us. How might we try to do that?

The starkness of discipleship: on being ready for the end-time

35-59 'Be dressed for action; have your lamps burning. You [are to be] like people expecting their Lord when he returns from the wedding, so that when he comes and knocks they immediately open up for him. Happy are those slaves whom the Lord finds still awake when he comes. Amen I tell you: he will put on his clothes, make them lie down to eat, and come and wait on them. Congratulations to them if he comes even in the second watch or even in the third watch and finds them like this.

But be sure of this: if the householder knew what time the burglar was coming, he wouldn't allow his house to be broken into. And so you must be ready, because the Son of Man is coming at a time when you don't think he will.'

Peter said to him, 'Lord, are you telling this parable to us or to everybody?'

And the Lord said to him, 'So who is the reliable and sensible steward, whom the Lord will appoint over his servants, to give out the food-allowance at the proper time? Congratulations to that slave whom the Lord when he comes finds doing this. Truly I tell you that he will appoint him in charge of all his possessions. If however that slave says in his heart, "My Lord is taking his time in coming," and begins beating the male and female slaves, and [starts] eating and drinking and getting drunk, that slave's Lord will come on a day when he does not expect, and at a time [that] he does not know – and he'll cut him in two and set his portion with the unbelievers.

'That slave who knows what his Lord wants, and hasn't prepared or acted in accordance with his will, shall be beaten many times. On the other hand, the one who did not know, but has done what deserves chastisement, shall be beaten fewer times. Everyone to whom God has given much, God will demand much from them. The one to whom God has entrusted much, God will demand much more from them.

'I have come to set fire to the earth, and what do I want, if it is already kindled? [or: 'how I wish it were already blazing']. I have a baptism to be baptised with – and how great is my distress until it is accomplished. Do you think that I came to give peace on earth? No, I tell you: I came to bring division. For from now on, there will be five in a single house, divided three against two and two against three; father will be divided against son, and son against father, mother against daughter and daughter against mother, mother-in-law against daughter-in-law, and daughter-in-law against mother-in-law.'

And he said to the crowds, 'When you see a cloud arising in the west, immediately you say, "A rainstorm is on its way" – and so it turns out. And when [you notice] the south wind blowing, you say, "It'll be a scorcher" – and it happens. Hypocrites [or: actors]! You know how to interpret the appearance of earth and sky, but you have no idea how to interpret this moment?

'Why don't you assess what is right on your own account? When you are going to the magistrate with your opponent, while you are travelling, take the trouble to settle with him, in case he drags you to the judge, and the judge hands you over to the constable, and the constable flings you into prison. I'm telling you, no way will you come out of there, till you have paid the last penny.'

There is some uncomfortable teaching here; some fragments of it appear in Matthew, but Luke has made much more of a discourse of it. In one way it seems to continue the previous discourse; but the sudden shift to 'readiness for the end' and the change of tone seem to justify making a new section of it.

There are one or two shocks:

- *the idea of the Lord (or Master) putting on his waiter's outfit and feeding his own slaves is decidedly unexpected. Perhaps Luke is trying to startle his affluent readers;*

- *the word Lord/Master shifts between Jesus and the slave-owner in an interesting and startling way, although when Jesus' hearers are warned that they'll be placed with 'unbelievers' if they are asleep when he comes, it is clear that we are not precisely speaking of real servants, but of disciples;*
- *Jesus asks if we think that he has come to bring 'peace on earth'. The answer is 'Yes', because that is what the angels indicated to the shepherds in 2:14;*
- *even Luke's grammar becomes rather jarring here, but it can't be done in English.*

How does Luke's teaching on wealth strike you? Uncomfortably? If so, why?

On repentance – the parable of the fig tree

13 1-9 At that time some people were there, telling him about the Galileans whose blood Pilate had mixed with their sacrifices. In reply he said to them, 'Do you think that these Galileans were worse than all other Galileans, that they suffered this? No, I tell you: unless you all repent, you will die in a similar way. Or what about the eighteen people on whom the tower at Siloam fell and killed them – do you think that they were worse sinners [or: debtors] than everyone else who lives in Jerusalem? No, I tell you: unless you all repent, you will die in just the same way.'

He told this parable: 'A person had a fig tree planted in his vineyard, and he came looking for fruit on it, and found none. He told the vinedresser, "Look – it's three years I've been coming to look for fruit on this fig tree and not finding it. So cut it down – why [should] it occupy [the ground] to no purpose?" But he replied, "Lord – let it go for this year too; give me a chance to dig it round and put manure on it, and [see] if it yields fruit in future . . . otherwise you can cut it down."'

Luke is the Gospel of repentance, and we have here a story and a parable that both emphasise the urgency of repentance. Jesus is told of some of his fellow Galileans who have been butchered by Pilate (just as he will in the end be butchered by Pilate), and he attacks the implied comment that they deserved it more than anyone else. Then he mentions some Jerusalemites who were killed in an accident, and applies a similar interpretation to them: **everyone** *needs to repent, and soon. Then he tells a fig-tree parable, which is possibly Luke's version of the difficult story in Mark 11; it also, however, echoes the angry parody of a love-song in Isaiah 5, about Israel as the Lord's unfruitful vineyard. Sinners, like fig trees, are given another chance – but not indefinitely.*

Luke is also, of course, the journeying Gospel, and the reader will notice that once again the two terminus points, Galilee and Jerusalem, are mentioned; currently Jesus is on his journey from the first to the second (although we might be pardoned for thinking here that he has already arrived).

(For private reflection, rather than public discussion) Are you on a journey of repentance?

The cure of a woman, crippled for eighteen years

10-17 He was teaching in one of the synagogues on the Sabbath. And look! A woman who had had a diseased spirit for eighteen years, and was bent over and unable to straighten up at all. When he saw her, Jesus addressed her and said, 'Woman – be freed from your disease'; and he laid his hands on her, and immediately she straightened up – and she glorified God. The ruler of the synagogue was annoyed that Jesus had healed on the Sabbath; and he told the crowd, 'There are six days when [we] have to work: so come and be cured on those days, and not on the Sabbath-day.'

The Lord answered him, 'Hypocrites: doesn't each of you on the Sabbath untie your ox or your ass from the trough and take them to drink? But this woman is a daughter of Abraham, whom – look! – Satan had bound for eighteen years: wasn't it necessary for her to be freed from this captivity on the Sabbath-day?'

When he said this, his opponents were all embarrassed; and the whole crowd rejoiced at all the glorious things that were being done by him.

This story displays two possible reactions to Jesus: the cured woman glorifies God, which, as we have already seen, is an appropriate reaction as far as Luke is concerned. The reaction of the synagogue-ruler is inappropriate: his target is Jesus, but it is the crowds whom he addresses, telling them that work is forbidden on the Sabbath, even though it is not **they** *who have been working. Jesus' response is stern, and aimed more widely than at just the ruler, since it is addressed to 'hypocrites' in the plural. Once again the battle-lines are drawn, and at the end of the story we see two possible reactions to Jesus: either embarrassment or rejoicing at glorious things. Which will you choose?*

Two parables (one male, one female) and a 'Lucan summary'

18-22 And so he said, 'What is the kingdom of God like, and to what shall I compare it? It is like a grain of mustard, which a man took and threw into his garden; and it grew and turned into a tree, and "the birds of heaven lived in its branches".'

And again he said, 'What shall I compare the kingdom of God to? It is like a leaven which a woman took and hid in three measures of flour until it was all leavened.'

And he was journeying through cities and villages, teaching, and making a journey to Jerusalem.

Luke often balances his references to men and to women, indicating that the gospel is for all humanity; so here we have a male gardener and a baker woman standing as icons of God. The 'and so' with which the first parable opens may suggest that it is linked with the preceding rejection in the synagogue: the man's gesture of 'throwing' the grain of mustard into the garden feels more like rejection, less like serious gardening. Either way, the point of the story lies in the restless power of God, which is also present in the 'journey' motif of the 'Lucan summary' which ties the two parables together.

The quotation about the 'birds of heaven' comes from Psalm 103:12.
What **is** *the kingdom of God like?*

The difficulty of getting into the kingdom of God

23-30 Someone said to him, 'Lord, is it [just a] few who are being saved?' He said to them, 'Keep struggling to go in through the narrow gate, because, I tell you, many will try to get in, and won't manage it, once the master of the house has got up and locked the door. And you'll begin to stand outside and knock on the door saying, "Lord, open up for us"; and he'll answer you, "I don't know where you people come from." Then you'll start saying, "We ate and drank in your presence, and you taught in our streets." And he'll tell you, "I don't know where you come from: Depart from me, all you doers of evil."

'Then there will be weeping and gnashing of teeth, when you see Abraham, Isaac and Jacob and all the prophets in the kingdom of God, and you people thrown outside. They'll come from east and west, and from north and south. And see – the ones who are going to be first are [now] last; and the ones who are going to be last are [now] first.'

The whole of Chapter 13 has sin and rejection as its deepest theme. Here our attention is more explicitly on who gets into the kingdom. For the first time this 'universal gospel' speaks of the inclusion of the Gentiles, and the concomitant exclusion of some of those who think they have an automatic right of entry. This is not necessarily addressed only to Jesus' Jewish hearers; Luke may also have the over-comfortable members of his church in view. Notice how an individual's question at the beginning provokes an address to a wider audience: 'he said to **them***'. This is not the first time that we have seen this technique in Luke's Gospel.*

'Depart from me, all you doers of evil' comes from Psalm 6:8.
Is *it just a few who are being saved?*

Pharisees, Herod, Jerusalem

31-35 At that moment, some Pharisees came up and said to him, 'Get out, and journey away from here, because Herod is wanting to kill you.' And he said to them, 'Go ['journey', of course] and tell that fox: "See, I am expelling demons and performing healings today and tomorrow, and on the third day I am being consummated." But today and tomorrow and the next day I ***must*** journey, because it is not possible for a prophet to die outside Jerusalem.

'Jerusalem, Jerusalem, she who kills the prophets, and stones those who are sent to her, how often did I want to gather your children, like a bird gathers her young under her wings, and you didn't want it. Look – your house is abandoned. I tell you, you won't see me until you say, "Blessed is the one who comes in the Lord's name." '

The 'journeying' theme is to the fore here, and it is made clearer than at any point in the Gospel so far that the journey must end in death: see the references here to 'consummated' (like the 'exodus' at the Transfiguration, it must be Jesus' Death and Resurrection), to dying in Jerusalem, and to killing the prophets. Once again there is the theme of rejection, symbolised by Herod, clearly, and by Jerusalem, and perhaps also by the Pharisees, who are on the face of it trying to help Jesus, but a) their advice would mean interrupting his journey, b) Jesus assumes that they are in regular contact with Herod, and c) all references to them thus far in the Gospel have led us to expect the worst. Notice the characteristic 'I ***must*** *journey': the word 'must' is only three letters in Greek, but it punches well above its weight in Luke-Acts.*

Jesus' reference to them saying 'Blessed is the one who comes . . . ' refers, of course, to his arrival in Jerusalem. See how Luke always gently reminds us of where the journey is headed.

Where is your journey headed?

The fifth 'disastrous dinner party'

14 1-24 And it happened as he was going into the house of one of the rulers of the Pharisees on a Sabbath to eat bread: and they were watching him carefully. And look! A man suffering from dropsy was before him; and in response Jesus said to the lawyers and Pharisees, 'Is it permitted to heal on the Sabbath or not?' They were silent. And he took him and healed him and let him go; and he said to them, 'If one of you has a son or an ox fall into a well, won't he immediately pull him out on the Sabbath-day?' And they couldn't manage any answer in response to this.

He told his fellow guests a parable, as he noticed how they chose the top places, saying to them, 'When someone invites you to a wedding, don't lie down in the top place, in case someone more honoured than you may have been invited by him; and when he arrives, the one who invited both you and him will tell you, "Give way to this man," and then you'll be embarrassed, and will start to occupy the bottom place! No – when you're invited, go ['journey', once more] and lie down in the bottom place, so that when the person who invited you comes he can tell you, "Friend, come up higher." Then you'll have glory in the presence of all those who are lying down with you. Because everyone who exalts themselves will be humbled, and those who humble themselves will be exalted.'

And he said to the one who had invited him, 'When you hold a breakfast or supper party, don't go inviting your friends or your brothers and sisters or your kinsfolk or your affluent neighbours; you don't want them to invite you in return, so that it becomes "tit-for-tat". No – when you have a party, invite poor people, crippled people, lame and blind. And you'll be blessed, because they have no way of giving you "tit-for-tat": your reward will come at the Resurrection of the dead.'

One of his fellow guests, when he heard this, said, 'Blessed is the one who eats bread in the kingdom of God.'

He said to him, 'A certain person was having a big party; and he invited many people. And he sent his slave at the time for the party, to tell the people who had been invited: "Come along, because it's ready now." And with one voice they all started to make excuses. The first one told him, "I've bought a farm, and I really ***have*** to go out and see it. Please, count me excused." And another one said, "I've purchased five pair of oxen, and I am going ['journeying'] to try them out. Please, count me excused." And another one said, "I have married a wife; and for that reason I can't come."

'The slave arrived and recounted all this to his lord. Then the householder was furious, and told his slave, "Quick – go out into the streets and alleys of the city; and bring here the poor and crippled and blind and lame."

'The slave said, "Lord, what you commanded has been done – and there is still room." And the lord said to the slave, "Go out to the roads and hedges, and ***force*** them to come in, that my house may be filled. For I'm telling you people that none of those men who were invited will taste my meal." '

This 'dinner party' is, of course, a complete disaster. As a matter of fact, the 'dinner' is just a loose setting that Luke provides for some very stark teaching on Jesus' part; as Luke tells it, we have to admit, Jesus undoubtedly started it, and he directs his fire absolutely everywhere: at the lawyers and Pharisees (who mean trouble, we know; but they haven't actually said anything at this point), at his fellow guests, at his host, and even at someone who makes a pious remark about eating in the kingdom of God.

The 'parable' about choosing the bottom place sounds remarkably pragmatic (better to be summoned upwards than booted downwards) – or perhaps Luke is sniping at wealthy Christians? Certainly there is humour in the story, and we should read it with something of a smile.

The host is told he's invited the wrong people. He should instead have invited the ritually impure (see Leviticus 21:18-20 for something like this list), as indeed the householder eventually does in the parable of the banquet, even though at least one of the invited guests had a scripturally warranted excuse (see Deuteronomy 24:5, 20:6).

One attractive feature of this passage is that the man with dropsy forms a 'Lucan pair' with the woman in the previous chapter.

Would **you** *invite Jesus to a dinner party?*

Be serious about discipleship: exhortation to the journeying crowd

25-35 Many crowds were journeying with him, and he turned and said to them, 'If someone comes to me and fails to hate their father and their mother and their wife and their children and their brothers and their sisters – yes, and even their own life – they cannot be my disciple. Whoever does not carry their own cross and come after me, can't be my disciple.

'For which of you who wants to build a tower, doesn't first sit down and calculate the expense, to see if they have sufficient to complete it? [This is] so as not to have all the spectators/onlookers start to make fun of him, if he lays the foundation and doesn't have the resources to finish it off: "This fellow began to build, and didn't have the resources to finish it off."

'Or what monarch, journeying to engage in war with another monarch, will not first sit down and consider if he is able, with ten thousand [troops], to encounter the one who is coming at him with twenty thousand [troops]. And if he can't, then while the other monarch is still a long way off, he sends an embassy and asks for negotiations for peace.

'In just the same way, any of you who does not say farewell to all their possessions ***cannot*** be my disciple.

'To sum up: salt is good; but if the salt loses its sharpness, how will it be seasoned? It's no good for the soil or for the dunghill – it's thrown out.

'Let them hear who have ears to hear.'

These are uncomfortable words. Luke's (and Jesus') view of discipleship is decidedly stark. Once again we notice 'journeying' and Jesus' attentive 'turning'. We cannot help being struck by the strong language of 'hating' the various members of one's family. We have all done that occasionally, of course; but what is meant here is the quite radical detachment that the two sets of brothers showed in Chapter 5, verse 11, and which is expressed in this passage as 'say farewell to all your possessions'.

The two parables, of the tower builder and the militant monarch, likewise express the importance of knowing what you are about, in terms of the experience of Jesus' hearers, who may have reflected that only in the previous chapter they had heard of a tower that was not especially well built, and fell down!

Are you serious about discipleship?

JESUS' TERRIBLE FRIENDS: AN INTRODUCTION, AND THREE STORIES (15:1-32)

Introduction

15 [1, 2] And they were getting close to him, all the tax collectors and sinners; [they wanted] to listen to him. And the Pharisees and the scribes grumbled, 'This fellow gives hospitality to sinners – and eats with them!'

Christians have consistently given 'scribes and Pharisees' a bad press; but it is important to remember what they were about. The Pharisees were a 'lay' organisation, who wanted to create an Israel to which the Messiah might come. To that end, they applied the Levitical laws of purity (intended for the priestly caste) to themselves; in particular, they aspired to a pure 'table-fellowship' – so that the Messiah might join them at their meals. Imagine their shock and horror when they saw Jesus, who was in some respects very close to them, associating with such absolutely disreputable people. But Jesus' 'terrible friends' were part of his message, that the kingdom of God is open to absolutely everybody. Including, of course, scribes and Pharisees, if they are open to God's love. That is the context of the three lovely stories that make up this chapter.

Do you sometimes feel that Jesus should have a more selective choice of friends?

A man rejoices at getting his sheep back

3-7 And he told them this parable: 'Suppose one of you has a hundred sheep, and loses one of them – won't he leave the [other] ninety-nine in the desert, and go journeying after the lost one till he finds it? And when he finds it, in his delight he puts it on his shoulders; and when he gets home, he summons his friends and neighbours, saying to them: "[Come and] rejoice with me, because I have found my lost sheep." I'm telling you, that's how much joy there'll be in heaven over a single sinner who repents, as opposed to ninety-nine righteous ones who see no need for repentance.'

This is an enormously challenging story. Remember the context in which it is told, of complaints that Jesus' friends were not religiously respectable (like the shepherds back in Chapter 2). Jesus' answer is that this is the way that God behaves. No shepherd with half an eye on the bottom line would do anything as unwise as what is suggested here, nor would he carry the miscreant home: sheep have twice as many legs as human beings, and are not designed to be carried. The point is that God behaves in that irrational way, because God loves all human beings, including, of course, the 'tax collectors and sinners' who flocked so enthusiastically to Jesus.

A woman celebrates with her girlfriends when she recovers her housekeeping money

8-10 'Or think of a woman who has ten drachmas: if she loses one drachma, won't she light a lamp and sweep the house, and hunt carefully until she finds it? And when she finds it, she summons her women friends and neighbours, saying, "[Come and] rejoice with me, because I have found the drachma that I had lost." I'm telling you, that's how much joy there'll be among the angels of God, over one sinner who repents.'

The previous story, of the sheep that was lost, appears also in Matthew's Gospel (18:12-14), where it is a tale about looking after members of the Christian body who go astray. Luke has turned it into a story of God's joy over sinners who repent, and has then hammered the point home by adding a story where God is presented as a woman who loses some of her precious (and pitifully small) housekeeping allowance and likewise throws a party. Luke repeats several of the same phrases ('summons friends and neighbours', 'rejoice with me', 'I'm telling you, that's how much joy there'll be') to emphasise that it is the same God we are talking about. So this is not only yet another story about repentance and forgiveness in Luke, but also yet another 'Lucan pairing'.

A scapegrace son is welcomed home – with a party!

11-32 He said, 'A certain person had two sons. And the younger of them said to his father, "Father, give me the portion of the property that falls to me." And he divided his life between them. Not many days later, the younger [son] gathered everything together and went abroad to a distant country; and there he squandered his property by living extravagantly.

'When he had spent the lot, a serious famine occurred throughout the country; and for the first time he was without resources, and so he went [journeyed] and joined one of the citizens of that country; and he sent him into the fields, to feed pigs; and he longed to stuff himself from the carob pods on which the pigs were feeding – and no one gave him permission. He came to himself and said, "How many of my father's employees have more than enough bread – and here am I, dying of hunger! I'll get up and journey to my father; and I'll tell him 'Father – I've sinned against God and sinned before you; I'm no longer fit to be called a son of yours. Make me like one of your employees.' "

'But while he was still a long way away, his father saw him, and had compassion on him; and he ran and fell on his neck and kissed him. The son said to him, "Father – I've sinned against God and sinned before you; I'm no longer fit to be called a son of yours . . . "

'The father said to his slaves, "Quick – bring out the Number One robe, and put it on him; and give a ring on his hand, and sandals on his feet; and bring the fattened calf, and kill it, and let's have a banquet and celebrate, because this son of mine was a corpse – and he has come alive again; he was lost, and has been found." And they began to celebrate.

'Now the elder son was in the field; and as he came nearer the house, he heard music and dancing. And he summoned one of the servants and asked what this was all about. He said, "Your brother has arrived, and your father has killed the fattened calf, because he got him back safe and sound."

'He was furious, and refused to go in. His father came out and started pleading with him. But he replied to his father, "Look! For so many years I've been slaving for you, and never disobeyed your commandment, and you never even gave me a goat to have a party with my friends. But when this son of yours comes, who ate up your life with prostitutes, you killed the fattened calf for him!"

'But he said to him, "Child, you're always with me, and everything that's mine is yours. We ***had*** to celebrate and rejoice, because this brother of yours was a corpse – and he is alive; and lost, and has been found." '

When Rembrandt painted this most famous of all Lucan parables, he portrayed the father with his arms round the son: the left hand is that of a man, and the right hand that of a woman. The artist had spotted that the parent in this parable is both father and mother.

It is an extraordinary story. The younger son is brutally rude and arrogant to his father, who is astonishingly docile. There is nothing at all to be said for the young man, **except** *that he decides to go home. Even the employment he* *finds, in a not wholly satisfactory attempt to stave off hunger, is horrifying to Jewish ears: looking after pigs. Set that against the behaviour of the Father, who was actually on the look-out, then ran to his son and kissed him and with every possible external attention restored to him his lost status as 'a son of mine' – and then, as in the two previous stories, the party begins.*

The story should have ended there, but that would mean leaving unanswered the complaints that started the chapter. They are now personified in the steaming, sulking, loitering-outside figure of the elder brother. There are some hints that he may stand for the Jewish authorities who were opposed to Jesus' indiscriminate hospitality. This ill-tempered elder son has apparently also forgotten that his Father had given him half of his 'life'. He speaks of not disobeying 'the commandment'; and father and son play the same game as Moses and God in Exodus 32:7, 11 at the time of the Golden Calf, where God and Moses each speak to the other of **'your** *people'. In just the same way the elder brother speaks of 'this son of yours' (like the lawyer at 10:37 and Martha at 10:40, he can't bear to give him a name), and God replies with 'this brother of yours'. The Golden Calf story is also alluded to in the mention of 'music and dancing' that had so annoyed the elder brother (see Exodus 32:19).*

With supreme artistry, Luke does not say whether or not the elder brother went in to the party. That is for you, the reader, to decide. What would you do?

The steward whom the Lord praised

16 1-9 He also said to his disciples, 'There was a certain wealthy man who had a steward. Now this steward had been charged with squandering his possessions, and he called him and said to him, "What's this I hear about you? Give an account of your stewardship, because you can no longer be a steward."

'The steward said to himself, "What am I to do, seeing that my Lord is taking away my stewardship from me? I don't have the strength to dig, and I'm [too] embarrassed to beg . . . ***I*** know what I'll do, so that when I'm removed from the stewardship they'll give me hospitality in their houses." And he summoned each of his Lord's debtors; and he said to the first one, "How much do you owe my Lord?" And he said, "A thousand gallons of olive oil." He said to him, "Take your documents, sit down, and quickly write five hundred." Then to the next one he said, "What about you? How much do you owe?" He said, "Ten thousand gallons of wheat." He says to him, "Take your documents, and write eight thousand." And the Lord praised the steward for his unrighteousness [or: 'praised the unjust steward'], because he had acted prudently. Because the children of this world are more prudent than the children of light with regard to their own generation. And I'm telling you, make yourselves friends of the Mammon of Iniquity [or: unjust wealth], so that when it runs out you may be given hospitality in the eternal tents.'

Like its predecessor, this is a deeply subversive story, challenging us to look at the world with fresh eyes. The man who was wealthy enough to have a steward (like some of Luke's intended audience, perhaps) is certainly not the hero of the story. If there must be a hero, then the only candidate is the steward, who is charged (perhaps falsely) with squandering his master's possessions, and who is dismissed without being permitted to offer his version of events, and who shows such a ready wit in organising allies for himself.

There are two other points to give salt to our reading of the story. First, the word that I have translated and capitalised as 'Lord' could mean no more than the 'master' of the steward; but it is possible to read the story as meaning that 'Jesus praised the unjust steward', which would be subversive indeed (it is bad enough if it is the steward's master).

Second, the conclusion of the story, 'make yourselves friends of the Mammon of Iniquity, so that when it (what?) runs out you may be given hospitality in the eternal tents', leaves the reader in a moral fog: is it a joke? a piece of practical advice? irony?

Now try fitting all that to the teaching that follows, and ask yourself: What is wrong with Money?

Loosely connected sayings, some of them concerning money

10-18 'The one who is reliable on the tiniest matter, is also reliable on a big issue; the one who is dishonest on the tiniest matter is also dishonest on a big issue. So – if you are not reliable in regard to dishonest wealth [or: unjust mammon] – who's going to entrust you with the real thing? And if you are not reliable on other people's affairs, who's going to give you what is your own?

'No servant can be a slave to two lords; for either he'll hate the one and love the other, or he'll be devoted to the one and look down his nose at the other. You can't serve God and Money.'

The Pharisees (being lovers of money) heard all of this, and they scoffed at him. And he said to them, 'You're the ones who justify yourselves before human beings – but God knows your hearts; because what human beings regard as top priority is an abomination to God.'

'The Law and the Prophets went up to John; but from then on, the good news of the kingdom is being proclaimed, and everyone forces their way into it [or: 'suffers violence']. But it is easier for heaven and earth to pass away than for a single serif [on a single letter] of the Law to fail.

'Every man who divorces his wife and marries another one commits adultery; and the man who marries a woman who is divorced from her husband also commits adultery.'

It is not easy to know what to say about these, hard to link them adequately. The first two sound as though they might be continuing the story of the steward: in both of them Jesus speaks of money/Mammon, but not in quite the ironic way that the story had led us to expect. The injunction to be reliable about other people's affairs is precisely what the steward disobeyed; and as for not being able to serve two masters, that seems to be precisely what the steward adroitly did! Luke's church must have listened uncomfortably to all this; but it is hard to see how it all fits.

The next paragraph charges the Pharisees (not at all justly) with being 'lovers of money'; and it is certainly as subversive as the rest of the teaching. Then comes the mysterious saying about the kingdom of God and violence: is it a good thing that people force their way in, or a bad thing that it suffers violence? Finally comes a characteristically strong statement from Jesus on divorce, in which the rights of the woman are firmly upheld.

All of which leads into yet another of Luke's subversive stories.

The wealthy man who went to hell

19-31 'A certain man was wealthy; he wore purple and linen, and he had sumptuous feasts every day.

'But a poor man called Lazarus was flung down at his gateway, covered with sores. And he wanted to fill himself on what fell from the rich man's table. Instead, the dogs came and licked his sores!

'It turned out that the poor man died, and was carried by the angels into the bosom of Abraham. The rich man died and was buried. And, in hell, he lifted up his eyes, since he was in torment; he sees Abraham a long way off, and Lazarus in his bosom. And he called him and said, "Father Abraham, have mercy on me, and send Lazarus to dip the tip of his finger in water and cool off my tongue, because I'm in pain in this flame." But Abraham said, "Child – remember that you received good things during your life; and similarly Lazarus got bad things. Now he's being comforted here, and you're in pain. And, as if all that were not enough, between us and you there's a huge chasm established, so that people who want to cross over from here to you can't, nor do they make the crossing from there to us." But he said, "So I'm asking you, Father, to send him to my father's house (you see, I've got five brothers), to warn them not to come into this torture chamber." Abraham says, "They have Moses and the prophets – let them listen to ***them***." He said, "No, Father Abraham: if someone journeys to them from the dead, they'll repent." He said to him, "If they don't listen to Moses and the prophets, they won't be convinced even if someone were to rise from the dead." '

This is another thoroughly subversive story. As soon as we read of the (unnamed) rich man's clothing and parties, we know there'll be trouble. Lazarus (whose name means 'God has helped'), by contrast, **is** *given a name, and his sufferings are described in unpleasant detail. Then comes a sudden reversal. Lazarus can't afford a funeral, so is instead transported straight to 'Abraham's bosom'. The rich man, on the other hand is buried properly, and Luke assumes as a matter of course that he goes to hell. He has not learnt his lesson, however, and some delightfully lively dialogue shows that he is still imperiously inclined (giving indirect orders to Lazarus), while Abraham carefully explains the facts of life. Abraham calls him 'child', as the Father did the Elder Brother in Chapter 15; this is perhaps picked up in the two senses of 'father' ('Father Abraham' and 'my father's house'),* *reminding us of a similar ambiguity about the word at 2:48-49. But the verdict is irresistible, and we tremble as we read.*

Does the story of Lazarus and the rich man challenge you? In what way?

Instructions to disciples

17 1-10 He said to his disciples, 'It is impossible that scandals should not come.
But woe to the one through whom they come. It is better for that person to have a millstone round their neck and be hurled into the sea, than that they scandalise one of these little ones. Mind yourselves!

'If your fellow-Christian commits a sin, rebuke them; and if they repent, forgive them. And if they commit a sin against you seven times a day, and seven times come back to you saying "I repent", you will forgive them.'

And the apostles said to the Lord, 'Increase our faith.' The Lord said, 'If you have faith like a mustard seed, you would say to this mulberry tree, "Be uprooted and plant yourself in the sea", and it would obey you.

'Suppose one of you has a slave ploughing or looking after the sheep, are you going to tell him, when he comes in from the field, "Come along right away, and lie down [for a meal]"? No – won't you tell him, "Make something for me to eat; put your livery on and wait on me while I eat and drink – and you can eat after that!"? Do you ***thank*** the slave because he did what was ordered? It's just the same with you people: when you've done everything that you were ordered, [just] say, "We are unprofitable slaves – we have done [only] what we ought to have done." '

These instructions, except for the last paragraph about the treatment of slaves which may have been directed at Luke's affluent audience, are found in Chapter 18 of Matthew, although not in quite the same order (this may be because of Matthew's tidy mind). And Luke characteristically adds an emphasis on 'repentance and forgiveness'. The 'uprooting of the fig tree' is in Mark (9:24), where it is in fact a mountain that is uprooted; perhaps Luke has combined this with the 'cursing of the fig tree' (Mark 11:12-14), which he does not include.

A 'Lucan summary' and a grateful Samaritan

11-19 And it happened as [he was] journeying to Jerusalem, that he himself was proceeding through the middle of [or: through the borders of] Samaria and Galilee.

And as he was entering a village, ten leper men met him; they stood far away, and raised their voices to him, 'Jesus, master, take pity on us.' He saw them and said to them, 'Go [journey], and show yourselves to the priests.' And it turned out that as they were on their way, they were made clean!

Now one of them, when he saw that he had been cured, came back, glorifying God in a loud voice; and he fell on his face at his feet. And he was a Samaritan! Jesus responded, 'Weren't [all] ten made clean? The [other] nine – where [have they gone]? Were none to be found returning to give glory to God, except this foreigner?' And he said to him, 'Up you get – continue your journey. Your faith has saved you.'

The 'Lucan summary' characteristically reminds us of the journey, and its (slightly confusing?) landmarks of Samaria and Galilee. The next story also continues the 'journeying' theme: the lepers are told to 'journey' (as is the grateful one). And there are other points at which we can detect the hand of Luke: the Samaritan ex-leper glorifies God, like the shepherds in Chapter 2. And the fact that he is a non-Jew, and, worse, a Samaritan, emphasises Luke's sense of the gospel moving out from its Jewish base to include 'every-one'.

When Jesus says to the foreigner 'your faith has saved you' what has ***he*** *received that the others had not received?*

What about the end-time?

20-37 When he was asked by the Pharisees, 'When is the kingdom of God coming?', he replied to them, 'The kingdom of God doesn't come with close observation. And they won't say "Look – here [it is]," or "There [it is]." For look! The kingdom of God is right inside you!'

And he said to his disciples, 'Days will come when you will long to see one of the days of the Son of Man – and you won't see it. And they'll tell you, "Look – there [it is], look – here [it is]." Don't go off in pursuit. For as lightning when it flashes lights from one end of the horizon to the other, so will the Son of Man be in his day. First, however, it is necessary for him to suffer much, and to be rejected by this generation. And as it happened in Noah's days, so it will be in the days of the Son of Man. They were eating, they were drinking, they were marrying and they were getting married – right up to the day when Noah went on board his Ark. Then the deluge came, and destroyed every one of them. Just like it happened in Lot's days: they were eating, they were drinking, they were buying, they were selling, they were planting, they were building. But on the day when Lot went out of Sodom, [the Lord] rained fire and sulphur from heaven, and destroyed every one of them. So it will be on the day when the Son of Man is revealed. On that day, if someone is on the rooftop, and their belongings are in the house, they should not go down to fetch them. Similarly, some-one who is in the field shouldn't come back. Remember Lot's wife. You see, everyone who looks to preserve their life will lose it, while everyone who [is prepared to] lose their life will revive it. I'm telling you: on that night, there'll be two people in one bed: one will be taken, and the other left. And there will be two women grinding in the same place; one will be taken, and the other left.'

They replied, 'Where, Lord?' He said to them, 'Where the body is, there the vultures will gather too.'

The material gathered together here is found elsewhere, mainly in Matthew 24, but also in Mark 13; in those Gospels, however, it comes nearer to the end. The one exception is the introductory verses, the exchange between Jesus and Pharisees. We have learnt in our reading that for Luke Pharisees mean trouble.

The disciples' question, 'Where, Lord?', is undeniably puzzling – but the answer is not particularly enlightening. Perhaps we should realise that we are dealing with the unknown.

What do you think that Jesus might have meant by saying 'The kingdom of God is right inside you'?

Two Lucan parables on prayer

18 1-14 He told them a parable about the need to pray all the time, and not give up. He said, 'A particular magistrate in a particular city had no respect for God, and no regard for human beings. Now there was a widow in that city; and she kept coming to him and saying, "Give me justice against my opponent." And for a time he refused. Later, though, he said to himself, "Perhaps I don't respect God, and have no regard for human beings – but because this widow is pestering me, I'll give her justice. Otherwise she'll end up by coming and giving me a black eye!" Do you think that God won't bring about justice [or: vindication] for his elect who shout to him day and night, even though he is slow in dealing with them? I'm telling you – he'll quickly bring about justice for them. Nevertheless, when the Son of Man comes, will he find faith on earth?'

He also told this parable to some people who trusted in their own righteousness, and were contemptuous of everyone else:

'Two people went up into the Temple to pray. One was a Pharisee, and the other was a tax collector. The Pharisee stood and prayed to himself as follows: "God, I give you thanks that I'm not like the rest of humanity: thieves, dishonest [or: unrighteous/ unjust], adulterers – or like this fellow, the tax collector. I fast twice a week; I give away a tenth of everything I possess."

'The tax collector, on the other hand, stood a long way off; he didn't even dare lift up his eyes to heaven. Instead, he beat his breast, and said, "God, be merciful to me, the Sinner." I'm telling you, he's the one who went to his house counted-as-righteous, not the other one. Because everyone who lifts themselves up will be put down; but those who put themselves down will be lifted up.'

These two parables are only found in Luke's Gospel. Both of them (rather unusually) are given headings, so that the reader knows what they are about. Both of them have to do with prayer, and both of them make use of a whole series of words connected with righteousness and justice: the word for opponent could nearly be translated 'the one who is against the righteous'. They are both good stories, memorably told and with a touch of humour (the widow's threat of a black eye, the Pharisee's tedious catalogue of his virtues); we can feel Luke's artistry at work here. The words for 'justice' and for 'opponent' both have the same root here.

What is wrong with the Pharisee's prayer? Do you sometimes sound like him?

Jesus and babies

15-17 They tried to bring babies to him also, for him to touch them. The disciples saw, and rebuked them. Jesus, however, called the babies to him and said, 'Let the little children come to me, and don't get in their way. You see, the kingdom of God consists of people like this. Amen, I tell you, whoever doesn't accept the kingdom of God like a little child, no way will they get into it.'

This charming story is also in Mark 10:13-16 and Matthew 19:13-15, except that Luke has omitted the detail that Jesus 'took them in his arms, laid his hands on them and blessed them'.

What does it mean for us to 'accept the kingdom of God like a little child'?

An affluent ruler asks about inheriting eternal life

18-30 And a certain ruler asked him, 'Good teacher, what am I to do to inherit eternal life?'

Jesus said to him, 'Why do you say that I am good? No one is good except One – namely God. You know the commandments: "Thou shalt not commit adultery; thou shalt not kill; thou shalt not steal; thou shalt not bear false witness; honour thy father and mother." ' But he said, 'I've kept all of these since my youth.' When Jesus heard [this], he said to him, 'You still lack one thing: whatever you have, sell it, and distribute [the money] to the poor, and you'll have treasure in heaven. And, here, follow me.' When he heard this, he became very sad. You see, he was extremely affluent.

When Jesus saw him getting so very sad, he said, 'How difficult it is for those who have possessions to journey into the kingdom of God! For it is easier for a camel to go in through the eye of a needle than for someone who is affluent to go into the kingdom of God.'

Those who heard [this] said, 'In that case, who can be saved?' He said, 'Things that are impossible for human beings are possible for God'.

Peter said, 'Look! We've abandoned our own and followed you.' He told them, 'Amen I tell you – there's no one who has left house or wife or brothers or parents or children, for the sake of the kingdom of God who doesn't receive many times over in this [present] age, and in the age that is coming, life eternal.'

This episode is also in Mark and Matthew; Luke has tidied up what he found in Mark, and perhaps also emphasised the detachment that disciples require, and the dangers of affluence (writing, perhaps, for a wealthy congregation); but otherwise he leaves it much as he found it, except that he turns Jesus' interrogator into a 'ruler'. We also notice that the question put to him by the ruler is identical to that on the lips of the lawyer who was rewarded with the disconcerting parable of the Good Samaritan.

How would **you** *answer the question, 'What am I to do to inherit eternal life?'*

Jesus warns the Twelve about what will happen at the end of the journey

31-34 He took the Twelve with him and said to them, 'Look – we're going up to Jerusalem; and everything written through the prophets will be accomplished for the Son of Man: he'll be handed over to the Gentiles, and be ridiculed, and insulted, and spat upon. And they'll flog him and then kill him – and on the third day he'll rise again.' And they didn't understand any of this – and the matter [or: 'word'] was hidden from them; and they couldn't grasp what was being said.

This is the third passion prediction (see 9:22; 9:44), though Luke makes much less of them than Mark does (see Mark 10:32-34). The attentive reader will note two changes that are characteristic of Luke. First, the prediction is narrowed to just 'the Twelve', and, second, there is his typical emphasis on fulfilling prophecy. It is Luke's way of saying that God is in charge. Luke also omits the disciples' blunder.

The disciples 'couldn't grasp' what Jesus said. Can you?

A blind man near Jericho gets his sight back

35-43 It happened as he drew near to Jericho a blind person was sitting begging beside
the way. He heard a crowd journeying through, and asked what it was. They told him, 'Jesus the Nazarene is passing by.' And he shouted, 'Jesus, Son of David, have pity on me!' And the people in front told him sharply to be silent. But he cried out all the more, 'Son of David, have pity on me!' Jesus stopped, and ordered him to be brought to him; when he approached, he asked him, 'What do you want me to do?' He said, 'Lord, that I may see again.' And Jesus said to him, 'See again. Your faith has saved you.' And straightaway he saw again, and followed him, glorifying God. And when they saw it, the whole populace gave praise to God.

This story is also in Mark 10:46-52 and Matthew 20:29-34; but Luke has made some characteristic changes. Mark sets the story at the moment when Jesus departs from Jericho, which is a bit puzzling. Luke locates it as part of the ongoing journey up to Jerusalem. He emphasises that the crowd was 'journeying'; he eliminates Mark's rather alarming disrobing on the part of the blind man, and emphasises the verb 'see again'. He changes the form of address from Rabbouni to Kyrie, and (how many times have we heard this phrase?) has the beggar 'glorifying God', and the 'populace' giving praise to God.

Also characteristic of Luke is the fact that the blind man's persistence gets him what he wants; and of course we remember that 'sight for the blind' was part of Jesus' 'mission-statement' at Nazareth, back in 4:18.

Do you find it difficult to be persistent with God?

Zacchaeus of Jericho

19 1-10 And he entered and passed through Jericho. And look! A man called
Zacchaeus; and he was a head tax collector; and he was affluent. And he

was trying to see Jesus ('which one is he?'); and he couldn't, because of the crowd, because he was small in stature. And he ran on ahead, and went up a sycamore tree to see him, because he was going to pass by it. And when he got to the spot, Jesus looked up and said to him 'Zacchaeus! Quick – down you come: because today I must stay in your house.' And he came down in a hurry, and joyfully gave him hospitality. And they all saw it, and complained, 'He's gone in to stay with a man who is a sinner.' Zacchaeus stood there, and said to the Lord, 'Look, Lord; I'm giving half of my possessions to the poor; and if I have defrauded anyone of anything, I'm giving it back fourfold!' Jesus said to him, 'Today salvation has come to this house, because this man is also a child of Abraham; you see, the Son of Man came to look for the lost, and to save them.'

This story is only in Luke. As in the previous episode, Luke simplifies the introduction in a way that emphasises the journeying theme. The man's name will give us a clue: it is an abbreviation of Zachariah, 'the Lord has remembered', so despite the fact that he has so much going against him as an 'affluent tax collector', we feel optimistic about the outcome of the story. There is the memorable detail about Zacchaeus' lack of height, and the unforgettable moment when everyone is looking at him up in the tree, waiting for Jesus' condemnation, which never comes (though we may imagine an eternal pause after Jesus first addresses him). Twice in the passage Luke uses his characteristic 'today'; Zacchaeus hurries, as Mary had done in Chapter 1, and his 'joy' reminds us that Luke is the Gospel of joy. We notice also, as always in Luke, the radical demands of hospitality, indicated by Zacchaeus' more than generous compensation for what he has done wrong. It is 'repentance in action'.

What strikes you most about this story?

The parable of the absentee landlord

11-27 As they listened to this, he told another parable, because he was near Jerusalem, and they thought that the kingdom of God was about to appear straightaway. So he said, 'A certain nobleman journeyed to a distant country, to accept his kingdom and return. He summoned his ten slaves, and gave them ten minae, and told them, "Do some trading while I'm away." Now his citizens hated him, and sent an embassy after him to say, "We don't want this man to rule over us." And it turned out, when he returned, having accepted his kingdom, he gave orders for these slaves to be called, the ones to whom he had given the money, to find out what they had earned in their trading. The first one came and said, "Lord – your mina has yielded ten minae." And he said to him, "Well done, good slave: because you turned out to be faithful on a tiny matter, assume authority over ten cities." And the second one came and said, "Here's your mina, Lord: it's made five minae." He told this one also, "You, too, be in charge of five cities." And the other one came and said, "Lord – here's your mina. I kept it hidden in a handkerchief, because I was afraid of you; you're a severe man – you take up what you didn't put down, and you harvest what you didn't sow." He said, "Out of your own mouth I condemn you, wicked slave. You knew that I'm a severe man, taking up what I didn't put down and harvesting what I didn't sow – so why didn't you give my money to a bank, so that on my arrival I could have claimed it with interest?" And he said to the bystanders, "Take the mina from him, and give it to the one who has ten minae." And they said to him, "Lord – he [already] has ten minae." "I tell you, it will be given to everyone who has, and from the one who has not, even what they have will be taken from them. But these enemies of mine who didn't want me to be king over them, bring them here and slaughter them in front of me." '

This is really a very audacious story. Luke tells us in the introduction that it's meant to correct misapprehensions about the kingdom of God, given that the journey has now almost reached Jerusalem. But the king, who is presumably meant to represent God, turns out to be a thoroughly unpleasant fellow, with more than a passing resemblance to Herod. His subjects loathe him; he rewards initiative, but (on his own admission) he is very severe in his dealings with slaves, and is something of a greedy capitalist; and, finally, his response to any kind of opposition takes the form of public murder.

The reader will have to pause and ask, 'What, then, is the kingdom of God like, and who is the God of Jesus Christ?'

The journey ends with the entry into Jerusalem

28-40 And with these words, he continued to journey onwards to Jerusalem.

And it happened, when he drew near to Bethphage and Bethany, near the mountain called 'Of Olive Trees', he sent two of the disciples, saying, 'Go into the village opposite; when you journey into it you'll find a colt tied, on whom no human being has ever sat. Untie it and bring it. And if anyone asks you why you are untying it, you'll say this, "The Lord has need of it." ' The ones who had been sent went off and found [things] as he had told them. As they were untying the colt, its masters [or: lords – *kyrioi*] said to them, 'Why are you untying the colt?' They said, 'The Lord has need of it,' and they brought it to Jesus, and they threw their garments over the colt and sat Jesus on it. As he journeyed, they spread their garments underneath him on the road. As he was now drawing near to the slope of the Mountain of Olives, the whole crowd of disciples began to rejoice and praise God at the top of their voices, for all the miracles they had seen: 'Blessed is the Coming One, the King in the Lord's name, in heaven peace and glory in the highest places.'

And some of the Pharisees in the crowd said to him, 'Teacher, speak severely to your disciples.'

And he answered them, 'I'm telling you – if they are silent, the stones will cry out.'

After a characteristic Lucan summary, with the familiar reference to a journey, Luke retains more or less what he found in Mark, but makes some typical changes. We notice the interplay between different senses of Kyrios/Lord *(the owners of the donkey and the Lord), which may remind us of a similar ambiguity about 'Father' in 2:48, 49. Jesus' ride on the donkey is described in terms of a journey. We also notice how the crowd 'began to rejoice and praise God', and how their welcoming song quotes Psalm 118.*

Do you find it easy to 'rejoice and praise God'?

Jesus, Jerusalem and the Temple

41-48 And as he drew near, when he saw the city, he wept over it, saying, 'If [only] you also had known on this day the things that lead to peace; but now it's hidden from your eyes. Because the day will come on you, and your enemies will throw up an earthworks alongside you, and they'll encircle you and hem you in from all sides, and they'll dash you to the ground, and your children within you because you didn't know the time of your visitation.'

And he went into the Temple; and he started to expel the sellers, telling them 'It is written: "And my house shall be a house of prayer" – but you've made it a den of thieves.'

And he was teaching every day in the Temple. The chief priests and the scribes were looking for a way to destroy him – and so were the Most Important People; and they could find nothing to do with him – because the whole populace hung upon his words.

The 'things that lead to peace' echoes 14:32 (the king going out to war), and appears in only these two places in the entire New Testament. The equivalent verb for the idea of 'visitation' is also in Luke 1:68, 78; 7:16. The quotation about 'my house shall be a house of prayer' is from Isaiah 56:7, and the 'den of thieves' is from Jeremiah 7:11. Luke has rather oddly (despite his interest in the Gentile mission) missed out the reference to the Gentiles in the first of these quotations, although Mark has it. Perhaps Luke thought that his readers would make the connection.

The Temple story is introduced by another 'Lucan summary': 'he was teaching every day in the Temple'. The 'Most Important People' (literally 'first') might perhaps be a dig at Luke's affluent church.

Do you think that Jesus might behave like this today if he visited your local church?

The battlelines are drawn: an awkward question and a dangerous parable

20 1-19 And it happened on one of the days, while he was teaching the people in the Temple, and giving the good news, the Chief Priest and the scribes came up to him, along with the elders; and they spoke, saying to him, 'Tell us, by what authority do you do these things? Or who is it that gives you this authority?'

He replied to them, 'Now I'll ask you something. So tell me – was John's baptism from heaven, or from human beings?'

They debated among themselves, 'If we say "from heaven", he'll say, "Why did you not believe him?"; but if we say "from human beings", the whole populace will stone us to death, for they are convinced that John is a prophet.' So they replied that they didn't know where it was from. And Jesus said to them, 'And I'm not telling you by what authority I do these things.'

He started to address this parable to the populace: 'A man planted a vineyard, and he leased it out to cultivators, and went abroad for a considerable time. And at the appropriate moment, he sent the cultivators a slave, for them to give him some of the fruit of the vineyard; but the cultivators beat him and sent him away empty-handed. And he did it again and sent them a second slave, but they beat him too, and when they had dishonoured him they sent him away empty-handed. And he did it again and sent them a third slave. And this one too they wounded and flung him out. The lord of the vineyard said, "What shall I do? I'll send my beloved son. Perhaps they'll respect him." But when the cultivators saw him, they discussed [it] with one another, "This is the heir – let's kill him, so that the inheritance may be ours." And they flung him out of the vineyard and killed him.

'So what do you think the lord of the vineyard will do to them? He'll come and destroy the cultivators and give the vineyard to others.'

When they heard it, they said, 'God forbid!' He looked at them and said, 'So what is this Scripture: "The stone which the builders rejected, this is the one that has turned into the cornerstone." Everyone who falls over that stone will be dashed to pieces; but the person on whom it falls, it will crush him.'

And the scribes and the chief priests sought to lay hands on him at that moment; and yet they were afraid of the people, because they knew that it was at them that he had spoken this parable.

The tone of the Gospel is now unmistakably menacing. Luke has left this more or less as he found it in Mark (12:1-12), though the alert reader may notice how he tidies things up, so that the parable (in which Jesus pulls no punches, as he adapts Isaiah 5 to the present situation) is told to the 'populace', a favourite Lucan word. Luke also makes it clear that it is Jesus to whom the parable refers, by speaking of the 'beloved son'.

Could Jesus have been a bit more 'diplomatic', do you think?

Three attempts to trap Jesus, and Jesus' adroit responses

20-47 They watched him carefully; and they sent spies, who pretended to be on the right side, to seize on something he said, so as to hand him over to the magisterial authority of the procurator. And they asked him, 'Teacher, we know that you speak and teach correctly, regardless of who you are talking to, but that you truly teach God's way: is it allowed for us to pay tribute to Caesar or not?'

He however detected their cunning, and said to them, 'Show me the denarius – whose image and likeness does it have?' They said, 'Caesar's'; and he said to them, 'So pay back Caesar's property to Caesar – and God's property to God.'

And they were unable to seize on anything he said, in the presence of the populace; and they were stunned by his response and fell silent.

Some of the Sadducees came up; these people deny that there is a Resurrection; and they interrogated him: 'Teacher, Moses wrote down for us that "if someone's brother dies, and [the brother] was married and childless, his brother should take his wife, and raise up seed for his brother". So – there were seven brothers. Number One took a wife, and died childless; and Number Two and then Number Three took her, and all seven of them took her, and they died, without leaving children. At last the woman died. So – in the "Resurrection", whose wife does she become? (You see, all seven had had her as wife!)'

And Jesus said to them, 'The sons of this world marry and are given in marriage – but those who are judged worthy of that [other] world, and worthy to reach the Resurrection, don't marry or get married; and neither will they die, because being children of the Resurrection they are on a par with the angels, and they're children of God. But Moses pointed out at the Bush that corpses are raised, when he says, "The Lord is the God of Abraham and the God of Isaac and the God of Jacob." But he's not the God of corpses – no, he's the God of the living, for they're all alive to him.'

Some of the scribes replied, 'Teacher, well said.' For they didn't dare interrogate him any longer.

He said to them, 'How do they say that the Messiah is David's son? For David himself says in the Book of Psalms,

"The Lord said to my Lord,
'Sit at my right
until I make your enemies
a footstool for your feet.' "

'So David calls him "Lord": how, then, is he his son?'

In the hearing of the entire populace, he told his disciples: 'Beware of the scribes who want to go about in long robes; they love being saluted in the public squares, and front seats in the synagogues, and top places at banquets. And they make a pretence of long prayers. These people will get a much more severe condemnation.'

Luke has left this more or less as he found it in Mark, except that he has shifted the question about the 'Great Commandment' back to Chapter 10, and placed it on a lawyer's lips; at this point he has simply left a couple of traces of it, the scribes' 'well said', and the reluctance to press his interrogations any further. He has, too, a much briefer version of Matthew's assault (23:1-36) on the scribes and Pharisees (although you might point out that Luke has already said his piece about the Pharisees in 11:39-44).

But we can feel the doom pressing in on Jesus, now that his journey is over and he has arrived in Jerusalem.

Do you want to stay with Jesus, now that he has reached this point?

A destitute widow

21 [1-4] He looked up and saw the people putting their gifts in the Treasury. They
were affluent; but he also saw a needy widow putting two tiny coins in there,
and he commented, 'Truly, I'm telling you, this poor widow put in more than all the

others. You see, all of these contributed to the gifts from out of their surplus, while she contributed to the gifts from out of what she ***didn't*** have. She put in all the life she had.'

Beyond a little bit of tidying, Luke has not changed very much of what he found in Mark 12:41-44; but as we read we need to recall that widows get an especially good press from Luke, and that Luke compares the widow to the Father of 15:12, who 'divided his life'. Luke's affluent congregation will no doubt have pondered these things.

Does this make you feel a bit uncomfortable?

An innocent remark about the Temple leads to a prediction of the end

5-36 And when some people remarked about the Temple, that it was adorned with lovely stones and votive-offerings, he said, 'All these things which you are looking at – the days will come when no stone will be left on another stone that will not be pulled down.' They asked him, 'Teacher, so when will this happen? And what's the sign when these things are about to take place?' He said, 'Watch out that you don't get misled. For many people will come in my name, saying, "I AM!" and "The Time Has Come." Don't go journeying after them; but when you hear of wars and revolution, don't get panic-stricken. For these things have to happen first – but the end is not immediately.'

Then he said to them, 'Nation will rise up against nation, and kingdom against kingdom; and [there will be] great earthquakes; and in places there will be famines and epidemics, and terrors and great signs from heaven. But before all this, they'll lay hands on you, and hunt you down, handing you over to synagogue and prison; [you will be] brought before kings and governors for the sake of my name. It will give you the opportunity to bear witness. So make it your policy not to practise your speech for the defence beforehand. For I shall give you eloquence and wisdom which none of your opponents will be able to resist or refute. What is more, you will be handed over by parents and siblings, cousins and friends – and they'll kill some of you, and you'll be loathed by everyone because of my name. Nevertheless, not a hair of your head will be destroyed: through your unflinching endurance you will take possession of your lives.

'But when you see Jerusalem encircled by armies, be sure that her devastation is close. Then let those who are in Judaea flee to the mountains, and let those who are inside Jerusalem get out; and those who are in the rural areas must not go into the city, because these are the days of her punishment, for all that is written to be fulfilled. Woe to those who are pregnant or who have children at the breast in those days, for there will be great distress on the land, and wrath on his people, and they'll fall at the edge of the sword, and they'll be taken captive to all the Gentiles. And Jerusalem shall be under the jackboot of the Gentiles, until the Times of the Gentiles are completed.

'And there shall be signs in the sun and the moon and the stars; and on earth there shall be anguish of nations, and perplexity from the roaring and raging of the sea. Human beings will stop breathing, in fear and anticipation of the things that are coming on the world – for the powers of heaven shall be shaken.

'And then they shall see the Son of Man coming on the cloud with power and great glory. When these things start to happen, look up, and lift your heads – because your redemption is approaching.'

And he told them a parable, 'Look at the fig tree (and indeed all trees): as soon as they bud, from the evidence of your eyes you know that the summer is now at hand. And so you also, when you see these things happening, be aware that the kingdom of God is at hand. Amen I tell you, no way will this generation pass away before everything happens. Heaven and earth will pass away, but my words will not pass away.

'Be careful not to get your senses dulled by being hung over, or drunk, or by everyday preoccupations. Otherwise that Day will come suddenly upon you, like a trap; for it will come on all the inhabitants of the earth [or: 'to all those who dwell on the face of all the earth']. Stay awake, all the time, asking to have the ability to escape all these things, and to stand before the Son of Man.'

Luke has taken over this long passage more or less as Mark left it, but making some characteristic changes of his own; 'famines and epidemics' for example, which sound the same in Greek, and 'terrors and great signs in heaven', which add to the general sense of foreboding. Luke adds 'prisons' to 'synagogues' as places where Christians might expect to be taken. Some scholars take the reference to 'Jerusalem encircled by enemies' as evidence that Luke wrote this on the basis of reports of the siege of Jerusalem that ended in AD 70, and likewise the predictions of trouble for Israel, and for 'this people' and for 'Jerusalem'. Some of the material Luke has already used in Chapter 17 (23, 24, 37), where it is about the delay in the coming of the Son of Man.

The reader may reflect, on hearing what Christians may expect in the shape of betrayal and death and hatred, that there has not been a century in the Church's existence, when this has not been the case. Can you face that prospect in your own life?

A 'Lucan summary' concluding Jesus' work in Jerusalem

37, 38 In the daytime, he would teach in the Temple; but at night he went out and camped on the Mountain called 'Of Olives'. And the whole populace would get up early in the morning [and come] to him in the Temple to listen to him.

We are now on the point of moving into the sombre and chilling story of Jesus' passion, and Luke brings to an end Jesus' ministry in Jerusalem (to which the Gospel had been aiming since Chapter 9, and in a sense from its very beginning) with one of his 'summaries'. He reminds us here of two themes of great importance to him. First, there is the Temple, where the Gospel started, and where it will end and Acts begins. Acts will not end there, however, but in Rome, having turned its back on Jerusalem. So it is that Luke deliberately surprises us with the information that Jesus has no permanent HQ in Jerusalem, but only a temporary base on the Mountain of Olives, from which direction the Messiah was popularly expected to come.

The second theme is that of the 'populace' (a favourite term of Luke) who have never been far from the surface of the narrative, open enough to the Gospel, if not fanatical about it, but often listening to Jesus.

What was it about Jesus that made the populace listen to him so attentively?

LUKE'S ACCOUNT OF JESUS' SUFFERING AND DEATH (22:1–23:56)

Introductory Lucan summary

22 1, 2 The feast of Unleavened Bread, called Passover, was drawing near; and the
chief priests and the scribes were looking for a way to destroy him; for they
were afraid of the populace.

This is very nearly exactly what Mark had written, with one or two small changes; in context, however, it functions as a 'Lucan summary', creating atmosphere, and signalling (as so often in Luke) the importance of the populace.

Judas' betrayal

3-6 Satan had entered Judas, the one called 'Iscariot', who was of the number of the
Twelve; and he went off and talked with the chief priests and captains, how to betray
[or: hand over] him. And they rejoiced, and made an agreement to give him money.
He gave his consent, and started looking for a good moment to hand him over [or:
betray], without a crowd to [bother] them.

Although Luke is largely following Mark, we shall notice at several points in the Passion Narrative that Luke and John seem to graze in the same paddock. One example is here, where he says that 'Satan had entered Judas', something we find also at John 13:2, 27.

Preparing the Passover meal

7-13 The day of Unleavened Bread came, the day on which the Passover had to be sacrificed; and he sent Peter and John, saying, 'Go [or: literally, 'journey'] and prepare
the Passover for us, so that we may eat.' They said to him, 'Where do you want us to
prepare [it]?' He said, 'Look! As you go into the city, a man will meet you who is carrying a water-pot. Follow him into the house into which he goes ['journeys', of course].
And you will tell the master of the house, "The teacher says to you, 'Where is the
chamber where I am to eat the Passover with my disciples?'." And he will show you a
large upstairs room, spread with couches. Prepare [the meal] there.'
They went off, and found it as he had said, and prepared the Passover.

Luke has made some small changes from what he found in Mark (14:12-17). In the latter, it had been the disciples who took the initiative; here it is Jesus, who singles out Peter and John. Luke also inserts his beloved 'journeying' word.

What do you make of the 'man . . . carrying a water-pot'?

This is my body . . .

14-20 And when the moment came, he lay down [to eat], and his apostles with him. And he said to them, 'I have eagerly desired to eat this Passover with you before I suffer. For I am telling you that I shan't eat it at all until it is fulfilled in the kingdom of God.' And he took a cup and gave thanks [or: did Eucharist] and said, 'Take this, and divide it among yourselves. For I'm telling you, from now onwards, I shan't drink from the produce of the vine, until the kingdom of God comes.' And taking bread, he gave thanks, broke and gave it to them saying, 'This is my body which is being given for you. Do this for my remembrance.' And the cup likewise after they had eaten, saying, 'This cup, the new covenant in my blood, is what is poured out for you.'

Luke calls Jesus' companions the 'apostles', where Mark had 'the Twelve'. He has also changed the order slightly: the mood is made perhaps slightly less sombre by the fact that he puts the prediction of his betrayal after the distribution of bread and cup. Luke also introduces a blessing of a cup before the bread, perhaps to underline that it is a Passover ritual.

Is this how you envisaged a Passover meal turning out?

Prediction of the betrayal, a squabble, and warnings

21-30 'But look! The hand of the one who is betraying me is with me at the table. Because the Son of Man is going on his journey in accordance with what has been appointed. But alas for that person through whom he is being betrayed.' And they started arguing among themselves who it would be that was about to do this.

And there was a quarrel, about which of them seemed to be Top [Apostle]. He said to them, 'The kings of the Gentiles act as lords over them, and those who are authorities over them are known as benefactors. With you it [must] not [be] so. No – let the top one among you become like the youngest, and the leader like one who serves. Tell me – who is top: the one who lies down, or the one who serves? Isn't it the one who lies down? Well, ***I'm*** in the middle of you as the one who serves.

'You people are the ones who have stuck it out with me in my trials. And I am assigning [a kingdom] to you, just as my Father has assigned a kingdom to me, that you may eat and drink at my table in my kingdom, and you may sit on thrones, judging the twelve tribes of Israel.'

Luke departs here from Mark: he inserts two characteristic phrases, 'journey', and 'in accordance with what has been appointed', to underline his conviction that Jesus (and his disciples) are 'on their way', and that God is in charge. He has also placed here something like the squabbling that arose in Mark 10:41-45 when James and John made their bid for power; but Luke has turned it round neatly in the direction of the washing of the disciples' feet that John reports at this point (John 13:4, 5, 12-17). Luke also places here the material about judging the twelve tribes of Israel, which Matthew places earlier (Matthew 19:28).

How would you describe the mood of this meal?

Prediction of Simon's lapse of faith

31-34 'Simon, Simon, see, Satan sought to sift you like wheat; but I prayed for you
that your faith should not fail. And then you in your turn, come back to yourself and
support your brothers [and sisters].'

He said to him, 'Lord – with you I'm even ready to journey to prison and to death!'

He said, 'I'm telling you, Peter, the cock won't crow tomorrow before you've denied, three times, that you know me!'

The series of s-sounds with which this section begins does not come out very well in English, but it reflects what appears to be deliberate alliteration in Luke's Greek.

The material does not appear quite like this in Mark (14:27-31). Characteristic of Luke is the double repetition of Simon's name (cf. 'Master, master' at 8:24, and 'Martha, Martha at 10:41); and it is interesting that Luke also has Jesus address him here by the nickname 'Rock'.

This is a story all about Simon Peter. What does it tell us?

Armed to the teeth?

35-38 And he said to them, 'When I sent you off without purse or bag or sandals, did
you lack anything?'

They said, 'Nothing.'

He said to them, 'Right – but now let anyone who has a purse take it, and the same with a bag; and anyone who doesn't have a sword should sell his cloak and buy one. For I'm telling you that this Scripture passage must be fulfilled in me: "And he was reckoned with the lawless"; you see, what is written about me is nearing accomplishment.'

They said, 'Lord, look – here are two swords.'

He said, 'It's enough.'

This baffling passage is only in Luke. It picks up the instructions about travelling light that we saw in 10:4, but seems to argue that things are now so bad that previous instructions are now to be disregarded, and they must invest in an arsenal. On the other hand, when they admit to having a small selection of weapons (only two!), Jesus tells them that it's sufficient. What do you think he meant?

Notice the characteristic Lucan notion that a 'scripture passage must be fulfilled'. This particular one comes from Isaiah 53:12, the fourth and last of the 'Songs of the Suffering Servant'.

'What is written about me is nearing accomplishment': this is one possible meaning of a phrase that has always stumped scholars.

Why did they have two swords?

Jesus prays to the Father

39-46 And he went out and journeyed, in accordance with his custom, to the Mountain of Olives; and the disciples followed him. When he got to the place, he said to them, 'Pray not to enter into temptation.' And he withdrew from them, about a stone's throw; and he fell on his knees and prayed, 'Father, if you wish, take this cup from me. But not my will – let yours be done.' And he arose from [his] prayer, and came to the disciples; and he found them asleep because of their grief, and he said to them, 'Why are you asleep? Arise and pray not to enter into temptation.'

Luke changes what he found in Mark (14:32-38); the story is no longer a triptych (three separate episodes of prayer); he adds 'in accordance with his custom', as he had when speaking of Zachariah's turn to sacrifice (1:9), and Jesus' first visit to Jerusalem for Passover (2:42). He also calls it (as so often before, and look at the first chapter of Acts) 'the Mountain of Olives' rather than Gethsemani. Quite unlike Mark's version, Jesus twice tells his disciples to 'pray' (Luke's is the Gospel of prayer, we remember). And Jesus is less evidently miserable here than he was in Mark's account. Charitably Luke ascribes the disciples' somnolence to 'grief', just as in 24:41 he will ascribe their lack of belief in the Resurrection to 'joy'.

Between 'let yours be done' and 'And he arose from [his] prayer', some early manuscripts have 'there appeared to him an angel from heaven, strengthening him. And being in an agony, he started to pray more intently. And his sweat became like drops of blood, falling on to the ground.' It was probably not what Luke originally wrote, however.

What is this story about?

The arresting party

47-51 While he was still speaking, look! A crowd, and the one called Judas (one of the Twelve!) approached them. And he drew near to Jesus, to kiss him. Jesus, however, said to him, 'Judas – is it with a kiss that you are betraying the Son of Man?'

When his companions saw what was about to happen, they said, 'Lord, are we to hit [someone] with a sword?' And one of them hit the Chief Priest's slave and cut off his ear (the right-hand one). Jesus responded, 'Let them be; that's enough!' And he touched the ear and healed it!

Again Luke offers a rather briefer account than what we find in Mark. It is only Luke, however, who comments on the inappropriateness of a kiss as an accompaniment of the betrayal. Then comes some violent (if wholly ineffective) resistance. Whoever it was (and unlike John, Luke is not telling) might argue, I suppose, that Jesus had only a few minutes earlier been speaking of the importance of being well armed. But then Jesus negates the gesture by healing the fairly trivial (though doubtless tiresome to the slave in question) wound that had been inflicted.

Jesus' reproof to the religious authorities

52, 53 Jesus said to the chief priests and captains of the Temple who had come upon him, 'You've come out with swords and clubs, as though [arresting] a bandit! But every day, when I was with you in the Temple, you never stretched out your hands against me. No – this is your hour, and the domain of darkness.'

This is an odd passage, for the most part only in Luke. It shows a Jesus who is very much in command, and with some gentle irony, or even humour ('I'm not really dangerous'). He refers back to 19:47 ('teaching daily in the Temple'), which was only in Luke; and Luke is the only one to make the enigmatic remark about 'your hour and the domain of darkness', which takes us back to the end of the temptation narrative (Luke 4:13).

Why did the arresting party think that they needed 'swords and clubs'?

Peter doesn't know Jesus

54-62 When they had arrested him, they took him and led him to the house of the Chief Priest. But Peter followed from a long way off. When they had kindled a fire in the middle of the courtyard, and they had sat down together, Peter sat in the midst of them.

A little slave girl saw him sitting facing the light. She looked closely at him and said, 'This one was with him, too.' But he disagreed and said, 'I don't know him, woman.'

And after a short time, someone else saw him and said, 'You're one of them, too!' But Peter said, 'Man, I'm not!' And an hour or so later, someone else insisted, 'For sure he was with him – he's a Galilean!'

Peter said, 'Man – I've no idea what you're talking about.'

And immediately, while he was still speaking, a cock crowed.

And the Lord turned and looked at Peter. And Peter recalled the Lord's comment, that he'd told him, 'Before the cock crows today, you'll deny me three times.' And he went out and wept bitterly.

This saddest of all stories is in all the Gospels, but Luke tells it in his own way. He places it slightly earlier than it was in Mark, and produces a most telling touch when he has Jesus (who appears from nowhere) turn and look at Peter, which is sufficient to remind him of what he has just done and said.

What is the significance of Peter's tears?

The mocking of Jesus

63-65 And the men who held him mocked him and beat him, and they covered him up and interrogated him, 'Prophesy, who's the one who struck you?' And they addressed him with many other impertinent remarks.

Luke places this episode slightly later than Mark does, and makes it lead into the interrogation by the religious authorities. In some ways this is closer to Matthew's version, although Luke is the only one to speak of 'impertinent remarks' (literally, 'blaspheming').

In the Sanhedrin

22[66]–23[1] And when day broke, the presbyterium of the populace gathered, chief priests and scribes; and they led him into their synagogue, saying, 'If you are the Messiah, tell us.' He said to them, 'If I tell you, you won't believe; but if I interrogate [you], you won't answer. But from now on, the Son of Man will be seated at the right hand of the power of God.'

They all said, 'So – you are the Son of God, then?' He said to them, 'It is you people who say that I am.' They said, 'What need do we still have of evidence? For we have heard from his mouth.' And the whole crowd of them got up and led him to Pilate.

Luke has shortened Mark's account, omitting the allegation about 'destroy this Temple and in three days I shall rebuild it', and going straight on to the difficult question: is Jesus, or is he not, the Messiah? It is no longer, according to Luke, the Chief Priest who finds Jesus guilty, but all of them. And it is hard, on this account, to know what Jesus is guilty ***of****!*

Jesus is accused before Pilate

2-5 They began to accuse him, saying 'We found this man subverting our nation and preventing them from paying tax to Caesar, and saying that he is a King-Messiah.'

Pilate interrogated him, 'Are you the King of the Jews?'

He answered, 'You say so.'

Pilate said to the chief priests and the crowds, 'I find no crime in him'; but they insisted, 'This man is stirring up the populace, teaching in all of Judaea, and starting from Galilee right up to this point.'

Luke gives a slightly different introduction to the scene between Jesus and Pilate. He makes the accusations against Jesus demonstrably false: the reader knows perfectly well that Jesus was not 'subverting' the nation or 'preventing them from paying tax to Caesar' or 'stirring up the populace'. But they are all the kind of thing that the affluent in society might unthinkingly say. He also adds his familiar 'journeying' theme, with the reference to Judaea and Galilee.

Jesus is sent to Herod

6-12 Pilate pricked up his ears, and asked if the fellow was a Galilean. When he found out that he was from Herod's jurisdiction, he sent him up to Herod, since he was also in Jerusalem at that time.

When Herod saw Jesus, he greatly rejoiced. For [he'd been] wanting to see him for a long time, because he'd been hearing about him, and he was hoping to see a miracle being done by him. He interrogated him at some length – but he didn't respond to him in any way. The chief priests and the scribes were standing there, vigorously accusing him. Herod, along with his troops, regarded him with contempt, and played a game with him, dressing him up in gorgeous clothing, and sending him back to Pilate. Herod and Pilate became friends with each other on that day; for they had previously been at enmity.

This passage is only in Luke, and once again we meet Herod, in whom Luke has more than a passing interest. Like John the Baptist and Jesus at the beginning, so now Herod and Pilate are brought together at the end. Herod's superficial interest in 'Jesus the miracle-worker' marks him out as someone who can't cope with who Jesus is for Luke, so it is not surprising that he plays his silly game and cements a trivial alliance.

We may contrast Herod, who 'was hoping' to see one of Jesus' party-tricks, with Cleopas and his companion in the following chapter, who 'had been hoping' that Jesus was to redeem Israel.

What is the difference between Jesus on the one hand and Pilate and Herod on the other?

Pilate is reluctantly forced to condemn Jesus

13-25 Pilate called the chief priests and the rulers, and the populace, and said to them, 'You brought me this person on the grounds that he is causing rebellion among the people, and look here – speaking for myself in your presence, I have examined this person, and I've found in him no evidence that he is guilty of the accusations that you are bringing against him. And nor did Herod (because he sent him up to us); and look – nothing worthy of death has been done by him. So I am going to have him flogged and release him.'

But they all cried out together, 'Take this one away; release Barabbas to us!' (This one had been flung into gaol because of a riot that had taken place in the city, and for murder.) Pilate addressed them again; he wanted to release Jesus. But they went on shouting, 'Crucify him, crucify [him].' He addressed them a third time, 'Why? What evil has this man done? I have found no capital crime in him. So I'm going to flog him and release him.' But they insisted, with loud shouts, demanding that he be crucified – and their shouts prevailed, and Pilate decided that their request should be granted. He released the one they had been demanding, the one who had been flung into gaol because of rioting and murder – and Jesus he handed over to their will!

Luke departs from Mark here, and runs a bit closer to John's account of the scene before Pilate. He shares with John the strong sense that Pilate tried very hard to release Jesus. Luke manages to convey this with the awkward sentence 'nothing worthy of death has been done by him'. Luke is also closer to John than he is to Mark in the reference to 'crying out' and to the demand for Barabbas rather than Jesus. On the other hand, it is Luke alone who makes it clear that Jesus' flogging, with monstrous injustice, is for being innocent-but-accused.

Jesus' companions on the way to death

26-32 And as they led him away, they took hold of Simon, a Cyrenean, who was coming from the field, and put the cross on him to carry it behind Jesus.

A great crowd of the populace was following him, and also [a crowd] of women, who were mourning him and weeping for him. Jesus turned to the women and said, 'Daughters of Jerusalem, don't be weeping over me. No – weep for yourselves and for your children. Because, look! Days are coming when they will be saying, "Congratulations to the women who are barren, and the wombs that have not given birth, and the breasts that have not suckled." Then they will start saying to the mountains, "Fall on us," and to the hills, "Cover us." Because if they do these things when the wood is green – what might happen when it's dry?'

And two other criminals were led out with him to be executed.

*Luke has grouped together three groups of companions for Jesus as he goes out to his execution. The first and the third are already in Mark, although Luke's account of Simon of Cyrene is less stark than Mark 15:21. The second group, however, the 'women of Jerusalem', who have the courage to show their affection for Jesus, is only in Luke, and is part of the evidence that makes people want to call Luke the 'Gospel of women'. Jesus' sensitive response to their mourning, and the characteristic Lucan note that he '***turned*** to the women', give the incident great emotional weight. The line about asking the mountains and the hills to bury them is already in Hosea 10:8, in the context of the destruction of the Northern Kingdom. Here it is clearly the destruction of Jerusalem that is in view.*

Jesus' companions at Skull Place

33-43 And when they came to the place that was known as 'Skull', there they crucified him, and the criminals, one on the right, and one on the left. 'When they divided his garments, they threw lots.'

And the crowd stood, watching. And the rulers sneered at him, saying, 'He saved others; let him save himself, if this is the "Messiah of God", the "Chosen One".' And the soldiers who came up also made a game of him, offering him sour wine, and saying, 'If you ***are*** the King of the Judaeans, save yourself!' There was also a placard on him, 'This is the King of the Judaeans.'

One of the crucified criminals started blaspheming him, saying, 'Aren't you the Messiah? Save yourself – and us as well!' The other scolded him in response and said, 'Have you no reverence even for God? Because you're under the same sentence; but we deserve it, because we are getting the going rate for what we did. But this man hasn't done anything wrong.' And he said, 'Jesus – remember me when you come into your kingdom.' And he said to him, 'Amen I tell you, ***today*** you will be with me in Paradise.'

Luke presents three possible reactions to Jesus: the 'populace' watch; the rulers (familiar Lucan term), soldiers, and one of his fellow criminals, turn the word 'save' on Jesus, to show that he's a fake; finally the other criminal gets him triumphantly and dramatically right, and turns into one of Jesus' 'terrible friends'. This perceptive murderer asserts that Jesus is indeed a King (or Messiah) and all but says that he is God. In addition the reader knows that whatever the rulers may think, Jesus is indeed 'Messiah of God' (9:20) and 'Chosen One' (9:35). The episode ends, with arresting solemnity, with 'Amen I tell you' and a striking Lucan 'today', and a most unexpected conclusion.

What does this episode say about Jesus?

The circumstances of Jesus' death

44-49 And it was now about the sixth hour, and a darkness came on all the earth until the ninth hour, because there was an eclipse of the sun. The veil of the Temple was torn in the middle, and Jesus cried in a loud voice, 'Father, into your hands I commit my spirit.' As he said this, he expired. When the centurion saw what had happened, he started to glorify God, saying, 'This person really was innocent.' And all the crowds who had come together for this spectacle, and had watched what took place, went back beating their breasts. All the men who were known to him stood a long way off, and also the women who had followed him from Galilee, watching these [events].

Luke is still clearly following Mark's account, but he makes one or two changes, where we can see his hand at work. He adds the detail about the eclipse of the sun, perhaps giving a scientific explanation for his educated readers. He omits Mark's terrible cry of abandonment ('My God, my God – why have you forsaken me?', Mark 15:34), and the sponge filled with vinegar (though the soldiers have given Jesus something like that earlier on). Jesus' last words are reported as a much more gentle quotation from Psalm 31:6. And the centurion, in a characteristic phrase, 'started to glorify God', and instead of the verdict 'Son of God', which in some ways is the climax of Mark's Gospel (Mark 15:39), we read, 'This person really was innocent'; and Luke adds the dramatic detail that the watching crowds (verse 48 picking up verse 35) 'went back beating their breasts'. Finally, where Mark had the disciples all run away, Luke is rather emphatic that 'all the men known to him' were, after all, still there, though he agrees with Mark that the faithful women were witnesses. And he does have the men standing 'a long way off'.

Where would you wish to be, at this moment?

How Jesus was buried

50-56 And look! A man called Joseph, who was a member of the Sanhedrin, and a good and just man (he had not voted for their decision and action), from Arimathea, a city of the Jews, who was waiting for the kingdom of God, this man approached Pilate and asked for the body of Jesus. And when he had taken it down, he wrapped it in a linen cloth, and placed him in a tomb hewn out of the rock, where no one had yet lain. And it was the Day of Preparation, and Sabbath was about to begin [literally, 'dawning'].

And the women who had followed with him from Galilee, saw the tomb, and [saw] how his body was placed. They went back and prepared spices and perfumes, and for the Sabbath-day they rested in accordance with the commandment.

Once again, Luke is following Mark, but with some shades of meaning of his own. He specifically exempts Joseph of Arimathea from any blame in Jesus' death. He follows Mark in saying that Joseph was 'waiting for the kingdom of God'. But in Luke that phrase has a special meaning. Basically it means to 'receive'; but in 2:25 Luke uses it of Simeon 'waiting for the comfort of Israel'; at 2:28 Simeon 'received' or 'took' Jesus into his arms; at 12:36 it refers to people 'expecting' their Lord when he comes back from the wedding. And in 15:2, it refers to Jesus' unfortunate propensity to lavish hospitality on undesirables. If in the previous passage Luke seems to have downgraded the women by emphasising that they weren't alone, he now makes handsome amends, by repeating that they had 'followed' (or 'been disciples') 'from Galilee'. He also points to their faithfulness and love, in preparing spices for anointing Jesus' body, to their status as witnesses (they saw 'how his body was placed') and their fidelity as Jews ('for the Sabbath-day they rested in accordance with the commandment'); for this very Lucan idea about the 'commandment', see also 1:6; 15:29; 18:20.

No body, but two men in white clothes

24 1-12 But on the first day of the week, in the deep dawn, they came to the tomb, bringing the spices they had bought. And they found the stone rolled away from the tomb; and when they went in, they did not find the body of the Lord Jesus. And as they were puzzling about this, look! Two men stood by them in dazzling clothes. They became fearful, and bowed their faces to the ground; [the two men] said to the women, 'Why are you looking for the Living One among the corpses? He is not here – no, he has been raised! Remember how he told you, while he was still in Galilee, that "the Son of Man must be delivered into the hands of sinners and be crucified and on the third day rise again".' And they recalled his words.

And when they returned from the tomb, they announced all these things to the Eleven, and to all the rest. They were the Magdalene Mary, and Joanna, and Mary of Jacob, and the rest of the women with them. They said these things to the apostles. And these words appeared to them like nonsense; and they didn't believe them. And Peter arose and ran to the tomb and stooped down and saw the cloths, and went off home, marvelling at what had happened.

Luke, for the last time, uses what Mark (16:1-8) had written, but makes several changes. There is no conversation about rolling the stone away; they simply find it so, and no dead body. Then they encounter 'two men', clearly angels, in an encounter that echoes the Transfiguration (9:28-36). The two men rebuke them for looking in the wrong place, and remind them that Jesus had actually predicted his Resurrection. There is here no mission to Galilee, no instructions to Peter and the disciples. And Luke has avoided Mark's astonishing ending, 'They said nothing to anyone – for they were afraid'.

In addition, Luke reports a visit by Peter to the tomb, with a characteristic Lucan phrase, 'marvelling at what had happened', but also using some words that will appear in John's version of the scene: 'ran', 'bent down and saw the cloths', 'he went off home (or: to himself)'.

Were the women right?

The journey from Jerusalem to Emmaus and (rather rapidly) back to Jerusalem (a liturgy?)

13-35 And look! Two of them on that day were journeying to a village that was sixty stades (seven or eight miles) distant from Jerusalem. And they were talking to each other about all these things that had happened. And as they talked, Jesus himself actually drew near and was journeying with them. Their eyes were prevented from recognising him. He said to them, 'What words are these which you are exchanging with each other as you walk?' And they stopped dead, looking sullen.

One of them, called Cleopas, answered him, 'Are you the only one visiting Jerusalem, and you don't know the things that have taken place in Jerusalem during these days?'

And he said to them, 'What sort of things?' They told him, 'Things about Jesus the Nazarene, who appeared as a man, a prophet, powerful in word and deed before God and before the entire populace? How they handed him over, our chief priests and rulers, to a death sentence, and they crucified him? We had been hoping that he was going to be the one to ransom [or: liberate] Israel. And now, some women from our lot have astonished us; they got to the tomb at dawn, and didn't find his body, and they came saying that they'd seen a vision of angels, who said he was alive. And some of those with us went off to the tomb; and they found it just as the women had said – but they did not see him.'

And he said to them, 'What ***fools*** you are! [So] lacking in imagination, [not] to believe all that the prophets had said! Wasn't it ***essential*** for the Messiah to suffer this and [so] enter into his glory?' And he started with Moses and with all the prophets, and explained the stuff about himself in all the scriptures.

And they drew near to the village to which they were journeying – and he pretended to be journeying further. But they pressed him, saying, 'Stay with us, because it is towards evening, and the day has already declined.' And he went in to stay with them. And it turned out, as he lay down [to eat] with them, he took the loaf, and blessed [it] and broke [it] and handed [it] over to them – and their eyes were opened wide, and they recognised him! And he vanished from them.

And they said to each other, 'Wasn't our heart burning within as he was talking to us on the journey? As he was opening up the scriptures to us?'

And they got up at that moment and returned to Jerusalem, and found the Eleven gathered, and their companions, who were [all] saying, 'The Lord really is risen, and he's appeared to Simon.' And they in their turn related the things that had happened on the way, and how he'd been recognised by them in the breaking of the bread.

This episode is only reported in Luke, and it may be helpful to make two points about it. First, it is a journey, perhaps a microcosm of the whole journey that is Luke-Acts, and indeed (for Luke) the entire Christian life. It starts, like the gospel, in Jerusalem, and, like the gospel, it ends there – but much has gone on. The journey started slow and plodding; its pace quickened up when Jesus 'journeyed with them'; it seemed to have come to a pleasant halt as the day declined – but it culminated in a rapid sprint back to Jerusalem. And that, it turns out, is only the beginning of a quite new journey.

Second, it is a Eucharistic service. Standardly, the Christian Eucharist begins with 'where the worshippers are', what in some traditions is called the 'Penitential Rite'. That is represented by the sullen disciples speaking to each other and (rather reluctantly) to Jesus of their disillusionment. Next comes the 'service of the word', Jesus taking them through the Scripture readings, and tying it together in a homily (though most preachers these days avoid addressing their congregations as 'fools', whatever their private opinions). Then, in the form of a request to Jesus to stay on, come the 'prayers of intercession'. This is then taken up in the service of communion (taking, blessing, and distributing bread) in which Christians have, ever since that Easter Sunday evening, momentarily recognised their Lord. Finally there is the dismissal, where the congregation is told to 'go in peace'. That is precisely what happens to Cleopas and his companion. As all Christians should be, they are animated by the liturgy they have attended, and go hastily on the journey for which the liturgy has equipped them. And the liturgy and the journey both take them back (at least from time to time), to the Church, 'the Eleven and those with them'.

Does Christian liturgy have the same effect on you that it had on these two sad disciples?

The real Jesus – not a ghost – appears

36-43 As they were saying these things, he himself stood in the middle of them, and he says to them, 'Peace [be] with you.' They were panic-stricken and terrified – they thought they were seeing a spirit! And he said to them, 'Why are you so disturbed, and for what reason do doubts arise in your mind? See my hands and my feet: it is me, in person. Feel me, and see that a spirit does not have flesh and bones, as you see that I have.' Saying this, he showed them his hands and feet. As they still didn't believe (it was too good to be true), and were [just] marvelling, he said to them, 'Do you have anything edible here?' They gave him a piece of grilled fish, and he took it, in front of them, and ate it!

This passage finds echoes in John's Gospel (see John 20:19-23 and 21:5,10). The point of it is twofold: first, that Jesus is different. He can suddenly appear in their midst; and they are clearly not sure that it is he. Second, he is real: he can be felt; he still bears (presumably) the marks of crucifixion; and he can eat. Resurrection, Luke is telling us, is not just a feeling that Jesus is 'still very much with us' – it is much more precise and purposeful than that.

The summary of the teaching of Luke's Gospel

44-49 He said to them, 'This was the meaning of my words, which I spoke to you while I was still with you, that everything written about me, in the Law of Moses, and in the Prophets, and in the Psalms, must inevitably be fulfilled. Then he opened their minds to understand the scriptures and he told them, 'So it is written that the Messiah suffered and rose from the dead on the third day; and repentance for the forgiveness of sins be preached to all the Gentiles, beginning from Jerusalem. You are witnesses of these things. And, look, I am sending you the Father's promise upon you. You [are to] settle down in the city until you are clothed with power from on high.'

Here Luke weaves together a good many themes from the Gospel which is now ending, themes that will also be part of the narrative of Acts that is about to begin. We may mention the following:

- *Jesus' words are explained in terms of a continuity with the message of the three sections (Law, Prophets, Psalms) of the Hebrew Bible, what we call the Old Testament;*
- *the idea of 'opening the mind' reminds us that not everyone in the Gospel has been able to see Jesus in this way; and we shall see that in Acts likewise there are those who fail to see Jesus as the fulfilment of the Hebrew scriptures;*
- *the heart of the matter is that the Messiah suffered and rose. At the end of Acts, Paul is about to suffer;*
- *the message, of both Jesus and the infant Church of Acts, is 'repentance for the forgiveness of sins';*
- *the message is both a journey and an invitation to a journey 'starting from Jerusalem'. It never loses touch with its roots, but proceeds to 'the ends of the earth' (Acts 1:8);*
- *the message, which was first delivered in the Temple, is now to go out to 'all the Gentiles (or nations)', which is what we shall see happening in Acts;*
- *the journey continues by means of 'witnesses': primarily witnesses to the Resurrection. In the first place, it will be 'the Twelve and those with them'; later the task is handed over to Stephen, Philip, Paul and any single reader of the Gospel and Acts who responds with an open mind;*
- *the journey is not under their control: for the moment, they must 'settle down in the city' and wait;*
- *the journey is under the control of 'the promise of my Father . . . power from on high', what elsewhere in Luke-Acts is called 'the Holy Spirit', whose journey this is.*

Which of these features of Luke's Gospel has most struck you in your reading of it?

Jesus leaves them; they survive

50-53 He led them out towards Bethany, and he raised his hands and blessed them. And it happened as he blessed them that he parted from them, and was being taken up to heaven. They worshipped him and returned to Jerusalem with great joy; and they were all the time in the Temple, blessing God.

This is a powerful ending. Three times the word 'bless' is used, echoing the four times it was used in the Infancy Narratives (1:42; 1:64; 2:28; 2:34). The last act of the Gospel is the same as its first, in the Temple, blessing God. Now, however, it is no longer an old man with no descendants, but a young group, on the point of expanding rapidly. They have also learnt the correct approach to Jesus, for Luke tells us that they 'worshipped' him, and the alert reader will recall 4:7, 8, when it was established from Scripture that 'you shall worship the Lord your God'. Luke is understated in his assertion of who Jesus is; but follow him carefully and you will see that he has a very lofty view of him indeed.

Acts of the Apostles

Acts of the Apostles

The racy tale that you are about to read is the second part of our two-volume narrative and it is likewise addressed to 'Theophilus'. If the Gospel was the Gospel of Jesus, you might say that Acts is the 'Gospel of the Holy Spirit'. Two ways in which you will notice the power of the Spirit: first, Acts is a journey, always 'on the move', until it reaches Rome; and even then it is restless – the last word (two words in English, only one in Greek) of the two volumes is 'without hindrance'. Second, in his account of the Pentecost incident, Luke represents this Holy Spirit as 'fire' and 'mighty wind'. Watch how this power is made evident throughout this extraordinary story.

Prologue

1 1-5 Theophilus: the first account I drew up about all the [things] which Jesus began to do and teach, from the day when he gave orders to the apostles whom he had chosen, through the Holy Spirit; and then he was taken up. He had showed himself alive to them, after his passion, by many convincing proofs, appearing to them through [a period of] forty days, and speaking the things that concern the kingdom of God. While he was staying with them, he directed them not to depart from Jerusalem, but to await 'the promise of the Father, which you have heard me [talking about]. For John baptised with water, while you will be baptised with the Holy Spirit, not many days from now.'

Luke here rapidly and skilfully summarises 'the story so far'. The two-volume work that we call 'Luke-Acts' (and an untranslatable particle in the Greek here makes it clearer than we can in English that we are now beginning Volume II) is addressed to the 'Most Excellent Theophilus'. This form of address is appropriate for one of the Equites, the second (but still decidedly exalted) rank of Roman society. The name 'Theophilus' might be that of a real person, perhaps Luke's well-to-do patron. Or, since it means 'Beloved by God' or 'Lover of God', it might be addressed to any Christian reader.

One aspect of Acts that we shall frequently notice is the way it echoes Volume I, the 'Gospel of Luke'. The first example of such an echo comes here, with the reference to 'forty days'. Just as Jesus prepared for his mission with forty days in the desert, he now prepares the Church for its mission with forty days of appearances. We note, too, the first mention of the Holy Spirit, whose chronicle Acts is, and the phrase 'the promise of the Father', referring to the Holy Spirit.

Notice that Resurrection is part of the 'given' of Acts, as it is of the New Testament as a whole.

The Ascension: final instructions, attentive prayer

6-14 So they came together, and asked him, 'Lord, is it at this time that you are re-establishing the kingdom for Israel?' He said to them, 'It is not your right to know times and seasons which the Father has fixed by his own authority. Instead, you will receive power when the Holy Spirit comes on you, and you will be my witnesses, in Jerusalem, and in all Judaea and Samaria, and until the end of the earth.'

As he said these things, while they looked, he was lifted up, and a cloud took him up, out of their sight. As they were gazing intently into heaven, while he journeyed, look! Two men were in their presence, in white clothes; and these men said, 'Men of Galilee, why do you stand looking into heaven? This Jesus, who was taken up from you into heaven, so he will come in [just the same] way you see him journeying into heaven.'

Then they returned to Jerusalem from the Mount called 'The Olive Grove', which is near Jerusalem, a Sabbath-day's journey. When they entered [the city] they went up to the upper room where they were staying: Peter and John and Jacob and Andrew, Philip and Thomas, Bartholomew and Matthew, Jacob of Alphaeus and Simon the Zealot and Judas of Jacob. All these were engaged unanimously in prayer, along with the women, and Mary the mother of Jesus, and his brothers.

The disciples do not really understand at present; this incomprehension continues a theme from the Gospel, of course. That will change when 'the Holy Spirit comes on you'; in a sense, Acts is the working out of this promise. Acts also shows how the apostles became Jesus' 'witnesses in Jerusalem and in all Judaea and Samaria' (reversing the order of the Gospel, where Jesus journeyed from Galilee through Samaria to Judaea and finally to Jerusalem) and 'as far as the end of the earth', which will be first Athens (Chapter 17) and finally Rome (28:30, 31).

Two favourite words of Luke that come in this text are translated here, 'gazing intently' and 'journeyed'. 'Went' is the more common translation of the latter, but does not reflect the weight that Luke puts upon it in the 'journeying Gospel'. 'A Sabbath-day's journey': orthodox Jews may not travel more than a thousand yards outside the city limits on the Sabbath-day. As in the opening of his Gospel, Luke is careful to show that the heroes of his story are observant Jews.

The list of apostles is the same as in Luke 6:14-16, but in a different order, and, of course, without Judas Iscariot. Some scholars feel that Luke puts the women 'in their place' by mentioning them last.

Note the word translated 'unanimously'; we shall see this again as a description of the infant Church.

Selecting a replacement for Judas

15-26 In those days, Peter stood up in the middle of the brethren and said (and the crowd of names together was about a hundred and twenty), 'Men and brothers, it was necessary for the scripture to be fulfilled which the Holy Spirit foretold through the mouth of David, regarding Judas, who became a guide to those who arrested Jesus, because he was numbered with us, and he had been allotted this ministry. So this fellow obtained a piece of land out of the wages of iniquity, and falling headlong he burst open in the middle, and all his guts poured out. This became known to all who dwell in Jerusalem, so that that piece of land was called in their own language 'Haceldama', that is 'Field of Blood'. For it is written in the Book of Psalms:

"Let his residence become a desert, and let the one who dwells in it not be"; and
"Let another take over his office-as-overseer."

'Therefore it is necessary that one of the men who came together with us all the time when the Lord Jesus came in and went out among us, beginning from the baptism of John until the day when he was taken up from us, should become with us a witness of his Resurrection.'

They set up two, Joseph called Barsabbas, who was nicknamed 'Justus', and Matthias. They prayed and said, 'You, Lord, knower of the hearts of all, show which one out of the two you have chosen, to take the place of this service and this apostolate from which Judas transgressed, to journey to his own place.' They gave them lots; and the lot fell on Matthias, and he was voted in with the eleven apostles.

Peter exercises here a leadership which he does not always have in Acts, initiating God's choice of a successor to Judas. We notice that once he has performed his task of making Eleven into Twelve, Matthias is never heard of again.

Twice in this passage Luke uses, what in Greek is a three-letter word, translated 'it is/was necessary'; and notice also the word 'foretold'. Both these words subtly convey the message that God is in charge; the Holy Spirit is irresistibly running the show.

The two quotations applied to Judas and the problems of his successor are from Psalm 69:25 and 109:8 respectively.

We also notice that the function of an apostle is to be a 'witness of his Resurrection'. Is that your function also?

Fire and wind at Pentecost

2 1-4 At the fulfilment of the day of Pentecost they were all together in the same place. Suddenly there came from heaven a sound, as of a violent wind rushing, and it filled the whole house where they were sitting, and divided tongues, as if of fire, appeared to them, and sat on each single one of them, and they were all filled with the Holy Spirit, and they began to speak in different languages, as the Spirit granted them to utter.

Now we 'see' the Spirit in action, with sound and sights (mighty wind, tongues of fire); we are meant to recall Jesus' baptism at Luke 3:22, with its own sound and sight (the Holy Spirit in bodily form, and the voice from heaven). The word 'fulfilment' is related to that which the evangelist uses at Luke 1:1; the work of God is being done. The fire and mighty wind are symbols of what we shall see in the rest of Acts, as the story of the Holy Spirit unfolds. The 'violent wind' blows throughout Acts, driving the story on, powerfully changing people's lives, driving Saul and Peter and the rest of them on the journey to the 'ends of the earth'; you can see it in the way intense opposition is overcome, in the signs and wonders and healings that accompany the gospel. 'Tongues of fire' stand as a symbol for the speeches that constitute one third of Acts of the Apostles. See how on that first Pentecost the gospel was preached to 'all the world', how Stephen and Peter and Paul cannot be prevented from speaking of Jesus to everyone they meet. Acts is the dramatic illustration of how the fire of the gospel spread round the Mediterranean world, of how the wind blew from Jerusalem to Rome, and then onwards down the centuries and across the world to wherever you are reading these words today.

Do you feel the fire and the wind in your life?

The gospel is preached to the entire world

5-13 There were Jews living in Jerusalem, devout men from all the nations under heaven. When this sound happened, the crowd came together and were confused, because each one of them heard them speaking in their own language. They were astounded and amazed, saying, 'Look! All these people who are speaking, aren't they Galileans? How do we each hear in our own language in which we were born? Parthians and Medes and Elamites and those who dwell in Mesopotamia, and Judaea and Cappadocia, Pontus and Asia, Phrygia and Pamphylia, Egypt and the parts of Libya round Cyrene, and Roman visitors, both Jews and proselytes, Cretans and Arabs, we hear them speaking in our [own] languages the great things of God.'

They were all amazed, and greatly perplexed, one saying to another, 'What's all this about?' But others said, mockingly, 'They are full of sweet [wine].'

Notice how the good news is already reaching 'to the end of the earth', and look at a map for all the places mentioned, to see how it makes a great circle round the Ancient Near East. The 'great things of God': the root is a favourite of Luke – see Luke 1:46, 58; 9:43; Acts 5:13; 10:46; 19:17.

The theme of initial rejection or mockery (in this case the allegation that the speakers are drunk) will reappear frequently in Acts. It is part of the energy of the Spirit that it arouses opposition as well as driving the story and the gospel forcibly onwards.

Peter's Pentecost speech

14-36 But Peter stood up with the eleven and raised his voice, and addressed them, 'Men of Judaea, and all you who are living in Jerusalem, let this be known to you, and give ear to my words. For these people are not drunk, as you suppose, for it is the third hour of the day. No – this is what was spoken through the prophet Joel:

"And it shall be in those days, says the Lord,
I pour out some of my spirit on all flesh;
and your sons and your daughters shall prophesy,
and your young men shall see visions,
and your elders shall dream in dreams.

"And on my servants, male and female, in those days
I pour out some of my spirit and they shall prophesy,
and I shall give portents in heaven above
and signs on the earth below,
blood and fire and smoky vapour.
The sun will be changed into darkness,
and the moon into blood
before the Day of the Lord comes, great and glorious.
And it shall be that all who call upon the name of the Lord shall be saved."

'Men of Israel, hear these words: Jesus the Nazarene, a man marked out from God to you by miracles and portents and signs, which God did through him in the midst of you, just as you yourselves know, this same man, by the predetermined plan and foreknowledge of God [when he had been] delivered up through the hand[s] of the lawless, you nailed and destroyed him. God raised him up, undoing the birth pangs of death, because it was not possible that he should be held fast by it. For David says, with regard to him:

"I saw the Lord before me throughout,
because he is at my right, so that I be not shaken.
Therefore my heart rejoiced
and my tongue exulted
and still my flesh shall dwell in hope.
Because you will not abandon my soul to Hades,
nor will you permit your Holy One to see destruction.
You made me know the ways of life.
You fill me full of joy with your face."

'Men, and brothers, it is allowable [for us] to speak to you with confidence about the patriarch David. He died and was buried, and his tomb is in our midst to the present day. Now, since he was a prophet, and since he knew that God, with an oath, "had sworn to him that the fruit of his loins would sit on his throne" [Psalm 132:11; 2 Samuel 7:12, 13] he spoke prophetically about the Resurrection of the Messiah, "He was not abandoned into Hades, nor did his flesh see destruction" [Psalm 16:10]. This is Jesus, whom God raised up; and we are all Jesus' witnesses. And so he has been exalted to God's right hand; he received the promise of the Holy Spirit from the Father, he poured out the Spirit; that is what you people are seeing and hearing. For David did not go up to heaven, but it is David who says [in Psalm 110:1]:

"The Lord said to my Lord: Sit on my right
until I make your enemies a footstool for your feet."

'So let the entire house of Israel know infallibly that God appointed him Lord and Messiah, this Jesus, whom you people crucified.'

The first of several speeches in Acts: like many ancient historians, Luke uses these speeches to interpret to the reader what he thinks is going on. At the same time, however, he writes in a way appropriate to the speaker.

The long quotations from Joel 2:28-33 and Psalm 16:8-11, and the reference to 'God's foreknowledge' emphasise that the Holy Spirit is directing operations. The rather complicated argument about David is meant to demonstrate that the scriptures really refer to Jesus.

As Luke does throughout Acts, Peter here emphasises Jesus' death, to which God's response is Resurrection, making Jesus 'Lord and Messiah'.

'God appointed him Lord and Messiah'. What difference does this make?

The powerful effects of the speech

37-41 When they heard [him], they were pierced to the heart; and they said to Peter and the rest of the apostles, 'What shall we do, brothers?' And Peter said to them, 'Repent, and let each of you be baptised in the name of Jesus Messiah, for the forgiveness of your sins, and you will receive the gift of the Holy Spirit. For the promise is to you, and to your children, and to all those a long way off, whomsoever the Lord our God shall summon.'

In many more words he testified, and he invited them, saying, 'Be saved from this crooked generation.' So those who accepted what he said were baptised; and there were added on that day about three thousand souls.

The preaching of the word has an immediate effect; and, as in the gospel, it comes in terms of 'repentance and forgiveness of sins'.

As in the early part of Luke's Gospel, one is given the impression of immense and immediate success: three thousand added in a single day.

Do Peter's words have the same effect on you?

Life in the early Church – 1

2 42–3 1a They were holding fast to the apostles' teaching, to the breaking of the bread and to communion, and to the breaking of the bread and the prayers. There came awe on every soul; and many portents and signs came about through the apostles. And all the believers were in the same place, and they held everything in common; and they sold their possessions and their belongings, and divided them [among] everybody according as anybody had need. Every day they persisted unanimously in the Temple, breaking bread at home. They received their share of food joyfully and in simplicity of heart, praising God, and having favour with the whole people. And the Lord was every day adding the number of saved to the same place.

This paragraph is the first of several examples in Acts of the 'Lucan summary', a device that we have seen the evangelist employ quite often in the Gospel, but which he uses more especially in Acts. Its function is to create atmosphere rather than report events. It is also Luke's way of telling the reader, 'this is what it should be like today'.

Notice the phrase 'in the same place (1:44)', and, later, 'to the same place' (3:1a). This is the fourth time in Acts that we have encountered this rather obscure expression (see also 1:15 and 2:1), which presumably is intended to emphasise the unity of the infant Church. See also the word translated as 'communion'. The Greek for it is 'Koinonia'; it is an idea of immense important in early (and not just early) Christianity, with a wide range of meanings, including unity, partnership, close relationship, sharing, and participation.

Does this describe what goes on in **your** *nearest Christian community?*

A beggar receives more than he had asked for

1b-10 Now Peter and John used to go up to the Temple at the hour of prayer, the ninth hour. And a certain man, who was crippled from his mother's womb, used to be carried, and they would place him every day by the gate of the Temple; [this was the gate] known as the Beautiful Gate. [The purpose was] for him to beg alms from the people going into the Temple. When he saw Peter and John on the point of going into the Temple, he asked to receive alms. Looking intently at him, Peter, with John, said, 'Look at us.' And he fixed his attention on them, expecting to receive something from them. But Peter said, 'Silver and gold are not at my disposal; but what I have, that I give you. In the name of Jesus Messiah the Nazarene, rise up and walk.' And taking hold of him by the right hand, he raised him up. Straightaway, his feet were strengthened, and his ankles; and he leapt up, and stood, and walked, and went into the Temple with them, walking and leaping, and praising God. And the whole people saw him walking and praising God. And they recognised him because he was the one who used to sit [begging] for alms at the Beautiful Gate of the Temple, and they were filled with astonishment and terror at what had happened to him.

Now the apostles are clearly carrying on the work of Jesus. In this scene, John is somewhat redundant, and his presence is always just a little awkward; it is Peter who is the centre of attention.

'Praising God': this is the effect of the Spirit on ordinary people. See Luke 2:20; 18:43; 19:37; Acts 2:47.

The 'whole people' is also an important theological idea for Luke. For example, they were waiting in astonishment outside the sanctuary while Zachariah talked with the angel Gabriel (1:21), and Simeon describes Jesus as 'the glory of your people Israel (2:32), and Jesus' accusers allege (23:5) that 'he stirs up the people by teaching them'.

Do you think that Christianity has lost its power to astonish?

Peter's second speech

11-26 As he held on to Peter and John, the whole crowd ran up to them, at the colonnade named after Solomon, utterly astonished. When Peter saw the people, he responded to them, 'Men of Israel, why are you amazed at this, or why do you look intently at us, as though it were through [our] own power and godliness that we had made him walk? The God of Abraham and the God of Isaac and the God of Jacob, the God of our ancestors, glorified his servant Jesus, whom you people handed over and denied to Pilate's face, when [Pilate] had passed a verdict of acquittal. But you lot denied the Holy One and the Just One, and demanded for yourselves the gift of a murderer. And the Prince of Life you murdered; God [then] raised him from the dead. Of this we are all witnesses. And by faith in his name, this man whom you see and know, his name has strengthened him, and the faith that is through him gave him this wholeness before all of you. However, as it is, brothers, I know that [it was] through ignorance [that] you acted; and the same for your rulers. But this was how God brought to fulfilment the things he had fore-announced through the mouths of all the prophets, the Messiah's suffering. So – repent, and turn, to have your sins erased, so that times of refreshment may come from the Lord and he may send you Jesus Messiah who was fore-appointed for you, whom heaven must receive until all the times of restoration which God spoke through the mouths of his prophets, holy from all time. Moses, for example, says, "The Lord your God will resurrect a prophet for you, from among your brethren, like me. You will listen to him according to all the things that he speaks to you. And it shall be that every person who does not listen to that prophet shall be rooted out from the people."

'And all the prophets from Samuel and his successors who spoke also announced these days. It is you people who are the children of the prophets, and of the covenant that God covenanted with your ancestors, saying to Abraham, "And by your seed all the families of the earth shall be blessed." For [to] you in the first place God resurrected his Servant and sent him, blessing you [through] each one of you turning away from your wickednesses.'

Peter's second speech; he is visibly growing in confidence, and we find ourselves asking if this can possibly be the same man as in the Gospel (see Luke 22:54-60). This is how the Spirit works. At the same time we notice the awkwardness of speech that Luke has given him, which I have tried to represent in the translation.

The burden of his speech is about how the Spirit works: the same God, operating in the same way, in the stories from the Hebrew Bible, in the life of Jesus, and in the life of the Church. See the cumbersome translation of words compounded with 'fore', which make exactly the same point. Another typical Lucan idea is that of 'repentance'. Repentance means 'changing your ways', turning your life round through 180 degrees, like the Prodigal Son in Luke 15:11-32 or Zacchaeus in Luke 19:1-10, or the thief to whom Jesus said, 'Today you will be with me in Paradise' (Luke 23:39-43).

Once again Peter insists on his hearers' responsibility for the death of Jesus, and on the apostles' role as witnesses to the Resurrection.

How is the crowd supposed to respond to the healing?

Opposition and success

4 1-4 As they were talking to the people, the priests and the captain of the Temple and the Sadducees approached him, greatly annoyed because they were teaching the people and proclaiming in the person of Jesus the Resurrection from the dead; and they laid hands on them, and placed them in custody until the next day. For it was already evening.

Many of those who heard the speech came to faith, and the number of men turned out [to be] about five thousand.

Now we see what Luke regards as a typical reaction on the part of the authorities: irritation and imprisonment, and another Lucan summary, to point the contrast.

Does Christianity today arouse the same measure of opposition and acceptance?

Peter's third speech – the power of the Holy Spirit

5-31 It happened on the next day that the rulers were gathered together: the elders and the scribes in Jerusalem, and Annas the High Priest, and Caiaphas and John and Alexander, and whoever were of high priestly stock. And setting them in the middle, they enquired, 'By what power, or in what name, did you do this?'

Then Peter, filled with the Holy Spirit said to them, 'Rulers of the people and elders, if we today are under investigation because of a kindness done to a sick man, [and] by what means this man was saved, let it be known to all of you, and to the entire people of Israel, that [it was] in the name of Jesus Messiah the Nazarene whom you lot crucified, whom God raised from the dead, that is how this man stands before you, cured. This is the stone, the one despised by you, the builders, that became the cornerstone. And there is no other name wherein salvation lies; for there is no other name under heaven which is given among human beings in whom we must be saved.'

Seeing the confidence of Peter and John, and grasping that these people were illiterate and untrained, they marvelled; and they recognised them as having been with Jesus – and seeing the man standing with them, the one who had been healed, they had no answer to give. They ordered them to leave the Sanhedrin and conferred with each other, saying, 'What shall we do to these people? For what has happened through their agency is a sign well-known and evident to all those who dwell in Jerusalem; and we can't deny it. Instead, to prevent further distribution to the people, let's threaten them not to speak in this name any longer to anybody.'

They summoned them and instructed them absolutely not to utter nor to teach in the name of Jesus. In response, Peter and John said to them, 'Consider whether it is right before God to listen to you rather than to God. For as for us, we cannot ***not*** speak the things that we have seen and heard.'

They added further threats and released them; they had found no grounds for punishing them. This was because of the people, for they were all glorifying God after what had happened. For more than forty years old was the man on whom this sign of healing had happened.

When they had been released, they went to their own, and reported all the things that the chief priests and elders had said. When they heard [it], unanimously they lifted up their voice to God and said, 'Master, you who made the heaven and the earth and the sea, and all that is in them, the one who said by the Holy Spirit through the mouth of our father David your servant:

"Why were the Gentiles arrogant,
and peoples think vain thoughts?
The kings of the earth have appeared,
and the rulers gathered for a [common] purpose
against the Lord and against his Messiah."

'For in truth, they gathered in this city against your holy Child, Jesus whom you anointed: Herod and Pontius Pilate, with the gentiles and the peoples of Israel, to bring about whatever your hand and your counsel had predestined [should] happen. And now, Lord, look upon their threats, and grant to your slaves to speak your word with all confidence, when you stretch out your hand for healing and signs and portents to happen through the name of your holy Servant Jesus.'

As they made their intercession, the place was shaken in which they were gathered, and they were all filled with the Holy Spirit, and they began to speak the word of God with confidence.

Like Jesus, the apostles now get brought before the authorities. Like Elisabeth (Luke 1:41) and Jesus (Luke 4:14, 15, 18), Peter is filled with the Holy Spirit (compare Acts 2:4; 4:31), and will not retract by an inch. He quotes Psalm 118, just as Jesus had done at Luke 20:17.

Notice, too, the insistence on the 'name' of Jesus, which we shall meet frequently throughout Acts.

The astonishing confidence of these apostles, and their lack of education, and the fact that they had known Jesus, taken together count as evidence for their central claim, that Jesus was indeed raised from the dead.

The authorities' response is to attempt to silence them. The attempt is foredoomed, and the disciples' prayer dramatically confirmed by an earthquake, the equivalent of the 'fire and wind' of Pentecost.

A question for the reader: as you go through Acts, what do you understand by being 'filled with the Holy Spirit'? Do we have here another Pentecost? Does Luke expect it to be frequently repeated?

Life in the early Church – 2

32-37 There was a single heart and soul in the group of believers. And not one of them would say that any of his possession was his own, but everything they had was in common.

With great power the apostles would give witness of the Resurrection of the Lord Jesus; and great grace was on all of them. For there was no one among them who was impoverished. For as many as were owners of lands or houses, they would sell [them] and bring the proceeds of what they had sold and they would lay [it] at the feet of the apostles; and distribution was made to each one according as anyone had need. Joseph who was surnamed Barnabas by the apostles, which when translated is 'Son of Comfort', a Levite, Cypriot by race, since he had a field, sold it, brought the money, and placed it at the feet of the apostles.

Another Lucan summary – a charming picture of the 'communism' of the early Church; though Luke knows perfectly well that it wasn't just as simple as this. See the dark story that follows.

How is the picture different from the previous one, at 2:42-47?

Ananias and Sapphira: you can't cheat the Holy Spirit

5 1-11 A certain man, Ananias by name, along with Sapphira his wife, sold a property, and misappropriated some of the purchase price, with the connivance of his wife, and bringing along a certain portion [of it] he laid it at the feet of his apostles. Peter said, 'Ananias, why has Satan filled your heart, that you should cheat the Holy Spirit and misappropriate part of the price of your land? [Was it not the case that] while it remained with you it remained, and that when it had been sold it was within your authority? Why did you put this business in your heart? It is not human beings whom you have cheated, but God.'

When Ananias heard these words, he fell down and breathed his last; and there came awe on all those who heard of it. The younger men wrapped him up and carried him out and buried him.

There was a delay of about three hours; and his wife came in, not knowing what had happened. Peter said to her, 'Tell me, was it for such-and-such a sum that you sold the field?' And she said, 'Yes, that was it.' Peter said to her, 'Why did you have a conspiracy to test the Spirit of the Lord? Look – the feet of those who buried your husband are at the door, and they will carry you out.' Straightaway she fell at his feet and breathed her last. The young men came in and found her dead, and carried her out and buried her by her husband. Great awe came upon the whole Church and on all who heard these things.

It is hard to imagine that we are meant to take this particularly seriously. There are several touches of dark humour here that suggest that we would do best to read it as a playful depiction of the major theme of Acts, that you cannot impede the work of the Holy Spirit. The alternative would be to regard the story as a chilling warning against dishonesty. We have to say that this is a very difficult passage. Why do you think it is hardly ever read in Church?

Life in the early Church – 3

12-16 Through the hands of the apostles, there were many signs and portents among the populace; and they were all together of one mind in Solomon's colonnade. None of the remainder [of the populace] dared to associate with them; but the people praised them. More than ever [the number of] those who believed in the Lord was increasing; [there were] crowds of men and of women. So they carried out the sick into the streets, and placed them on beds and mattresses, so that as Peter went [by], even [just] his shadow might overshadow one of them. And the group of cities in the vicinity of Jerusalem assembled, bringing sick people and those tormented by unclean spirits, who were all cured.

Yet another Lucan summary. The new element here is that of healing. The apostles continue the work of Jesus in the Gospel. (See, for example, Luke 3:33, 38; 5:12-26, etc.). It is important not to get too dispirited or too condemnatory about the present state of the Church. Rather we should recognise the unfailing action of the Holy Spirit, even today.

Have you seen the Spirit active in your own life? In the life of the Church?

The irresistible work of the Spirit

17-42 The High Priest and all those who were with him rose up, the ones who are the sect of the Sadducees; they were filled with fanaticism, and they laid hands on the apostles and placed them in the Public Prison. But the angel of the Lord by night opened the gates of the gaol, and led them out, saying, 'Go, stand up and in the Temple speak to the people all the words of this life.'

They obeyed, and went into the Temple just before dawn, and began to teach.

[Meanwhile] the High Priest and his people arrived, and they summoned the Sanhedrin, and the whole Council of Elders of the sons of Israel, and sent to the guardhouse to have [them] brought. The minions arrived, but failed to find them there; they went back and reported, 'We found the prison securely locked, and the sentries in position at the gates; but when we opened up we found no one inside.' When they heard these words, the Captain of the Temple and the high priests were puzzled about them – what could this mean? Then someone arrived and reported to them, 'Look – the men whom you put in prison are standing in the Temple, teaching the people.' Then the captain went off with his minions and brought them along; but without violence – because they were afraid of the people. [They didn't want] to be stoned.

They brought them and put them in the Sanhedrin. And the High Priest interrogated them, 'Didn't we give you strict orders not to teach in this name? And look! You have filled Jerusalem with your teaching, and you want to bring this man's blood on ***us***!' Peter responded (and the apostles) and said, 'We must obey God rather than human beings. The God of our ancestors raised Jesus, whom you had murdered by nailing him to the cross. This Jesus God elevated to his right hand as Prince and Saviour, to provide repentance for Israel, and forgiveness of sins. And we are witnesses of these things; and [so is] the Holy Spirit which God gave to those who obey him.'

When they heard, they were infuriated, and wanted to destroy them. But someone rose up in the Sanhedrin, a Pharisee called Gamaliel, a teacher of the Law, who was held in high regard by the whole people. He ordered [them] to put the men outside for a short time.

Then he said to them, 'Men of Israel, take care what you propose to do to these men. For before these present days, Theudas appeared, claiming to be somebody, and a number of men, something like four hundred, favoured him. He was assassinated; and all those under his command were dispersed. Then there arose Judas the Galilean, in the days of the census, and he got the people to follow him in rebellion. He too was destroyed, and all those under his command were scattered. And as for the present matter, I warn you, keep away from these people, and let them go. Because if this plan or this work is of human origin, it will be destroyed, but if its origin is divine, you will be unable to destroy them. Be careful that you do not turn out as God-fighters.'

They went along with his advice, and summoned the apostles. They flogged them, instructed them not to speak in the name of Jesus, and set them free. So they went their way rejoicing from the presence of the Sanhedrin, because they had been considered worthy to be dishonoured for the sake of the name, and all day long, in the Temple and at home, they never stopped teaching and gospelling the Messiah Jesus.

The authorities' resistance is as unsuccessful as that of Pharaoh in the original Passover. The 'angel by night' is meant to make us recall Exodus 12:42, and the irrational opposition of the authorities is meant to deprive us of all sympathy for them.

The apostles cannot be prevented from their task of being 'witnesses', whatever the authorities do. Gamaliel has seen the problem clearly.

What is **your** *task as 'witness'?*

Racial tensions in the early Church

6 1-6 In these days, as the disciples multiplied, there arose a complaint, Hellenists
against Hebrews, because their widows were being neglected in the daily distribution. The Twelve summoned the group of disciples and said, 'It is not desirable for us to abandon the word of God to wait at tables. Instead, brothers [and sisters], select seven men of attested merit from among you, full of the Spirit and of wisdom, whom we shall appoint; as for us, we shall devote ourselves to prayer and the ministry of the word.'

This speech was pleasing to the whole group, and they chose: Stephen, a man full of faith and the Holy Spirit, and Philip and Prochorus and Nicanor and Timon and Parmenas and Nicolaus, a proselyte of Antioch, whom they set before the apostles. They prayed over them, and laid hands on them.

Now there arises a spot of racial tension, Greek-speakers against speakers of Aramaic. Luke gives 'the Twelve' a central role; it is they, for example, who find a solution, in terms of the 'Seven' (another significant number). The Seven, like Peter, Elisabeth and Jesus, are to be 'full of the Spirit', and are to be appointed by the 'Twelve' on the recommendation of their fellow Greek-speakers. The seven who are chosen all have impeccably Greek names; but it is striking that the only two who are ever mentioned again, Stephen and Philip, turn out to be preachers, rather than officials at the soup-kitchen.

How does the Holy Spirit deal with the racial tension?

Life in the early Church – 4

7 The word of God increased, the number of disciples in Jerusalem multiplied very greatly; and a great crowd of priests came under obedience to the faith.

Another Lucan summary (note the strange, but to Luke important, title for the Church: 'the word of God') introduces the crisis over Stephen, one of the 'Seven'. He is accused, as Paul will be later, of blaspheming Moses and God; like Jesus (in Mark 14:56, 57, but not in Luke's Gospel) he is accused by false witnesses.

Stephen's success and death; another 'tongue of fire'

6[8–]7[53] Now Stephen, full of grace and power, was performing portents and great signs among the populace. And some people rose up from the synagogue that was called 'Libertines' – Cyreneans and Alexandrians and of those from Cilicia and Asia, arguing with Stephen. They did not have the resources to resist the wisdom and the Spirit with which he spoke. Then they secretly instigated men, who said, 'We heard him saying blasphemous things against Moses and God.' They aroused the people and the elders and the scribes, and they approached and dragged him off and took him to the Sanhedrin. Then they set up false witnesses, who said, 'This man is endlessly speaking words against this Holy Place and against the Torah. For we heard him saying that this Jesus the Nazarene will destroy this place and will change the customs that Moses handed down to us.'

They all looked intently at him, all those who were sitting in the Sanhedrin; and they saw his face, just like the face of an angel.

The High Priest said, 'Is this so?' But he said, 'Men, brothers and fathers, listen. The God of glory appeared to our ancestor Abraham when he was in Mesopotamia, before he lived in Haran, and said to him, "Come out from your country and from your kinsfolk, and come to the country that I shall show you." Then coming out of the land of the Chaldees, he went to make his home in Haran. And from there, after the death of his father, he changed his home to this country, in which you now have your home. And he did not give them an inheritance in it, nor even a foot of ground; and he promised 'to give him it for a possession, and to his descendants after him', though he had no child. This is how God spoke: "Your descendants shall be homeless in a country that belongs to others. And they shall enslave them and mistreat them for four hundred years. And the nation that enslaves them I shall judge," said God, "and after this they shall come out and worship me in this place." And he gave Abraham a covenant of circumcision; and so he fathered Isaac, and circumcised him on the eighth day: and Isaac [did the same for] Jacob, and Jacob [for] the Twelve Patriarchs.

'The patriarchs were jealous of Joseph; and they sold him into Egypt. And God was with him, and rescued him from all his tribulations, and gave him grace and wisdom before Pharaoh, King of Egypt, and he appointed him ruler over Egypt and over his entire house. And there came a famine over all of Egypt and Canaan, and great tribulation; and our ancestors could not find fodder, but Jacob heard that there was food in Egypt, and sent our ancestors on reconnaissance. And on the second [mission] Joseph was made known again to his brothers; and Joseph's family became known to

Pharaoh. And Joseph sent and summoned Jacob his father, and all his kinsfolk, about seventy-five souls; and Jacob went down to Egypt, and he and our ancestors died. And they were brought back to Shechem, and placed in the tomb that Abraham had bought, for the price of silver, from the children of Emmor at Shechem. As the time of the promise drew near which God had made to Abraham, the people grew and multiplied in Egypt, until "there arose another king over Egypt, who did not know Joseph". This [new king] did some sharp practice on our race, and mistreated our ancestors, to have their infants exposed so that they [should] not be kept alive.

'At that point, Moses was born, and he was divinely beautiful. He was nurtured for three months in his father's house; but when he was put out, the daughter of Pharaoh rescued him, and brought him up as a son for herself. And Moses was educated in all the culture of the Egyptians, and he was powerful in his words and deeds. But when his forty-year period was done, [the idea] arose in his heart to see his brothers, the sons of Israel. And seeing someone being maltreated, he came to their aid, and wrought vengeance for the one who was being oppressed, [by] striking the Egyptian. He thought that his brethren understood that God was giving them salvation through his hand; but they did not understand. On the next day, he turned up as they were fighting, and tried to reconcile them [to bring them] to peace, saying, "Men, you are brothers! Why are you maltreating each other?" But the one who was maltreating his neighbour repudiated him, saying, "Who appointed you ruler and judge over us? Do you want to murder me, the way you murdered the Egyptian yesterday?"

'Moses fled at this remark, and ended up homeless in the land of Midian, where he produced two sons. And when forty years were fulfilled, there appeared to him in the desert of Mount Sinai an angel, in [the] flaming fire of a thorn bush. Moses marvelled at the vision when he saw it; when he approached to look at it, the Lord's voice came, "I am the God of your ancestors, the God of Abraham and Isaac and Jacob."

'And Moses was all atremble and did not dare to look. And the Lord said to him, "Untie the sandal [from] your feet; for the place on which you stand is holy ground. Seeing I have seen the maltreatment of my people in Egypt, and I have heard their groan; and I have come down to rescue them. And now, come, I am sending you to Egypt."

'This Moses, whom they denied, saying, "Who appointed you as ruler and judge?" – this Moses God sent as Ruler and Redeemer, [by] the hand of [the] angel who appeared to him in the bush. This [was the one who] led them out, performing portents and signs in the land of Egypt, and in the Red Sea, and in the desert for forty years. This is the Moses who said to the sons of Israel, "God will raise up a prophet for you from among your brothers, [a prophet] like me." This [Moses] is the one who was in the Assembly in the desert, with the angel who spoke with him on Mount Sinai (and with our ancestors), [Moses] who accepted to give us living words. [This was the Moses] to whom our ancestors were reluctant to become subject; instead, they rejected him, and in their hearts turned [back] to Egypt, telling Aaron, "Make gods for us who go before us. For this Moses, who led us out of the country of Egypt, we do not know what has happened to him."

'And they made a calf in those days, and brought up sacrifice to the idol; and they rejoiced at the work of their hands. And God turned, and handed them over to worship Heaven's Army, as it is written in the scroll of the prophets:

"Did you not offer me sacrificial offerings,
for forty years in the desert, House of Israel?
And you took along the tent of Moloch
and the constellation of your god Rompha,
the statues which you had made to worship them;
and I shall move your home beyond Babylon."

'The tent of witness was for our ancestors in the desert, and the One who spoke to Moses had commanded, to make it according to the model which he had seen. [That was] what our ancestors in their turn brought in, with Joshua, when they restrained the Gentiles, whom God expelled before the face of our ancestors . . . right down to the days of David, who found grace before God, and asked to find a dwelling for the house of Jacob. But Solomon built a house for it nevertheless; the Most High does not make his home in [buildings] made by hand. As the prophet says:

"The heaven is my throne
and the earth is the footstool of my feet.
What kind of a home will you build for me, says the Lord,
or what is the place of my rest?
Is it not [that] my hand made all these things?"

'You stiff-necked people, and uncircumcised of heart and ears, you people always resist the Holy Spirit, as your ancestors so also you. Which of the prophets did your ancestors not persecute? And they killed those who foretold the coming of the Just One, whose betrayers and murderers you people became, you who received the Torah by the directions of angels, and failed to keep it.'

Stephen's defence consists in a rereading of the nation's history, in terms largely of the way God's word has invited Abraham, Joseph and Moses to go on unexpected and uncomfortable journeys. It also recalls to the listeners the occasional infidelities of the people. The way Stephen tells the story leaves a huge gap from the entry into the Promised Land to the reigns of David and Solomon, where the story abruptly ends. This speech has far more 'biblical echoes' than anything Peter has said so far, and it makes two points, as far as Acts is concerned. First, the word of God is for ever on the move; second, there is a history of resistance to that word. These two furnish the premises of a conclusion that is only partly spelt out: the Temple is not definitively God's dwelling-place. The reader should keep an eye on this conclusion as the story of Acts develops.

The quotation about 'sacrificial offerings' is from Amos 5:25-27; 'the heaven is my throne . . .' is Isaiah 66:1, 2.

There is no mealy-mouthed diplomacy in Stephen's speech. When should Christians hold their peace, and when should they speak out?

Stephen dies; Saul tries to destroy the Church

7 54–8 3 When they heard this, they were infuriated in their hearts, and they gnashed their teeth at him. But being full of the Holy Spirit, looking intently at heaven, he beheld the glory of God, and Jesus standing at the right hand of God and he said, 'Look – I see the heavens opening, and the Son of Man standing on the right hand of God.' But they shouted with a loud cry and stopped their ears, and rushed as one man against him, and they threw him out of the city and stoned him.

And the witnesses stored their garments at the feet of a young man called Saul. They stoned Stephen, who was making invocation and saying, 'Jesus, Lord, do not hold this sin against them.' Saying this, he fell asleep. And Saul agreed with his murder.

On that day a great persecution took place against the Church in Jerusalem; and they were all scattered up and down the country of Judaea and of Samaria. And some pious men buried Stephen and made loud lamentation over him.

Meanwhile Saul was trying to destroy the Church, going up and down the houses. He dragged [away] both men and women and handed them over to imprisonment.

This episode, linking the scattering of the early Church to the death of Stephen, and the death of Stephen to the death of Jesus, at the same time evokes the programme outlined in 1:8: 'You will be my witnesses in Jerusalem and in the whole of Judaea and Samaria.' Almost the central message of Acts is that you cannot prevent the work of the Holy Spirit. We notice, however, that the apostles are not 'scattered': they remain in Jerusalem, to give the infant Church the stability that it needs. At the same time the Saul theme is played, quietly, reminding us once again that the Holy Spirit is not to be frustrated.

Why does Luke mention Saul at this stage, do you think?

Life in the early Church – 5

4-8 So those who were scattered went about gospelling the word. Philip [for example] went down to a city of Samaria and preached the Messiah to them. The crowds unanimously paid attention to what Philip said when they heard and saw the things that he did. For many of those who had unclean spirits came out shouting in a loud voice, and many who were lame and paralysed were cured. And there was much joy in that city.

This is almost a 'Lucan summary', creating atmosphere, but using Philip (who we thought was waiting at table!) as a kind of example of the early preaching and its effects. Note that Luke is quite vague about where it happened. One oddity here is that the reader feels that it ought to be the unclean spirits, rather than their owners, who 'came out shouting in a loud voice'; but that is not what the Greek says. Some scholars feel that this and other similar looseness of expression suggest that Acts of the Apostles was not finally revised.

'Joy' for Luke is a mark of the presence of the Holy Spirit. Do you think that it is a mark of Christians in general?

Simon the magician is impressed by the power of the Holy Spirit

9-13 A man called Simon, who had practised magic [or: who was a foremost practitioner of magic], was already in the city. He amazed the race of Samaritans, alleging that he was someone special; and they all paid attention to him, from the least to the greatest, saying, 'This man is the power of God which is called Great.'

They paid attention to him because he had amazed them for quite a time with [his] magic tricks. But when they came to believe Philip, who was gospelling them about the kingdom of God and the name of Jesus Messiah, they started to get baptised, both men and women. Simon also came to believe, got baptised, and attached himself to Philip, because he saw signs and great miracles happening – he was amazed.

The reader notices that the word 'amazed' is now used for the third time. Like 'joy' it is evidently an important idea for Luke, indicating the presence of the Holy Spirit. We also observe the artistry with which Luke has set up the dénouement of the Simon story, which now continues.

What is the difference between practising 'magic' and 'signs and great miracles'?

Simon the magician surrenders to the Holy Spirit

14-25 Now when the apostles in Jerusalem heard that Samaria had received the word of God, they sent Peter and John to them. These [two] came down and prayed for them that they might receive the Holy Spirit. For [the Spirit] had not yet fallen on any of them; but they were only baptised in the name of the Lord Jesus. Then they laid hands on them, and they received the Holy Spirit.

Simon saw that it was through the laying on of hands by the apostles that the Spirit was given, and he offered them money, saying, 'Give me also this power, so that anyone I lay hands on may receive the Holy Spirit.' Peter said to him, 'May your cash and you go to hell, because you thought you could secure the gift of God with money. You have no part or share in this matter, for your heart is not straight before God. So repent from this vice of yours, and ask the Lord to see if the intention of your heart will be forgiven you. For I see that you are in bitter gall, and the chains of unrighteousness.' Simon answered, '[Please will] you turn to the Lord in prayer for me, so that nothing may come upon me of the things that you have seen.'

So they bore witness and spoke the word of the Lord. Then they returned to Jerusalem, and they gospelled many villages of the Samaritans.

So this part of the story ends; notice how the gospel is unflinchingly preached, despite internal and external problems, partly thanks to the central group of apostles (of whom, evidently, Peter is not the leader, since 'the apostles' send him and John into Samaria). Now Philip's story continues, the gospel spreading ever wider. This time it is to Africa that it goes – but see also how this wave of evangelisation has its roots in the racial problems that originally caused the appointment of the deacons, nearly three chapters ago.

Where has Simon gone wrong? How is it to be put right?

The gospel reaches Africa

26-40 The angel of the Lord spoke to Philip, saying, 'Rise up and go southwards, on to the road that goes down from Jerusalem to Gaza.' (This is desert.) He arose and went. And look! An Ethiopian man, a eunuch, a man of influence with Candace, Queen of the Ethiopians (he was in charge of her entire treasury), who had come with the intention of worshipping in Jerusalem, was now returning. He was seated in his chariot and reading the prophet Isaiah. The Spirit told Philip, 'Approach and hang on to the chariot.' Philip ran up, and heard him reciting Isaiah the prophet and said, 'Do you know what you are reading?' He said, 'But how can I, unless someone guide me?' He invited Philip to get up and sit with him. The portion of Scripture he was reading was this:

'Like a sheep to the slaughter he was led.
And like a lamb that is dumb before the one who shears him,
so he does not open his mouth.
In his humiliation his verdict was denied him.
Who will describe his generation?
Because his life is taken from the earth.'

The eunuch responded and said to Philip, 'This is my question to you: about whom does the prophet say this? About himself or about some other?' Philip opened his mouth, and starting from this scripture, he gave him the gospel of Jesus. As they journeyed on the way, they came to some water, and the eunuch said, 'Look! Water! What stops me from being baptised?'

And he gave orders for the chariot to stop, and they both went down into the water, Philip and the eunuch, and he baptised him. And when they came up out of the water, the Spirit of the Lord snatched up Philip, and the eunuch did not see him any more, for he was going on his way, rejoicing. Meanwhile Philip was found at Azotus, and he went through and gospelled all the cities until he reached Caesarea.

Another extraordinary story, giving us a flavour of what is really going on in Acts. Four times the word for 'journeying' is used in the Greek (8:26, 27, 36, 39), including the striking phrase 'as they journeyed on the way' (though it was impossible so to translate them all into English). It is a little glimpse of how the gospel spreads all over the world (Azotus, Caesarea, even Africa). It continues the theme of the Holy Spirit triumphing over all obstacles, in particular the storyline that started with the racial tensions between Greek- and Hebrew-speakers. That theme will now open out into the Christian life and ministry of one whom at present we know only as Saul. He will come to dominate the second half of Acts.

Finally, it is worth noting that we never hear anything more of the eunuch, and not much of Philip; they have served the narrator's purpose.

The quotation from Isaiah 53 is a familiar one in the New Testament – but this is one of the rare cases where it is explicitly linked to Jesus.

What was it that made the eunuch rejoice?

Saul encounters Jesus

9 [1-19a] Meanwhile, Saul was still breathing murderous threats against the Lord's disciples. He approached the High Priest and asked him for letters to Damascus, for the synagogues, so that if he should find any who were of The Way (both men and women) he might handcuff them and take them to Jerusalem.

Now as he journeyed, he happened to be drawing near to Damascus. Suddenly a bright light from heaven shone about him. Falling on to the ground, he heard a voice saying to him, 'Saoul, Saoul, why are you persecuting me?' He said, 'Who are you, Lord?' He [said], 'I am Jesus, whom you are persecuting. [Some manuscripts here add: 'It is hard for you to kick against the goad.' And in fear and trembling he said, 'Lord, what do you want me to do?' But the Lord said to him, ' . . .] But up you get, and go into the city, and it will be told you what you must do.' The men who were journeying with him stood speechless. They had heard the voice, but saw nobody. Saul arose from the ground; and when he opened his eyes he could see nothing. Taking him by the hand they led him into Damascus; and he was three days without seeing – and he neither ate nor drank.

Now there was a disciple in Damascus named Ananias, and the Lord said to him in a vision, 'Ananias.' He [said], 'Here I am, Lord.' The Lord [said] to him, 'Arise and go to the street called Straight, and look in Judas's house for a man of Tarsus called Saul. Look! He is at prayer, and he has seen in a vision a man called Ananias coming in and laying hands on him, so that he may see.' Ananias replied, 'Lord – I have heard from many people about this man, how much evil he has done to the saints in Jerusalem. And here he has a commission from the high priests to handcuff everyone who calls on your name.' The Lord said to him, 'Go, because this one is a chosen vessel to carry my name before Gentiles and kings and children of Israel. For I shall show him how much he must suffer for the sake of my name.' Ananias went off and entered the house and laid hands on him and said, 'Brother Saoul, the Lord has sent me, Jesus, who appeared to you on the way by which you came, so that you may see again and be filled with the Holy Spirit.' And immediately there fell from his eyes [something] like fish-scales, and he saw again. He arose and was baptised; he took food and regained his strength.

This is an excellent story, related with elegant economy by Luke, who regards it as so important that he tells it twice more, putting it as a first person narrative on Paul's lips, first to Jews (in Chapter 22), and then to distinguished Gentiles (Chapter 26). Notice the theme of journeying, the importance of visions, and yet Luke's restraint in reporting them. The reversal, from arresting officer to 'Brother Saul', that Paul experiences is characteristic of Luke; the identity of Jesus and the Church is something that becomes very important in Paul's later writings. The 'name' is a very important idea in Acts; we have seen it quite often already. Some people have argued for the authenticity of this episode from the fact that Saul's name is preserved in its Semitic form ('Saoul'). Above all, notice how Jesus dominates the scene, and how right Paul is to address him as 'Lord.'

This is the first explicit mention in Acts of Paul's mission to the Gentiles, and we should note it with care. We note also that it is Ananias to whom the message is entrusted. We may also admire Ananias's courage in approaching the rather alarming person of Saul.

'Who are you, Lord?' What is the full answer to this question, according to Luke?

Saul begins his mission: rejection on all sides

19b-30 He was with the disciples in Damascus for some days, and immediately he began to preach Jesus in the synagogues, saying, 'This man is [the] Son of God.' All those who heard him were amazed, and started saying, 'Isn't this the one who at Jerusalem ravaged those who call upon this name, and came here on purpose to handcuff them and take them to the high priests?' Saul, however, was all the more empowered, and confused the Jews who lived in Damascus, demonstrating that 'He [Jesus] is the Messiah'.

When a fair number of days were fulfilled, the Jews plotted to murder him. Saul knew their plot. They watched the gates day and night, in order to murder him. The disciples, however, took him by night; they let him down through the wall, winching him down in a hamper.

When he got to Jerusalem he attempted to join the disciples – and they were all afraid of him. They didn't believe that he was a disciple. Barnabas, however, took hold of him, led him to the apostles, and explained to them how he had seen the Lord on the way, and that he had spoken to him, and how he had spoken boldly in Jesus' name in Damascus. And he was with them, going in and out of Jerusalem, and speaking boldly in the Lord's name. And he was also arguing with the Greek-speakers – but they attempted to murder him. The brethren however knew about it, and led him down to Caesarea – and they sent him off to Tarsus.

So Luke gets Saul off-stage for the moment; but it is a significant moment, continuing the remarkable story of the character who will dominate most of the rest of the book. This second part of the story of his encounter with Jesus contains a number of themes that are important in Acts: preaching that Jesus is Messiah, the power given to evangelists, preaching first to synagogues, the threat of violence, and the solidarity of the Church.

Paul encounters suspicion from his fellow-Christians and attempted murder on the part of his fellow-Jews. Why does the gospel bring rejection?

Life in the early Church – 6

31 And so the Church, through the whole of Judaea and Galilee and Samaria, was at peace. It was building up, and journeying in the fear of the Lord; and it was filled with the comfort of the Holy Spirit.

This is another 'Lucan summary'; see how the author creates a mood, and also reminds us of the command given in 1:8 about being 'my witnesses in Jerusalem and in all Judaea and Samaria'. As before, the mood he creates is slightly at odds with reality: we have just seen hints of internal and external problems in the Church. Above all, though, Luke insists on the activity of the Holy Spirit.

The 'summary' also provides a cushion, separating Paul's narrative from a story where the reader's attention is more on Peter.

This book is called 'Acts of the Apostles'. Which apostles have we seen 'acting' so far?

Peter heals Aeneas and Tabitha

32-43 It happened that as Peter went through everywhere he also went down to the saints who dwell at Lydda. There he found a man called Aeneas, who for eight years had been lying on a stretcher; he was paralysed. And Peter said, 'Aeneas, Jesus Messiah heals you. Arise and make your own bed.' Immediately he arose. All those who lived in Lydda and Sharon knew about it; and they turned to the Lord.

In Joppa there was a lady-disciple named Tabitha. Translated, the name means 'Gazelle'. She was full of good works and of acts of charity that she performed. It happened in those days that she fell sick and died. They washed her [corpse] and put her in an upstairs room. Since Lydda was near Joppa, the disciples, hearing that Peter was there, sent two men to him, asking, 'Don't delay to come across to us.'

Peter arose and went with them. When he arrived they took him up to the upstairs room; and all the widows came to him, weeping and showing [him] tunics and garments that 'Gazelle' had made when she was with them. Peter flung everybody out, and fell on his knees and prayed; and he turned to the body and said, 'Tabitha, arise.' She opened her eyes, and seeing Peter, sat up. He gave her [his] hand and raised her up. Calling the saints and the widows he gave her [to them] alive. It became known through the whole of Joppa; and many believed in the Lord. It happened that for a good few days he stayed in Joppa, with Simon the Tanner.

These two 'healing stories', the first of them done explicitly in Jesus' name, the second echoing the story of Jairus's daughter in Luke 8 and Mark 5, serve to focus the reader on Peter as precisely continuing the mission of Jesus. That is what Acts is about. Now comes a very important moment, which we might call 'the conversion of Peter'.

What do the healing stories show?

The conversion of Peter to the Gentile mission

10 1-48 There was a man in Caesarea, Cornelius by name, a centurion of the 'Italian' cohort. He, along with his entire household, was pious and a God-fearer, doing many acts of charity to the people, and praying constantly to God. At about the ninth hour he saw clearly in a vision a messenger of God coming to him and addressing him, 'Cornelius.'

He looked intently at him, and, becoming fearful, said, 'What is it, Lord?' He said to him, 'Your prayers and your acts of charity have ascended as a memorial offering before God. Now – send some men to Joppa, and summon one Simon, who has the surname Rock. He is staying as a guest with a certain Simon the Tanner, who has a house alongside the sea.'

When the messenger who had spoken to him had departed, [Cornelius] summoned two of the house slaves, and a devout soldier from among those who were attached to him; he explained everything to them, and sent them off to Joppa. On the next day, as they were en route, and approaching the city, Peter went up to the roof to pray, at about the sixth hour. He was hungry, and he wanted to eat. And as they were preparing [the meal] a trance came over him, and he sees heavens opening, and a container coming down, like a large linen cloth with four corners being let down on the earth. In this container there were all the animals and creepy-crawlies of the earth, and the birds of the sky. A voice came to him, 'Arise, Peter, kill and eat.' But Peter said, 'No way, Lord; I have ***never*** eaten anything profane or unclean.' [The] voice [spoke] to him again, a second time, 'What God has made clean, you are not to call profane.' This happened three times; and the container was immediately taken up to heaven. As Peter was scratching his head [about] what the vision might [mean], look! The men who had been sent by Cornelius [were] enquiring for Simon's house, and stood at the gate, and they called and enquired, 'Is Simon with the surname "Rock" here?' and as Peter reflected about the vision, the Spirit said, 'Look! Three men who are looking for you. Up you get now, go down, and travel with them. Have no doubt that it is I who have sent them.' Peter went down to the men and said, 'Look! I am the one whom you seek. What is the reason for your being here?' They said, 'Centurion Cornelius, a good man and a God-fearer, who is of good reputation among the whole nation of the Jews, was directed by a holy messenger to send for you [to come] to his house, and [for him] to hear words from you.' So he invited them in and entertained them.

The next day he arose and went out with them; and some of the Joppa Christians went with him. The next day he entered Caesarea. Cornelius was expecting them; he had invited his kinsfolk and his close friends. When Peter arrived Cornelius met him; he fell at his feet and worshipped him. Peter, however, raised him up, saying, 'Up you get – I am also a human being [just like you].' And chatting with him he went in, and found that many people had come together. He said to them, 'You people know that it is unlawful for a Jewish man to associate with or approach someone of another nation. Yet God has taught even me not to call anyone profane or unclean. So when I was sent for, I came without refusing. Therefore may I ask you on what grounds you sent for me?' And Cornelius said, 'Four days ago to this hour I was praying the prayers of the ninth hour in my house. And look! A man stood before me in resplendent clothing and says, "Cornelius – your prayer has been heard, and your acts of charity remembered before God. So send to Joppa, and summon Simon who is surnamed Peter. He is a guest of Simon Tanner, by the sea." So immediately I sent for you; and you have done a lovely thing in coming. So now all of us are present, before God, to hear everything that the Lord has enjoined on you.'

Peter opened his mouth and said, 'In truth I recognise that God is not one to show partiality – in every nation, those who reverence God and do justice are acceptable to

God. The message which he sent to the children of Israel, gospelling peace through Jesus Messiah (he is the Lord of all) – you people know the thing that happened throughout the whole of Judaea, beginning from Galilee, after the baptism which John proclaimed, Jesus of Nazareth, how God anointed him with the Holy Spirit and power, who went about doing good, and healing all those who were tyrannised by the devil, because God was with him. We are witnesses of everything that he did, both in the area of the Judaeans, and in Jerusalem [itself]. He is the one whom they murdered, by nailing to a tree. He is the one whom God raised on the third day, and granted to him [the gift] of becoming visible, not to all the people, but to the witnesses whom God had appointed beforehand, that is us. We are the ones who ate and drank with him after he was raised from the dead. And he instructed us to proclaim to the people, and to give testimony that this is the one appointed by God as judge of [the] living and [the] dead. He is the one to whom all the prophets bear witness, for everyone who believes in him to receive forgiveness of sins through his name.'

While Peter was still uttering these words, the Holy Spirit fell upon all those who heard the word. And those of the Circumcision Party who were believers, who had come with Peter, were astounded that even on the Gentiles the gift of the Holy Spirit could fall. For they heard them speaking in tongues and extolling God's greatness. Then Peter responded, 'Surely no one can refuse water for these people to be baptised? They have received the Holy Spirit just as we did.' And he gave orders for them to be baptised in the name of Jesus Messiah.

Then they asked him to remain for some days.

*As once before, Luke seems to be emphasising the awkwardness of Peter as a speaker. The first sentence of the major speech is hardly a sentence at all, and it is impossible to find one's way through it. The last sentence of the same speech has a very awkward order. We should again consider the possibility that Luke is trying to catch Peter's awkward diction (or a style of speaking appropriate to the character). Other Lucan touches include the 'fore' idea hidden in 'appointed be***fore***hand' and 'speaking in tongues and extolling God's greatness', which remind us of Pentecost and Mary's Magnificat.*

This episode is one of immense importance in the Church's history. The question of whether or not non-Jews could be admitted was a fearsomely difficult one, and might have destroyed the Church at its very beginning. We could perhaps call this 'Peter's conversion'; and like Saul's 'conversion' Luke regards it as of sufficient importance to tell it again, in Chapter 11. The issue is still painfully alive in Chapter 15 (the 'Council of Jerusalem'). Since the beginning of his Gospel, Luke has been preparing us for the admission of the Gentiles – see Luke 2:32; 24:47; Acts 1:8; 9:15, and it seems entirely natural to us. We should never forget, however, that this was a very neuralgic issue.

The Holy Spirit here enables Peter to face and overcome his own prejudices, and to take a brave step that was going to land him and the Church in hot water. Are there areas in your life where the presence of the Spirit is required, to give you courage to face what must be faced, no matter how painful?

Peter is challenged by the Church; his defence

11 1-18 The apostles and the brethren who were throughout Judaea heard that the Gentiles had received the word of God. And when Peter went up to Jerusalem, the people of the Circumcision took issue with him, saying, 'You went into [the houses of] men with foreskins – and you ate with them!' Peter started up and explained it to them point by point.

'I was in the city of Joppa, and in a trance I saw a vision, a container coming down, like a big sheet with four corners being let down from heaven – and it came up to me. As I gazed intently at it, I contemplated it and saw the four-footed animals of the earth, and the wild beasts and the creepy-crawlies and the birds of heaven. I also heard a voice saying to me, "Arise, Peter, kill and eat." And I said, "No way, Lord, because profane or unclean [food] has never entered my mouth." The voice replied a second time from heaven, "What God has made clean you are not to call profane!" This happened as many as three times, and everything was pulled up to heaven again. And look! Straightaway three men approached the house where we were. They had been sent to me from Caesarea. The Spirit told me to go with them without argument. These six fellow Christians came with me, and we entered the man's house. He [then] reported to us how he had seen the messenger standing in his house and saying, "Send to Joppa and summon Simon who has the surname Peter, who will speak words to you by which you and your entire household will be saved." As I began to speak, the Holy Spirit fell on them, just as [it had] on us at [the] beginning; and I remembered the Lord's word, how he had said, "John baptised with water, but you people will be baptised by the Holy Spirit." So if God has given them the identical gift that he gave to us who believe in the Lord Jesus Messiah, who was I to thwart God?'

When they heard this they were silent, and they glorified God, saying, 'Indeed God has given the Gentiles the repentance that leads to life.'

This is such an important moment that Luke reports it twice, in third and first persons; or three times, if you include what Peter says in Cornelius's house, more if you include his speech in Chapter 15 to the 'Council of Jerusalem'. The opening lines, detailing the complaint of the 'Circumcision Party', sound like the beating of a menacing drum. However, what happened at Cornelius's house and its aftermath is a classic instance of the work of the Holy Spirit in Acts, effortlessly surmounting all obstacles, especially the major problem of the admission of non-Jews into the Church. When Luke tells us that Peter reported the circumstances 'point by point' that is high praise – for that was how the evangelist described his own aim at the beginning of the two-volume work.

It may console us in our era, when Christianity is still divided, to notice that the intervention of the Holy Spirit does not automatically solve all problems. Notice how the gospel is restricted to 'Jews only', at least initially, in the episode that follows.

Are there similarly painful issues that the Holy Spirit is inviting the Church to face and solve today?

Continuing aftershocks from the death of Stephen; the gospel is preached to the Gentiles

19-26 So those who had been scattered as a result of the oppression that happened in connection with Stephen came through as far as Phoenicia and Cyprus and Antioch, speaking the word to nobody other than Jews. Some of them were men of Cyprus and Cyrene, who came to Antioch, gospelling the Lord Jesus to the Greek-speakers. The Lord's hand was with them, and great was the number that believed and turned to the Lord. The report about them came to the ears of the Church in Jerusalem, and they sent Barnabas to go through as far as Antioch. He came, and saw God's grace; he rejoiced and encouraged them all to remain true to the Lord with devotion of heart, because he was a good man, and full of the Holy Spirit and of faith. And a fair crowd was added to the Lord. He came out to Tarsus to look for Saul; and when he found him he took him to Antioch. For a whole year they gathered with the Church and taught [them]. Calling disciples 'Christians' [or 'Messianists'] first happened in Antioch.

In charting the move away from Judaism, Luke plays on us his favourite 'three-card trick', distracting our gaze to 'Phoenicia', 'Cyprus' and even 'Cyrene' in Africa, when all the time his interest is only in Antioch. We have seen this device of his before, and will meet it again. Now the gospel moves gently away from 'Jews only' to 'Greek-speakers' and includes all those who could call Jesus 'Messiah'. Luke has effortlessly linked the stories of Peter and Saul by means of Barnabas, who is an accredited witness because he is 'full of the Holy Spirit', like Elisabeth, Jesus, Peter, and Stephen before him.

Luke tells us that Barnabas 'saw God's grace'. What do you think this means?

The 'collection' for Christians in Jerusalem

27-30 In those days, prophets came down from Jerusalem to Antioch. One of them, called Agabus, arose and foretold through the Spirit that there would be a great famine over the whole inhabited world. This happened under Claudius. Each of the disciples, according to their prosperity, determined to send to their fellow Christians who lived in Jerusalem. They did this and sent [it] to the elders, through the agency of Barnabas and Saul.

The three-card trick again, perhaps: Barnabas comes first, but it is Saul in whom Luke will soon start to show primary interest. Jerusalem is still very important in Luke's understanding of the Church, as this episode indicates: prophets come from there, and in return 'food parcels' are sent back. For Luke this has the happy effect of bringing Barnabas and Saul together, and of getting Saul to Jerusalem. With his reference to an event that took place in Claudius's reign, Luke also reminds 'Theophilus' that this Christian story takes place in the real Roman Empire.

We know from Paul's letters that he thought it very important for the wealthier Christian congregations in the Greek cities to make a collection for the Christians in Jerusalem. Why is this important in the unfolding of the 'Gospel of the Holy Spirit'?

Peter imprisoned and released

12 [1-19] At just that moment King Herod laid hands on some people from the Church to maltreat them. He had James, John's brother, put to death with a sword. Seeing that the Jews approved of [this step], he proceeded to have Peter arrested (it was the days of Unleavened Bread). He took him into custody, and handed him over to four detachments of soldiers to guard him. [Herod's] intention was to bring him before the people, after the Passover. So Peter was under guard in the gaol; and prayer for him was eagerly going up to God from the Church.

When Herod was just on the point of bringing him forward, on that very night, Peter was sleeping between two soldiers, immobilised with two sets of handcuffs; and there were guards before the door keeping an eye on his cell. And look! The Lord's messenger approached; and a light shone in the building. Striking Peter's side, he aroused him, saying, 'Quick! Up you get.' And the handcuffs fell off his hands, and the messenger said to him, 'Get dressed and put on your sandals.' And he did so. And he says to him, 'Put on your cloak and follow me.' And he went out and followed; and he had no idea that what the messenger was doing was the real thing – he thought he was seeing a vision! But they went through the first guard, and through the second, and they came to the iron gate that gave on to the city, which opened for them of its own accord. They emerged and went one street further on; and immediately the messenger left him. Peter came to himself and said, 'Now I know for sure that the Lord has sent his messenger, and has rescued me from the power of Herod, and from all that the people of the Jews expected.'

When he realised [this] he went to the house of Mary, John's mother (he was the one who was surnamed 'Mark'), where there were a good number gathered together in prayer. When he knocked on the door of the gatehouse a little slave girl approached to answer. Her name was Rhoda; and when she recognised Peter's voice, in her joy she didn't open the door, but ran and announced that Peter was standing at the gate! They said to her, 'You're crazy!' But she insisted that it was so, and they said, 'It's his angel.'

Meanwhile Peter carried on knocking. They opened and saw [that it was] him, and were astounded. He motioned to them with his hand to be silent, and reported how the Lord had led him out of prison, and said, 'Report this to James and the brethren.' And he went out and travelled to another place.

When day broke, there was considerable consternation among the soldiers: what had happened to Peter? Herod [initiated a] search for him, and, failing to find him, interrogated the guards, and ordered them to be led away. And he went down from Judaea to Caesarea and spent time there.

This is a remarkable story: a breathless adventure at its beginning, with some high comedy over the slave girl relieving the tension halfway through (and the reader will remember the last time that Luke had Peter and a slave girl together, at Luke 22:56), and, finally, a calm ending. 'Herod' is Herod Agrippa, grandson of Herod the Great, and he died in AD 44. By the end of the story, Herod, who had been 'on a roll' at the beginning, with one vote-catching execution behind him, and another in prospect, has been easily defeated; and while Peter is moving freely about the place, Herod has to make an undignified departure to Caesarea. Luke is quietly showing us how the Holy Spirit works. See also how skilfully Luke has linked the start of this episode with the preceding story, which brought together the Christians of Antioch and Jerusalem. Notice, too, some echoes of the death of Jesus, with the reference to Passover, always a tricky time in Jerusalem; and presumably this is now one year after Jesus died, so the memory will have been fresh and expectations high. Another echo is of the light that shone round those shepherds in Luke's second chapter. The evangelist keeps all kinds of threads together.

The Holy Spirit vindicates Peter rather than the powerful people like Herod. Have you noticed examples of this in your own life?

The death of Herod

20-23 He was very angry with the people of Tyre and Sidon. They came to him as a body; they had persuaded Blastus, who was Gentleman of the Royal Bedchamber, and sued for peace, because their country supported itself [by importing grain] from the King's country. On the appointed day, Herod, arranged in [his] royal finery, and sitting on the rostrum, addressed them publicly. The people cried out, 'The voice of God, not a human being.' Straightaway, the angel of the Lord struck him, because he had not given glory to God, and he expired, eaten by worms.

This story may owe something to Ezekiel's abuse of the 'Prince of Tyre' for his presumption (Ezekiel 28:2, 6, 9). But in its rough outline it is found also in the Jewish historian Josephus, and it completes the story of Herod's downfall; the reader will think of what was predicted in the Magnificat. From being in control, Herod is now history. The story is exceptionally well told. Contrast it now with the 'Lucan summary' that follows, and note the way in which Luke picks up the story of Barnabas and Saul, and prepares us for their ministry, which is shortly to start.

What is Luke's attitude to the rich and powerful? What is God's attitude?

The Church of all nations and many cultures

12[24]–13[3] The word of God increased and multiplied. Barnabas and Saul returned to Jerusalem, having fulfilled their service; they took John, who was surnamed Mark, along with them.

There were in Antioch, in the Church there, prophets and teachers: Barnabas and Simeon (called Niger), and Lucius the Cyrenean, Menahem who was foster-brother of Tetrarch Herod, and Saul. As they worshipped the Lord, and fasted, the Holy

Spirit said, 'Set apart for me Barnabas and Saul for the work to which I have summoned them.' Then they fasted and prayed and laid hands on them, and sent them on their way.

As occasionally happens in Luke-Acts, there appears to be some confusion: we had supposed John-Mark to be in Jerusalem with his mother, and Barnabas and Saul to have already returned to Jerusalem. But Luke is more interested in setting up the missionary team than in getting the times and places exactly right.

Very gently the passage hints at the catholic nature of the Church in Antioch. No less than five cultures or languages are represented, it seems: Aramaic (Barnabas, Saul), Hebrew (Simeon, Menahem), Latin (Niger), Greek (Lucius), and (somewhat vaguely) African (Cyrenean). With the statement that Menahem was foster-brother to the Tetrarch Herod, our mind goes back to the previous episode; and our admiration for the work of the Holy Spirit increases.

The Holy Spirit tends to make the Church all-embracing, rather than exclusive. Do you think that Christians are sufficiently catholic?

The gospel is more powerful than magic

4-12 Having been sent out by the Holy Spirit, they went down to Seleucia, and from there they went to Cyprus. And, being at Salamis, they proclaimed the Word of God in the synagogues of the Jews; and they had John as their assistant. They went through the whole island as far as Paphos; and they found a man who was a magician, a Jewish pseudo-prophet of the name of Bar-Jesus. He was with the proconsul Sergius Paulus, a man of some intelligence. This man sent for Barnabas and Saul, and demanded to hear the word of God. Elymas (for so his name is understood) the magician resisted them, seeking to divert the proconsul from the faith. But Saul (who is also Paul), filled with the Holy Spirit, gazed intently at him and said, '[You are] full of all cunning and all villainy, son of the devil, enemy of all righteousness, will you not stop [attempting to] divert the Lord's straight ways? And now look! The hand of the Lord is upon you, and you will be blind; you shall not see the sun until an appropriate time.'

Straightaway there fell on him mist and darkness, and he needed guides to get about. Then the proconsul, having seen what had happened, came to faith, overwhelmed by the Lord's teaching.

Saul (now starting to be given the name by which we know him best) is seen here for the first time as a full-blown apostle. From now on he outstrips Barnabas; and the episode before Sergius Paulus reminds the reader of Moses' feats of magic against the Egyptian necromancers in the presence of Pharaoh. The account of Sergius's conversion also fits with Luke's general notion of commending Christianity to a Roman audience. We may observe that Elymas's fate is precisely the opposite of what happened to Saul when he first heard the voice of Jesus.

Another theme to notice here is that of the 'journey', an idea very important to Luke. We must not think in terms of a 'travelogue' so much as of a theological idea, of these apostles being Jesus' witnesses 'to the ends of the earth'. So he goes from Antioch down to Seleucia, its port, then across to Cyprus, and the length and breadth of the island: we should, however, be marvelling less at Paul's travelling, and more at the power of the Spirit which it demonstrates.

The gospel is the power of the Holy Spirit, not fakery and trickery. Is it possible that the resurgence of beliefs in magic and paganism is connected with the decline of Christianity in the Western world?

Paul's first speech – in the synagogue at Pisidian Antioch

13-41 Having put out from Paphos, Paul and his group arrived at Perga in Pamphylia; but John deserted them and returned to Jerusalem. Meanwhile they went through from Perga and arrived at Pisidian Antioch. They entered the synagogue on the Sabbath-day, and sat down. After the reading of the Torah and the Prophets, those in charge of the synagogue sent to them saying, 'Brothers, if you have some word of comfort for the people, speak.' Paul arose, and, motioning with his hand, said, 'Men of Israel, and you who are God-fearers, listen! The God of this people Israel chose our ancestors and made the people great during the stay in the land of Egypt, and with uplifted arm led them out of that [land]. And for about forty years he put up with their moods in the desert. He destroyed seven nations in the land of Canaan, and gave their land as [Israel's] inheritance, for about four hundred and fifty years. And after that he provided judges, down to Samuel the prophet. After that they asked for a king, and God gave them Saoul son of Kish, a man of the tribe of Benjamin, for forty years. And after he had removed him [from the throne] he raised up David as their king; and he authenticated David, saying, "I have found David the son of Jesse, a man after my heart, who will carry out all my wishes."

'It was from David's seed, in accordance with [his] promise, that [God] brought Jesus as a saviour for Israel, with John the Baptist acting as his harbinger, prior to his entry, preaching a baptism of repentance for the whole people of Israel. When John had finished his course, he said, "Who do you suppose I am? I am not [The One]; he is coming after me, the one whom I am not worthy to untie the sandals of his feet."

'Brethren, children of the race of Abraham, and the God-fearers among you, it is to us that this message of salvation has been sent out. For those who live in Jerusalem, and their rulers, failed to know him; and they fulfilled the prophets' words that are read every Sabbath-day when they condemned him. And they found no capital crime, so they asked Pilate that he should be done away with. And when they had accomplished everything that had been written about him, they took him down from the cross and put him in a tomb. But God raised him from the dead; and he appeared for several days to those who had come up with him from Galilee to Jerusalem: these are the people who are now his witnesses to the people. And ***we*** are gospelling ***you*** the good news of the promise made to the ancestors. God fulfilled it for their children, when he raised Jesus up, as it says in the Second Psalm, "You are my Son – I have fathered you today." And that he raised him from the dead [in such a way that] he would never again return to corruption, he declared, "I shall give you David's holy promises." Therefore in another place he says, "You will not allow your Holy One to see corruption." For David in his own generation served God's purpose; then he slept, and was added to his ancestors, and saw corruption. But the One whom God raised did not see corruption.

'So, let it be known to you, brethren, that it is because of this that forgiveness of sins is being proclaimed to you – and from all the things from which you could not be justified by the Law of Moses, in him "everyone who believes is justified". So – watch out that it doesn't happen to you, what was spoken in the prophets:

"See, you scoffers; wonder and disappear.
For I am working a work in your days,
a work that you will never believe,
even if someone tells it to you in detail." '

Paul is from now on clearly the leader of the mission, and this is his first speech in Acts. It is a careful argument from Scripture, appropriate to a synagogue audience (though we may notice that its account of the history of Israel is quite as truncated as that offered by Stephen in Chapter 7). In some ways it does not sound much like Paul, as we know him from his letters, except for the Old Testament basis of the argument, and, towards the end, the link of 'faith' and 'justification'.

The line 'I have found David the son of Jesse . . . ' is from 1 Samuel 13:14; 'I shall give you David's holy promises' is Isaiah 55:3; 'you will not allow your Holy One to see corruption' is Psalm 16:10; and 'See, you scoffers . . . ' is Habakkuk 1:5. I have put 'everyone who believes is justified' in quotation marks because it sounds like Paul quoting himself.

It is worth checking the travels of Paul on a map; notice, for example, that there are two Antiochs, and that this speech has been delivered in Antioch in Pisidia, not Syrian Antioch.

Why does Paul, like Stephen before him, argue from the history of Israel?

Resistance to the Holy Spirit

42-52 As they went out, they invited them for the next Sabbath, for a discussion of these words. When the synagogue had broken up, many of the Jews and of the proselytes who worshipped there followed Paul and Barnabas; they spoke to them, and convinced them to continue in God's grace.

On the next Sabbath, almost all the city was gathered to hear the word of the Lord. When the Jews saw the crowds they were filled with fanaticism, and tried to contradict the things that Paul was saying – they defamed him. Paul and Barnabas, however, spoke fearlessly, and said, 'It was obligatory that the word of God should be spoken to you people first; since you have rejected it, and since you do not judge yourselves worthy of eternal life, look! We are turning to the Gentiles; for so the Lord has commanded us:

"I have set you [as] a light [for the] Gentiles,
so that you may mean salvation to the end of the earth." '

When the Gentiles heard this, they rejoiced, and they glorified the word of the Lord; and those who were set in the way of eternal life came to faith. The word of the Lord spread through the whole area; but the Jews incited female worshippers of high repute and the first men of the city, and they aroused persecution [against] Paul and Barnabas, and they expelled them from their district. They simply shook the dust off their feet against them, and came to Iconium. And the disciples were filled with joy and the Holy Spirit.

This is the first example of a pattern that we shall encounter frequently in Paul's ministry in Acts: the gospel is preached first to the synagogue. Often it meets with success at first; then, however, it is rejected, and the missionaries turn to the Gentiles, who are thirsty for it. Disciples expect persecution, and even rejoice in it. 'Joy' and 'the Holy Spirit' belong very close together, in Luke's view.

The reference to 'a light [for the] Gentiles, etc.' is from Isaiah 49:6. Alert readers will remember the phrase on Simeon's lips at the very beginning of Luke's Gospel (Luke 2:32).

Why are the disciples 'filled with joy and the Holy Spirit'?

The preaching causes divisions in Iconium

14 1-7 It happened in Iconium as before: they went into the synagogue of the Jews, and spoke in such a way that a crowd of both Jews and Greeks came to faith. But the Jews who were unbelievers instigated and poisoned the minds of the Gentiles against the brethren. So they spent a fair time speaking boldly, with the Lord bearing witness to the message of his grace, and allowing signs and portents to occur through their agency. The city crowd was divided: some were on the Jews' side, while others were with the apostles. Then the Gentiles and Jews made an attempt, with [the complicity of] their leaders, to maltreat them and stone them; when they became aware of it, they fled to the cities of Lycaonia – Lystra and Derbe, and the area round about; and they were gospelling there.

This episode brings another of Luke's themes to the fore: persecution always has the opposite effect to that which the persecutors intend. This has continued to be true in the history of the Church. So Augustine could say, 'The martyrs were bound, imprisoned, scourged, racked, burnt, rent, butchered – and they multiplied', and Tertullian, 'We multiply whenever we are blown down by you; the blood of Christians is seed.' Because the Spirit is in charge of events, the stoning of Stephen brought about a wider preaching of the gospel. The same is now happening in the life of Paul.

What is the effect of persecution?

Paul and Barnabas (almost) deified

8-18 At Lystra, there was a man who had no power in his feet; he had been lame since [he left] his mother's womb, and had never walked. This man heard Paul speaking. [Paul] looked at him intently, saw that he had [enough] faith to be saved, and said in a loud voice, 'Rise up, and stand straight on your feet.' And he leapt up and walked.

And when the crowds saw what Paul had done, they lifted up their voices in the Lycaonian language, saying, 'Gods have come down to us in the form of human beings.' And they started calling Barnabas 'Zeus' and Paul 'Hermes', since he was the chief speaker. And the priest of the Zeus that was before the city brought bulls and garlands to the gates, along with the crowds. And he wanted to offer sacrifice. But when the apostles Barnabas and Paul heard, they tore their garments and rushed out into the crowd shouting and saying, 'Men – why are you doing this? We are also human beings, with feelings just like yours; and we are gospelling you to turn away from these useless gods to the Living God, "who made heaven and earth, and everything in them". [This God], in bygone generations, allowed all the Gentiles to travel by their own ways – and yet he did not leave himself without witness, conferring benefits, giving you rains from heaven, and seasons of fruitfulness, filling your hearts with food and cheerfulness.'

And with this speech he only just managed to stop the crowds from sacrificing to them.

We notice that Paul has not yet fully displaced Barnabas; for it is Barnabas who is named first. But it is Paul who does the speaking. Here we have his third speech in Acts. The first was to serious-minded Jews; the second indicated the move from Jews to non-Jews; this one, finally, is to over-excited Gentiles.

Do you think that Paul and Barnabas might have been tempted to accept this offer?

An attempt at murder helps to spread the gospel

19-28 Some Jews came from Antioch and Iconium and they persuaded the crowds, and stoned Paul, and dragged him out of the city, thinking he was dead. The disciples surrounded him, and he got up and went into the city. The next day he went out with Barnabas to Derbe. They gospelled that city, and made a good few disciples, then returned to Lystra, Iconium and Antioch, where they strengthened the souls of the disciples, encouraging them to remain in the faith, 'because we have to enter the kingdom of God through many tribulations'. They installed elders for them in each Church; they prayed and fasted and offered them to the Lord in whom they had come to believe.

Then they crossed Pisidia and came to Pamphylia; they spoke the word in Perga and came down to Attalia. From there they sailed to Antioch, where they had been commended to the grace of God for the work that they had fulfilled. When they arrived and summoned the whole Church, they reported what great things God had done with them, and that he had opened a door of faith to the Gentiles. They spent no small period of time with the disciples.

*See once again Luke's narrative skill. Paul has a remarkable (but effortless) escape from death, which in no way deters him. He even goes **back** into the city, and only moves on the next day. This now allows the two of them to revisit Churches they have previously founded, building up the necessary ecclesial infrastructures. Then more journeying (though Luke does not indicate much of what they did in the various places) until they come back to square one, with the important exception that the Gentile mission is now well and truly under way.*

Why do Paul and Barnabas move so rapidly?

What about circumcision?

15 1-21 And some people coming down from Judaea started teaching the brethren, 'Unless you were circumcised [according] to the custom of Moses, you can't be saved.' Paul and Barnabas had a good deal of disagreement and argument with them; and it was arranged that Paul and Barnabas, and certain others of them, should go up to Jerusalem [to talk] to the apostles and elders about this issue.

So the Church sent them on their way, and they went through Phoenicia and Samaria. [As they went] they gave a detailed report of the conversion of the Gentiles; and they caused great joy to all their fellow Christians. When they reached Jerusalem, the Church, apostles and elders welcomed them. They related what great things God had done with them; but some of the Pharisee party who had joined the faith stood up and said, 'You must circumcise them and instruct them to keep the Law of Moses.'

The apostles and elders gathered to see about this affair. After a good deal of argument, Peter stood up and told them, 'Brethren – you [all] know that from early days God made his choice among you, that through my mouth the Gentiles should hear the word of the gospel and come to faith. And God, the knower of hearts, bore witness to them, giving them the Holy Spirit, just as [he had] to us. And God made no distinction in faith between us and them when he purified their hearts. So now why are you testing God, by putting a yoke on the disciples' neck, which neither our ancestors nor we had the strength to bear? On the contrary, through the grace of the Lord Jesus we believe that we are saved in just the same way as them.'

The whole group was silent as they listened to Barnabas and Paul recounting what signs and portents God had done through them among the Gentiles. After they had finished speaking, James responded, 'Brothers, listen to me. Simeon has explained how God first deigned to acquire from among the Gentiles a people for his name. And the prophets' words are in tune with him, as it is written, "After this I shall turn, and I shall rebuild David's tent which had fallen, and I shall rebuild the parts of it that had been torn down; and I shall put it to rights, so that the rest of humanity may seek the Lord, and all the nations on whom my name has been invoked, says the Lord, who does these things that have been known from all time."

'So my verdict is: not to cause trouble for those of the Gentiles who have turned to God, but to write to them to keep away from pollution by idols, and from fornication, and from meat that has been strangled, and from blood. For from the earliest generations Moses has those who proclaim him in every city, in the synagogues each Sabbath-day.'

This is a very important moment in Acts. The issue, bluntly stated by the intruders from Judaea, is whether you have to be circumcised in order to be a Christian. The meeting at Jerusalem is meant to find a way out: there were strong views on both sides. For Luke, narrating what has happened is a way of listening to God: Acts itself is a narrative listening, and so is Peter's story; but it is also the case with Paul and Barnabas (we notice that Paul normally gets mentioned first in this episode). Unusually their speech is not reported: 'They related what great things God had done with them . . . recounting what signs and portents God had done through them among the Gentiles'. Now it all rather turns on which way James will jump; he is, after all, the brother of the Lord, and might be thought to represent the more 'conservative' view-point (i.e. in favour of compulsory circumcision), and so it is uncertain how he will react. As it turns out, his speech is not all that coherent; but clearly he is doing his best to find a compromise, using a text from Amos (9:11, 12) for the purpose, while not surrendering so much of his heritage that the Pharisee Christians would feel uncomfortable. It may be relevant to note that Luke has him use 'Simeon', the Semitic form of Peter's original name. Some scholars feel that Luke may have smoothed things over a bit here. The puzzling opening remark from Peter's speech, that 'you know that . . . God made his choice among you . . . that through my mouth the Gentiles should have the word of the gospel and come to faith' seems not to fit with what we have seen already. Nor does it fit with Galatians 2:7, where it is agreed that Paul is to go to the Gentiles and Peter to the Jews. Moreover Luke does not offer any evidence from those opposed to the Gentile mission, nor Paul's (no doubt spirited) defence of the mission to the Gentiles. Perhaps in abbreviating his account Luke has followed his practice of emphasising the unity rather than the divisions of the Church.

Once again, it is theologically important, and relevant to the matter in hand, that Paul and Barnabas journey ('to the end of the earth') 'through Phoenicia and Samaria'. This both provides them with useful support from the wider Church and enables them to draw on a useful range of pastoral and missionary experience. Perhaps there is something here for the Church of our own day to learn.

What is the importance of this Jerusalem meeting, do you think?

The Church authenticates the mission of Paul and Barnabas

22-35 Then the apostles and the elders, along with the entire Church, decided to choose men from their number and send them to Antioch with Paul and Barnabas: Judas called Barsabbas, and Silas. These were prominent among the brethren; and they wrote this letter for them to carry:

> The Apostles and the Elder Brethren, Greetings to the Gentile Brethren in the territories of Antioch, Syria and Cilicia. Since we have heard that some people from here have disturbed you with what they said, unsettling your souls with things that we had not commanded, we have reached a unanimous agreement to choose men and send them to you along with our beloved Barnabas and Paul, people who have handed over their lives for the name of Our Lord Jesus Christ. So we have sent Judas and Silas (and the others) to announce this verbally. For we and the Holy Spirit have decided to put no greater burden on you than these (which are necessary): to abstain from things offered to idols, and blood, things strangled, and sexual vice. If you keep yourselves from these, you will do well. Farewell.

So they were sent off, and they came to Antioch; and gathering the group, they handed over the letter. They read it, and rejoiced at the encouragement. Judas and Silas, being prophets themselves, comforted the Christians and strengthened them with much talking; and having spent some time, they took their leave of the brethren [and went back] to those who had sent them. Paul and Barnabas spent time in Antioch, teaching and gospelling, with many others also, the word of the Lord.

The last phrase, 'the word of the Lord', is of immense importance in Acts. The reader notices that the letter and the theological argument were not enough by themselves. What counts is the personal contact, which means a willingness to travel. It is possible to see here a lesson for the Church of our day. We should also observe Luke's emphasis on Church infrastructures: the 'apostles and elders' have to validate the policy decisions taken by missionaries 'in the field'. Otherwise we are not Church.

The quarrel between Paul and Barnabas

36-41 After some days, Paul said to Barnabas, 'Let us return and visit the Christians in each city where we proclaimed the word of the Lord, to see how they are getting on.' Barnabas, however, wanted to take with them John called Mark; and Paul insisted that they should not take him along, since he had abandoned them in Pamphylia, and had not gone to work with them. A sharp disagreement arose, and they separated from each other. Barnabas took Mark and sailed to Cyprus, while Paul chose Silas, and set out, having been commended to the Lord's grace by his fellow Christians. He went through Syria and Cilicia, strengthening the Churches.

Paul is now quite clearly calling the tune. Not for the last time in his missionary work, he has a row, on a matter of principle, with a fellow missionary. Luke's Paul (and the Paul who reveals himself in his letters) is gratifyingly human. We may find ourselves longing to know what really caused John Mark to disappear.

Do you find it encouraging that those first Christians were liable to quarrel with each other?

Paul's sensitivity to cross-cultural issues

16 1-5 He reached Derbe and Lystra. And look! There was a disciple there named
Timothy, the son of a Jewish woman who was a believer, but a Greek father;
Timothy was vouched for by the Christians in Lystra and Iconium. Paul wanted him
to accompany him; he took him and circumcised him, because of the Jews in those
parts – for they all knew that he had a Gentile father. As they journeyed through the
cities, they handed down to them the decisions for them to observe, that the apostles
and elders in Jerusalem had decided upon.

So the Churches were strengthened in the faith, and every day they increased in number.

This 'Lucan summary' concludes an important section, in which Luke neatly brings together some issues of great importance to his understanding of the story. These include the 'journeying' theme, obviously; the appointment of Timothy as successor to Barnabas; the need for the awkward and painful circumcision, which dramatically highlights the sensitivity of the Jewish-Gentile issue; the need to enforce the compromise that has been arrived at in Jerusalem; the central position of the Jerusalem Church. Finally, the summary tells us that despite the uncomfortable issues involved, the Spirit's work is proceeding from strength to strength.

How the Spirit guides the mission

6-9 They came through Phrygia and the Galatian region, having been prevented by the Holy Spirit from speaking the word in Asia. They came down towards Mysia and tried to journey to Bithynia – and the Spirit of Jesus did not permit them. They bypassed Mysia and came down to Troas. And a nocturnal vision appeared to Paul, a Macedonian man standing, beseeching him and saying, 'Come over into Macedonia and help us.'

Two important ideas lurk in this passage: first, as so often in Acts, note the liberal sprinkling of place names. It is quite a good idea to trace them on a map, and, perhaps with the help of commentaries, look at the difficulty about what is meant by 'Galatia'. But it is important not to worry too much about it; what most interests Luke here is the 'journey' that the gospel is following, rather than precise geographical detail. Second, see how three times the trajectory of the mission is adjusted in response to divine intervention: the 'Holy Spirit', the 'Spirit of Jesus' and 'a Macedonian man', all serve to direct the gospel as it makes its huge (psychologically if not geographically) leap into Europe.

Does the Holy Spirit still guide us today? How?

Paul's first European mission: Philippi

10-13 When he had seen the vision, we immediately tried to go out to Macedonia; we inferred that God had called us to gospel them. We put out from Troas and ran a straight course for Samothrace, and the next day to Neapolis, and thence to Philippi, which is a leading city of the district of Macedonia, a [Roman] colony.

On the Sabbath-day we went outside the city, along a river, where we thought there was a prayer-place. We sat down and spoke with the women who came together.

This passage is the first of the four 'we' passages that we find in Acts, and it continues a few lines further, down to the beginning of the strange story of the slave girl. The four stories are at: 16:10-17, 20:5-15, 21:1-18, and 27:1–28:16. The reader might care to reflect on why Luke switches so abruptly to writing in the first person plural. There are various possible explanations: a) that this was how you narrated sea voyages in the ancient world, to make them more direct and hence more exciting; b) that this is simply the way that Luke liked to tell the story; c) that Luke was at this stage making use of some kind of written source, such as someone's travel diary; d) that Luke is here signalling to the reader that he was at this point in the story a companion of Paul. The last seems the most obvious, but you can make up your own mind about what he is doing here. Scholars are far from agreed on the subject.

Since it was a 'Sabbath-day', we assume that it was **Jewish** *women who were meeting by the river (although it turns out that Lydia was not Jewish but interested in Judaism). Once again we see Paul's familiar pattern of going first to the Jews.*

What is the reason for going first to the synagogue?

Lydia demands to be allowed to offer hospitality

14, 15 A particular woman was listening. Her name was Lydia, and she was a dealer in purple cloth from the city of Thyatira, and a God-fearer. The Lord opened her heart to pay attention to the things that Paul was saying. When she and her household had been baptised, she begged [us], saying, 'If you have decided that I am a believer in the Lord, come into my house and stay there'; and she prevailed on us.

Once again we see the familiar pattern: Paul preaches first to the Jews, as the reference to 'Sabbath' indicates; although it is interesting that here in Philippi he seems to have targeted primarily Jewish women – and Lydia is not even Jewish. As in the Cornelius story, so here we have not just an individual but an entire household coming to faith. This is something we shall see again soon, with the story of the gaoler/prison commissioner of Philippi. It may make us reflect on how evangelisation should be done.

Should the gospel be preached primarily to individuals or primarily to households?

Trouble in Philippi, and the effortless resolution of it

16-40 As we journeyed to the prayer-place, it happened that a slave girl encountered us. She had a spirit of divination, and she provided her owners with a tidy income by her prophesying. She dogged Paul's footsteps, and ours, and cried out, saying, 'These people are servants of the Most High God. They are proclaiming the Way of Salvation to you.'

She did this over several days. Paul was at the end of his tether; he turned round and told the spirit, 'I command you, in the name of Jesus Messiah, to come out of her.' And it went out of her at that [very] moment. When her owners realised that their chance of income had gone away, they seized hold of Paul and Silas, and dragged them to the agora, before the authorities. And taking them to the praetors, they said, 'These people (who are Jews) are turning our city upside down; and they are proclaiming customs that it is not permissible for us (who are Roman [citizens]) to admit or to practise.'

The crowd joined in the attack on them; and the praetors tore off their clothes and ordered them to be caned. They laid a large number of strokes on them, and threw them into prison, and ordered the prison commissioner to keep a very careful eye on them. When he received this order, he flung them into the innermost prison, and he fastened their feet to the stocks. Round about the middle of the night, Paul and Silas were praying and singing hymns to God, and the [other] prisoners were listening to them. Suddenly, there was a huge earthquake, [which] shook the foundations of the prison. Immediately all the gates were opened and everyone's chains were unfastened. The prison commissioner woke up, saw the doors of the prison open, and drew his sword. He was just on the point of killing himself (because he thought that the prisoners had escaped). Paul, however, cried out in a loud voice, saying, 'Don't do yourself any harm – for we're all here.' He asked for light, and rushed in. Trembling, he fell at the feet of Paul and Silas; he led them out and said, 'My Lords: what must I do in order that I may be saved?' They said, 'Believe in the Lord Jesus, and both you and your household will be saved.' And they spoke the word of the Lord to him, along with all those in his house. Even at that time of night he took them in, washed [away] the results of their beating, and he and all his people were baptised right away. He took them to his house, set food before [them], and with his whole household rejoiced, because he had found faith in God.

When day came, the praetors sent the lictors, saying, 'Release those people.' The prison commissioner reported these words to Paul: 'The praetors have sent for you to be released. So out you go, and go off in peace.' Paul however said, 'They have publicly flogged us without a proper trial – although we are Roman citizens; they have flung us into gaol, and now they want to get rid of us without any fuss! No way – they can come and get us out themselves!'

The lictors reported these statements to the praetors, who were alarmed to hear that they were Roman [citizens]. They came and begged them; they took them out and asked them to leave the city. When they left the prison, they went to Lydia; they saw the Christians [in her house], comforted them, and left [the city].

Here is another story that gives us Luke's understanding of how the Holy Spirit works. First there is a victory, in that Paul effortlessly exorcises the servant girl who has correctly identified them. Next comes an apparent setback: opposition from those who are financially threatened leads to flogging and imprisonment. From then on, however, it is all success: Paul and Silas entertain their fellow-prisoners by singing hymns; they are miraculously released; Paul orders the gaoler not to commit suicide, and receives him and his household into the Church; Paul lays down the law to the local authorities, who are embarrassed, and reduced to begging the evangelists to get out of town! Finally Paul does condescend to leave; but it is in his own good time, not theirs, and only after reassuring the infant Church in Lydia's house. We may also notice the change in meaning of 'Lord': the gaoler uses it to address Paul and Silas, but they use it only for Jesus. In a sense this is a little vignette of the entire battle that is Acts of the Apostles: who is Lord round here?

Who **is** *Lord round here?*

Persecution brings the gospel to Athens

17 1-15 Travelling through Amphipolis and Apollonia, they came to Thessalonica, where there was a synagogue of the Jews. In accordance with [his] custom, Paul went into them, and for three Sabbaths he held discussions with them on the basis of the scriptures, explaining [them] and demonstrating that it was inevitable for the Messiah to suffer and rise from the dead, and that 'This is the Messiah, Jesus, whom I am proclaiming to you.'

Some of them were persuaded, and they threw in their lot with Paul and Silas; there was a good number of Greek [God-]fearers, and not a few of the leading women. The Jews got jealous; and taking along some degenerates who hung about the market place, they called in Rentamob, and set the city in an uproar. They attacked Jason's house, and wanted to bring them before the assembly; but they didn't find them, so they dragged Jason and some of the Christians to the politarchs, shouting: 'These are the ones who are upsetting the [entire] world – and here they are, and Jason has given them hospitality! And all these people are acting against Caesar's decrees, saying that there's an alternative king in [this] Jesus.'

They succeeded in unsettling the crowd and the politarchs; when they heard this they took bail from Jason and the others, and let them go.

The Christians sent Paul and Silas out [of the city] to Beroea, then and there, by night. When they got there, they visited the synagogue of the Jews. These were more open-minded than those in Thessalonica, and they received the word with all eagerness; every day they would examine the scriptures [to see] if it was so. Many of them therefore came to faith; and there were a good number of prominent Gentile women, and men.

However, when the Jews from Thessalonica found out that Paul had preached the word of God in Beroea as well, they came [along], and there also they upset and disturbed the populace. Then and there the Christians sent Paul off, to travel to the coast; and Silas and Timothy waited there. Those who were conducting Paul escorted him to Athens; and they departed, with an order to Silas and Timothy to get to him as soon as possible.

Jason has appeared rather from a clear sky, and it seems that Luke supposes that we know who he is. Once again we see the familiar pattern of Acts: preaching leads to persecution, which brings about the spread of the gospel, to Athens and then Corinth, where Paul had one of his most successful ministries. We have come a long way from Jerusalem and Judaea, and are now at 'the end of the earth', at least in the sense that Athens was the commercial centre of the ancient world.

Paul in Athens

17[16–]18[1] While Paul was waiting for them in Athens, he was exasperated to see that the city was full of idols. So he held discussions in the syngogue with the Jews and God-fearers, and every day in the agora, with anyone who happened to come along. Some of the Epicurean and Stoic philosophers fell in with him, and some said, 'What is this rag-picker on about?' Others said, 'He seems to be a proponent of outlandish deities' (because he was giving the gospel message of Jesus and the Resurrection).

They took him and led him to the Areopagus, saying, 'Can we know what this new teaching is to which you are giving utterance? For you are imparting certain outlandish matters into our hearing. So – we want to know what is the meaning of it.' (All Athenians, and the foreigners passing through there, had no time for anything but talking or hearing about the latest [fad]).

Paul stood in the middle of the Areopagus and said, 'Men of Athens, you seem to me exceptionally devout. For as I was coming through [this city], and examining the objects of your worship, I also found an altar on which was inscribed "To the Unknown God". Therefore what you worship without knowing is what I am proclaiming to you. The God who made the universe and everything in it, being the Lord of heaven and earth, does not dwell in temples that human hands have made, and is not served by human assistance, as though he had need of anything. For it is he who gives life and breath and everything to all. Out of one [person] he made the whole human race to dwell over the entire face of the earth, having set the appointed times and fixed boundaries of their habitation, [for them] to seek God, [to see] if they might grope their way to finding him. For he is not far off from each one [of us]. For in him we live, and move, and are; and as some of your poets say, "We are of his family." So, being of God's family, we should not think that the deity is like gold or silver or stone, or something fashioned by human technology or thought. So God, overlooking the times of ignorance, now commands people everywhere to repent, for he has appointed a day on which he is going to judge the world in righteousness, by means of a man whom he appointed, and he has given an assurance to all by raising him from the dead.'

When they heard 'resurrection from the dead', some of them sneered; but others said, 'We'll hear you again on this matter.'

So Paul went out of their midst; but some men joined him, including Dionysus the Areopagite, and a woman called Damaris, and others along with them. After this he left Athens, and came to Corinth.

Once more we see the pattern, that Paul first attends the synagogue, and normally (though apparently not in Athens) gets rejected and turns to the

Gentiles. Here, though, the pattern is modified; for Luke reports a speech that would seem well crafted for his intellectual Athenian audience, and yet it is only minimally successful. We notice, however, that Luke uses Athens as the springboard for Paul's very fruitful ministry in Corinth.

The mysterious Jason in Thessalonica is one of Luke's 'loose ends'. Another feature of Luke here is, I suspect (it is hard to be sure, but I have so translated it) the slightly pompous invitation to the Areopagus, and Paul's rather stilted speech when he gets there.

What was it that brought Paul's speech in the Areopagus to such a sudden halt?

Paul arrives in Corinth: the familiar patterns repeated

2-8 [In Corinth] he found a Jew called Aquila, who was a native of Pontus. He had recently come from Italy with his wife Priscilla, because Claudius had decreed that all Jews should depart from Rome. [Paul] came to them because they were fellow-professionals (their trade was tent-making); and with them he lived and worked.

Every Sabbath he would hold discussions in the synagogue, trying to convert both Jews and Greeks. When Silas and Timothy came down from Macedonia, he was wholly absorbed in preaching, testifying to the Jews that Jesus was the Messiah; but they resisted and abused [him]. So he shook out his clothes and told them, 'Your blood be on your heads. I am clear of responsibility – from now on, I shall travel to the Gentiles.'

He went away from there and entered the house of a God-fearer called Titus Justus, whose house was adjacent to the synagogue. Crispus, the head of the synagogue, came to faith in the Lord, with his entire household, and many of the Corinthians heard, and believed, and were baptised.

Corinth was not a promising place for Paul's mission; it was a rich and thriving and multiracial society, a byword in its day for sexual activity of various kinds. Yet it was here that Paul stayed for a year and a half. Once again, we notice, he goes first to the synagogue, and not without success, since his 'fellow-professionals', Priscilla and Aquila, are fairly prominent in his letters. Nevertheless, this time Paul has apparently come to the conclusion that he is never going to get anywhere, although, as we shall see, he continues to go to the Jews first. Here Luke makes his point by having Paul echo Ezekiel 33:3-5, which Matthew picks up in his Gospel, at 27:25, that terrible moment when Jesus' own people reject him before Pilate.

Why was Paul so successful in Corinth?

What happened in Corinth

9-17 The Lord told Paul in a vision at night, 'Don't be afraid: speak up, and don't be silent, because I am with you, and no one will attack you to do you harm – because I have many in this city who are my people.' He settled [there] for a year and six months, teaching God's word among them.

When Gallio was proconsul of Achaia, the Jews combined against Paul, and took him to court, saying, 'He incites people to worship God in a way that is contrary to our Law.' When Paul was about to open his mouth, Gallio said to the Jews, 'If it were some evil crime or villainy, then, [my] Jewish [friends], I should reasonably put up with your complaint. If, however, the argument is about a discourse, and vocabulary, and law that is all your own, then ***you*** [are the ones who] must see to it. I have no desire to sit in judgement on these matters.' And he threw them out of court. They all took Sosthenes, the head of the synagogue, and beat him up in front of the tribunal. None of this was of any concern to Gallio.

This Gallio was brother to Seneca, the Roman philosopher who was Nero's tutor; inevitably some later Christians dreamed up a correspondence between Paul and Seneca. An inscription at Delphi dates Gallio's time in Corinth to AD 51 or 52. When Gallio supposed Christianity to be just another Jewish sect, that would have been to their advantage, since Judaism, though considered rather odd because of insisting on only one God, had the status of a 'permitted religion', and was therefore exempt from taking part in imperial worship.

Do you think that Luke likes to show the Roman authorities as basically well disposed to Jesus and his followers?

Paul moves on; return to the Holy Land

18-22 Paul remained many more days; he said goodbye to the Christians and sailed off to Syria, with Priscilla and Aquila in tow, having cut his hair at Cenchreae (for he had a vow). They arrived at Ephesus, and he left them there; meanwhile he went into the synagogue and held discussions with the Jews. However, when they asked him to stay a bit longer, he did not give his consent, but bade them farewell and said, 'I shall come back to you, if God wills.' He set sail from Ephesus and reached Caesarea. He went up [to Jerusalem] and greeted the Church [there]; and then he went down to Antioch.

Why has Paul suddenly left Timothy and Silas, Priscilla and Aquila? The reader may notice the apostle's tendency to split with his fellow workers; he was not altogether an easy man. Cenchreae, where he shaved his head, was the eastern port of Corinth. We observe that at Ephesus Paul has continued his practice of going to the synagogue first.

Why does Paul never spend very long in places?

Back to Asia Minor

23 Having spent some time, he went to one place after another in the Galatian and Phrygian regions, and strengthened all the disciples.

This is another 'Lucan summary', getting Paul off stage, perhaps to prepare for Apollos's visit to Corinth, the background to the controversy that emerges in Paul's first letter to the Corinthians.

Apollos in Corinth

18[24]–19[1a] A Jew by the name of Apollos, of Alexandrian origin, an educated man, arrived at Ephesus; he was very good on the scriptures. He had been taught the Way of the Lord, and was brimming with enthusiasm; he was speaking and teaching all about Jesus, [quite] accurately – but he only knew about the baptism of John. Apollos began to express himself freely in the synagogue. Priscilla and Aquila heard him; they got hold of him and explained the Way more accurately to him. Because he wanted to cross over to Achaia, the Christians wrote a letter, encouraging the disciples to welcome him. He arrived, and by [God's] grace helped the faithful greatly. For he vigorously refuted the Jews in public, showing through the scriptures that Jesus was the Messiah.

Now while Apollos was in Corinth, Paul went through the inland parts, and came to Ephesus.

Apollos is in Ephesus while Paul is in the Holy Land and Paul comes to Ephesus while Apollos is in Corinth; 1 Corinthians tells us about the divisions based on their two factions in Corinth. Was Ephesus too small for the two of them? Luke gently but firmly points out that Apollos's background and teaching may have been a bit deficient – only John's baptism, and perhaps not much on the Holy Spirit.

Later on in Corinth there was (at least) an Apollos-party and a Paul-party, with quite serious divisions between them. Are you encouraged or discouraged by the discovery that the early Church also had its divisions?

The coming of the Holy Spirit

1b-7 He found some disciples and said to them, 'Did you receive the Holy Spirit when you came to faith?' They said to him, 'We hadn't even heard if the Holy Spirit exists!' And he said, 'What were you baptised into?' They said, 'Into John's baptism.'

Paul said, 'John baptised [with] a baptism of repentance, telling the people to believe in the One coming after him – that is Jesus.'

When they heard this, they were baptised [in] the name of the Lord Jesus. When Paul laid his hands on them, the Holy Spirit came on them, they spoke in tongues, and they prophesied. The men were about twelve in number.

This is not the first time that Acts has spoken of the 'coming of the Holy Spirit', but other than at Pentecost, we have not really grasped what it was. At Pentecost it was tongues of fire, the sound of a mighty wind, and speaking in languages that everyone could understand. Clearly for the early Church the coming of the Holy Spirit was something tangible. Here it is represented as a matter of 'speaking in tongues' and 'prophesying', which may not take us much further. Evidently, though, it was something about which there could be no doubt and we need to bear this in mind as we continue our journey through this 'Gospel of the Holy Spirit'.

The coming of the Holy Spirit was obviously something that no one could doubt. What do you think it involved? Is it something that is still available today?

Paul's exploits in Ephesus

8-20 Going into the synagogue, he spoke freely for three months, holding discussions, and trying to convince [them] about the kingdom of God. But as some people were obstinate, and disbelieved, and reviled the Way before the people, he withdrew from them, and took the disciples on their own, and held discussions with them every day in Tyrannus's lecture hall. This lasted for two years; the result was that all those who lived in Asia, both Jews and Greeks, heard the word of the Lord. Through Paul's agency, God worked miracles that were quite out of the ordinary. For example, the sick had facecloths or handkerchiefs that had touched him taken to them, and their diseases left them, and evil spirits departed.

Some of the wandering Jewish exorcists attempted to name the name of the Lord Jesus, saying, 'I adjure you, by Jesus whom Paul proclaims.' There were seven sons of Sceva, a Jewish Archpriest, who were doing this. The evil spirit answered and said to them, 'Jesus I recognise and Paul I know – but who are you people?' And the man in whom the evil spirit was, leapt on them, and overmastered them all, so that they fled, naked and wounded, from that house. All the Jews and Gentiles who lived in Ephesus came to know of this; awe fell on all of them, and the event magnified the name of the Lord Jesus. Many of those who had come to faith came, acknowledging and declaring their acts. Several of those who had practised magic brought their scrolls, and burnt them before everybody; and they added up the price of them – it came to more than fifty thousand silver pieces! So by the Lord's might the word increased and grew.

This adroit combination of 'Lucan summary' and the story of the sons of Sceva creates an impressive atmosphere, of the gospel effortlessly overcoming every possible obstacle and reaching out to all humanity ('all those who lived in Asia . . . all the Jews and Gentiles who lived in Ephesus'). The facecloths and handkerchiefs that had touched Paul remind us of the effects of Peter's shadow (5:15). Notice, once again, the emphasis on the 'name of the Lord Jesus'. Notice, too, how 'Lord' has become a divine title for Jesus: contrast Luke 1:46, where it clearly referred to God. Now it is apparently 'God or Jesus' or 'God in Jesus'. Paul is still, we observe, going to the Jews first.

Is it important that, once again, Paul is victorious over magic?

Towards Jerusalem and Rome

21, 22 When these things were fulfilled, Paul resolved to pass through Macedonia and Achaia, and so journey to Jerusalem. He said, 'After I have been there, it is necessary for me to see Rome as well.' He sent two of his assistants, Timothy and Erastus, to Macedonia; meanwhile Paul himself stayed on for a time in Asia.

Is Paul splitting up yet again with his apostolic assistants? Luke does not say so, but we cannot help asking. Once again we notice the theme of travelling, and the fact that the gospel never stops anywhere, but presses on to Jerusalem and to Rome, where Acts will end, having arrived, presumably, at 'the end of the earth'.

Trouble averted in Ephesus

23-41 At about that time there was a fairly considerable disturbance with regard to the Way. For someone called Demetrius, a silversmith, who made silver shrines of Artemis, and provided the craftsmen with a good deal of business, called them all together, along with others who worked in related trades, and said, 'Men, you know that our livelihood depends on this trade. You [can] see and hear that this fellow Paul has been misleading vast numbers of people with his arguments, not just here, but almost everywhere in Asia. He says that [statues] made by human hands aren't gods! The risk is that not only will our profession come into disrepute, but also the temple of the great goddess Artemis will be reckoned as nothing, and it will be stripped of its majesty, which Asia, and [indeed] the whole world, worships.'

They heard him, and were filled with anger, and shouted out, 'Great is Artemis of the Ephesians'; and the city was filled with confusion. Unanimously, they rushed to the theatre, and dragged off the Macedonians Gaius and Aristarchus, Paul's travelling companions. Paul wanted to go into the crowd, but the disciples wouldn't allow him. Some of the Asiarchs, who were friendly towards him, sent to him and begged him not to venture into the theatre. People were shouting different things, for the assembly was in uproar, and most people had no idea why they had come together. Some of the crowd gave instruction to Alexander, as the Jews pushed him to the front. Alexander gave a signal that he wanted to make [his] defence to the people. When they realised that he was Jewish, a single slogan arose from the whole lot of them; for about two hours, they shouted, 'Great is Artemis of the Ephesians.'

The Secretary quietened the crowd and said, 'Ephesians, is there anyone who does not know that the city of Ephesus is the guardian of the Temple of the Great Artemis and of the image that fell from heaven? Since this is undeniable, you must show restraint, and do nothing reckless. For you brought these men, who are neither temple-robbers nor blasphemers of our God. So if Demetrius and his fellow professionals have a case against someone, the courts are in session, and there are proconsuls – let them accuse each other. If, however, there is anything further you wish to know, it will be settled at the statutory assembly. In fact we run the risk of being charged with sedition for [what has gone on] today, since there is no charge to which we shall be able to respond regarding this commotion. And having said these things, he dismissed the assembly.

Why has Luke given a relatively large section to this account of civil disorder at Ephesus? Perhaps to indicate to 'Theophilus', the archetypal Roman reader, that the disturbances that surrounded this new 'Way' are not just inner-Jewish problems; they also have implications for pagan religion. Demetrius's claim that Paul preaches against idols 'almost everywhere in Asia' suggests that the apostle was quite impartial about whom he annoyed: Jews with his claims about Jesus as Messiah, and pagans with his strict monotheism. And we have already heard Paul arguing this case in Athens. We also notice, not for the first time, that Luke presents Roman officials as inclined to protect Christians. At the same time, however, Luke wants to make it clear that the troubles are not the Christians' fault. It serves to stand as an example for many such problems that must have occurred in cities throughout the Mediterranean as Christianity made its way westwards.

Is Christianity still offensive to all sides?

Paul's travel plans changed by attempted murder

20 1-6 After the trouble had died down, Paul sent for the disciples and comforted them. [Then] he took leave of them and left to travel to Macedonia. As he went through those parts, he comforted them with much talking, and reached Greece, where he spent three months. As he was about to sail to Syria, there was a plot against him on the part of the Jews, and he decided to go back through Macedonia. He was accompanied by Sopater, son of Pyrrhus, a Beroean; of the Thessalonians there were Aristarchus and Secundus, Gaius from Derbe, and Timothy; the Asians were Tychicus and Trophimus. These people went ahead of us and waited for us at Troas. We left by boat from Philippi after the days of Unleavened Bread, and reached them at Troas within five days. We spent a week there.

This is the beginning of the second 'we' passage. The reader notices that, once again, the context is that of travel, including a sea voyage, and that there is the flurry of names (not all of them known to us) that we have come to expect in Acts. The Church of Acts is catholic in that it signals a broad mixture of cultures within its ample bosom.

Why does Luke so frequently emphasise that Paul and the early Christians observed the Jewish festivals?

Eutychus and the dangers of long sermons. Farewell to the elders of Ephesus

7-38 On the first day of the week, when we had gathered to break bread, Paul gave them an address, since he was due to leave the next day; and he prolonged his discourse till midnight; there were many lamps in the upper room where we had gathered. A young man called Eutychus was sitting at the window, and sank into a deep sleep as Paul talked longer and longer. Finally overcome by his somnolence, he fell down from the third storey, and was taken up dead. Paul went down and threw himself upon him. He embraced him and said, 'Don't be distressed – there is life in him.' He went up and broke bread and ate, having chatted for a long time, until daylight. They took the boy alive, and were comforted in no small measure.

Meanwhile we went on ahead to the boat and sailed to Assos. The plan was that we should take him on board there. For he had arranged it so – he was going to travel on foot. When he met us at Assos we took him on board and came to Mitylene. From there we sailed the next day and reached [a spot] off Chios. The following day we approached Samos, and the day after we came to Miletus. Paul had decided to sail past Ephesus, so as not to waste time in Asia. For he was hurrying to be in Jerusalem for the day of Pentecost, if possible.

From Miletus he sent to Ephesus and summoned the elders of the Church. When they arrived, he said to them, 'You know how from the first day that I came to Asia, I spent the whole time with you, serving the Lord with all humility and tears, and the trials that happened to me with the Jews' plots. You know how I did not keep silent about anything that is profitable, and proclaimed to you and taught you both in public and at home, testifying to Jews as well as Greeks [about] turning to God in repentance, and [about] faith in our Lord Jesus. Now look – I am bound in the Spirit to travel to Jerusalem, not knowing what will happen to me there, except that in each city the Holy Spirit testifies to me, telling me that imprisonment and anguish lie in wait for me. As for myself, I regard my life as in no sense precious to me, so long as I can complete the race, and the ministry that I have received from the Lord Jesus, to spread the witness of the gospel of God's grace. Now look – I know that none of you, among whom I have gone about proclaiming the kingdom, will ever see my face again. So I call you to witness, this very day, that I am innocent of the blood of all. For I never held back from announcing God's entire plan to you. Look after yourselves; look after the whole flock in which the Holy Spirit made you overseers to shepherd God's Church, which he got through the blood of his own [Son]. I know that after my departure ruthless wolves will come in to you. They will not spare the flock; and men will arise from among you who will utter travesties [of the truth], so as to draw away the disciples after them. So, stay awake. Remember that for three years, day and night, I never stopped admonishing each one with tears. Now I am offering you to God, and to the message of God's grace. God is able to build up, and to give the inheritance to all who have been sanctified. I never desired anyone's silver, or gold, or clothing. You [of all people] know that it was my own hands that took care of my needs, and of my companions. In every way I have shown you that [you] must strive to help the weak, and remember the words of the Lord Jesus. He himself said, "Happiness consists in giving rather than receiving." '

Saying this, he fell to his knees, and prayed with all of them. There was much weeping on the part of all, and they fell on Paul's neck and embraced him. They were especially saddened by his remark that they were destined to see his face no more. And they escorted him to the boat.

There is much in this episode that is characteristic of Paul: talking freely about himself as an example; his insistence on the centrality of the gospel ministry; his obsession with Jesus; his intense conviction about what is right. At the same time there is much that Luke regards as typical of the work of the Holy Spirit in general. Like Peter (9:36-41) and Jesus (Luke 7:11-17; 8:40-56), Paul brings someone back to life, for example. And there is the role of the Holy Spirit in appointing 'overseers' or 'bishops' to the Churches. There is the expectation that disciples will be persecuted and seduced from the faith. There is also the sadness that comes with the realisation that Paul is making his final farewell. He is on his way to Jerusalem, where there is likely to be trouble; although, as we know, Jerusalem is not his final destination. He is quite right, however, in saying that he will not see the elders of Ephesus again.

Do you get the feeling that the story is now rushing to its end?

From Miletus to the Holy Land

21 1-14 When we set sail and drew away from them, we steered a straight course to Cos, and the next day to Rhodes, and from there to Patara. [There] we found a boat that was crossing over to Phoenicia; we went aboard and sailed away. We sighted Cyprus, and leaving it to port, we sailed for Syria, and came down to Tyre, since that was where the vessel was unloading its freight.

We searched for the disciples and stayed here a week. They told Paul through the Spirit not to embark for Jerusalem; but when our time was up, we left on our journey. All of them, including the women and children, escorted us out of the city; and we fell on our knees at the shore, and prayed and parted from them; then we went on board the boat, while they returned home.

Meanwhile we continued our voyage from Tyre, and reached Ptolemais. [There] we greeted the brethren, and spent a day with them. The next day we departed and came to Caesarea. We entered the house of the Gospeller Philip. He was one of the 'Seven', and we stayed with him. He had four virgin daughters who spoke the word of God. We remained for [a few] more days; [then] someone came down from Judaea, a prophet called Agabus. He came to us, took Paul's girdle, bound his own hands and feet, and said, 'Thus says the Holy Spirit: "The man whose girdle this is, the Jews shall bind after this fashion in Jerusalem, and they shall give him over into the hands of Gentiles." '

When we heard this, both we and the locals begged him not to go up to Jerusalem. Then Paul responded, 'What are you doing, weeping and breaking my heart? For I am prepared not just to be arrested, but even to die on behalf of the Lord Jesus.' Since he could not be persuaded, we all held our peace and said, 'The Lord's will be done.'

This important passage combines two Lucan themes. First, there is the familiar travel story (it is the third 'we' passage), with plenty of place names, and an itinerary that we can check against the map. Second, however, and this is a part of the 'Gospel of the Holy Spirit', there is a note of impending doom. At Tyre Paul is warned (and should he have obeyed the Holy Spirit?) not to go up to Jerusalem; then there is another tearful farewell. Then at Caesarea there is yet another prophetic warning, and Paul's companions endeavour to dissuade him. But, like Jesus in Luke's Gospel, he has to go on with the journey, at all costs (see Luke 9:31, 51; 13:31-33), and no tears will dissuade him. His final remark sounds like Paul's authentic voice (see, for example Philippians 1:21-26; 3:7-11). Agabus we have already met, making another correct prediction at 11:28.

Why does Paul insist on continuing his journey, do you think?

Arrival in Jerusalem: a tense encounter with James

15-26 After this, we made our preparations and were on our way up to Jerusalem. Some of the disciples from Caesarea came with us. They brought one Mnason, a

Cypriot, a disciple of long standing, with whom we had been lodging. When we reached Jerusalem, the brethren welcomed us gladly.

On the following day, Paul went in with us to James; and all the elders were there. He greeted them, and explained in detail everything that God had done among the Gentiles through his ministry. When they heard [it], they glorified God, and said to Paul, 'Do you see, brother, how very many there are who have come to faith among the Jews? And they are all ardent observers of the Torah. They have been given information about you, that you were teaching rebellion against Moses, telling all the Jews in the Diaspora not to circumcise their children, and not to follow our way of life. So what about it? They will certainly hear that you have arrived. Therefore do what we tell you. We have four men who have taken a vow. Take them along with you; get yourself purified, and pay for them to have their heads shaved. Then they'll all know that there is nothing in the stories they've heard about you, and that in fact you are still keeping the Torah. With regard to the Gentiles who have come to faith, we have written, giving our verdict that they should avoid meat sacrificed to idols, and [meat that still has the] blood, and [meat that was] strangled, and sexual misbehaviour.'

Then Paul took the men, on the very next day; he had himself purified with them, and he went into the Temple, giving notice that the days of purification were completed, until the sacrifice had been offered by each one of them.

We might have been expecting fireworks at this meeting; it was clearly a tense and formal affair. Not only is Paul encountering James the brother of the Lord, but it is the 'liberal' Gentile mission meeting the 'conservative' Jewish Christian tradition. In addition, both sides have their supporters present at the meeting; and we already know how prickly Paul can be. The threatened explosion does not materialise, however, and Paul acquiesces like a lamb to their demands. He is made aware that his own supporters are outnumbered; he will in any event have known how tense things were in Jerusalem at festival-time – and this was just such an issue as to light the fuse. We have already seen how aware he is of the delicacy of the issues involved, as when he circumcised Timothy (16:3), the vow he took at Cenchreae (18:18), and his insistence, already mentioned, on keeping the Jewish feasts (20:6, 16; 27:9). At the same time, we must remember that Paul's insistence on the mission to the Gentiles, and on tempering for them the Law's demands, did create enormous tensions among those first Christians, especially, it seems, in Jerusalem. On his side, of course, Paul will be glad to have known that they implicitly acquit him of the charge of 'preaching rebellion against Moses'. He never did that – see Romans 9-11, for example.

Can we learn from this meeting how to deal with fellow-Christians who disagree with us on important issues?

Trouble in the Temple

27-30 When the seven days were almost up, the Jews from Asia spotted him in the Temple, and stirred up the crowd; and they laid hands on him and said, 'Help!

Israelites! This is the fellow who's teaching everyone everywhere against Israel and the Torah and this Temple. And now he's brought Gentiles into the shrine and has defiled this holy place!' The reason was that they had already seen Trophimus from Ephesus in the city with him; and they thought that Paul had brought him to the Holy Place. The whole city was aroused; the people rushed together, and they got hold of Paul and dragged him out of the Temple. And immediately the gates were closed.

> *This is an important moment. The reader knows that the troublemakers had misread the situation, or exploited it for their own purposes. Paul was not such a fool as to have defiled the Temple – nor would he have thought of doing so. Now, for the last time, Luke leaves the Temple where he had set the opening and closing scenes of his Gospel (and many scenes in between), and the opening scene (and many subsequent scenes) of Acts. This is the end; the gospel, however, continues its charted course 'to the end of the earth'.*
>
> *Was it really true that Paul was teaching 'against Israel and the Law and the Temple'?*

Paul rescued by Roman soldiers

31-36 As they attempted to kill him, a report went up to the tribune of the cohort that the whole of Jerusalem was in an uproar. He immediately took some soldiers and centurions, and came down on them at the double. They saw the tribune and the soldiers, and stopped raining blows on Paul. Then the tribune approached, arrested him, and gave orders that he was to be bound in double chains. He asked who he was and what he had done. Different [people] in the crowd said different things; and because of the noise, he couldn't get at the facts. So he had him brought to the barracks. But when Paul got to the steps, the soldiers, because of the force of the crowd, were actually carrying him. For the mob was behind him, shouting, 'Away with him!'

> *For Luke, violence and unjustifiable arrest is to be expected for those who preach the gospel of the Spirit. He may also have been glad to point out to his Roman readers that it was imperial troops who had saved Paul from being lynched.*

Second account of Paul's conversion; the help of a friendly tribune

21 37–22 29 As they were just about to enter the barracks, Paul said to the tribune 'Is it permissible to say something to you?' He said, 'Do you know Greek? Aren't you the Egyptian who started a rebellion some time ago, and led the four thousand assassins out into the desert?' Paul said, 'I am a Jew; but I'm also an inhabitant of Tarsus in Cilicia – citizen of a city of some significance. I ask you, let me speak to the people.' He let him, and Paul stood on the steps, and

motioned with his hand to the people. A great silence descended, and he spoke to them in the Aramaic language: 'Brethren and fathers, listen now to my defence before you.' When they realised that he was talking to them in Aramaic, their silence became more intense. He said, 'I am a Jewish man, born in Tarsus in Cilicia, but brought up here in Jerusalem, educated at the feet of Gamaliel, in accordance with the strictness of the Torah of our forefathers. I was just as fanatical for God as you people are today. I persecuted this "Way" to death; I arrested and handed over both men and women, as the High Priest and the entire Presbyterium can bear me witness. I had letters from them, and travelled to our brethren in Damascus, so as to bring the people who were there also in chains to be punished. However, as I was travelling, and getting near to Damascus, round about noon, suddenly a great blaze of light shone round me, and I fell to the ground, and heard a voice saying to me, "Saoul, Saoul, why are you persecuting me?" I answered, "Who are you, Lord?" He said to me, "I am Jesus the Nazarene, whom ***you*** are persecuting." Those who were with me saw the light; but they did not hear the voice of the one who was speaking to me. I said, "What shall I do, Lord?" The Lord said to me, "Arise, go to Damascus, and there you will be told about all the things that you have been ordered to do." Since I could not see, because of the radiance of that blaze of light, those who were with me led me by the hand into Damascus. Ananias, a devout man, and an observer of the Torah, who is vouched for by all the Jews who live there, came to me, stood over me, and said, "Saoul, brother, receive your sight back." And at that moment my sight came back [and I saw] him. He said, "The God of our forefathers has predestined you to know his will, and to see the Just One, and to hear a voice from his mouth, that you are to be a witness, to all people, of the things that you have seen and heard. And now, why do you delay? Up – get yourself baptised, and wash away your sins, calling on his name."

'When I returned to Jerusalem and was praying in the Temple, I fell into a trance, and I saw him saying to me, "Hurry – leave Jerusalem quickly, because they will not listen to your testimony about me." And I said, "Lord, they know that in all the synagogues I was committing to prison and flogging those who believe you, and that when the blood of Stephen (your witness) was poured out I myself was at hand, and approving, and looking after the clothes of those who killed him." And he said to me, "Go – because I am sending you a long way, out to the Gentiles." '

As they yelled and cast their garments and threw dust in the air, the tribune ordered him to be taken into the barracks, telling [them] to examine him with whips, to find out on what grounds they were screaming out against him. However, as they stretched him out for the flogging, Paul said to the centurion who was standing there, 'Is it permissible for you to flog a Roman [citizen] who has not been condemned?' When the centurion got the message, he went up to the tribune and reported to him, 'What are you going to do? This man is a Roman [citizen].'

The tribune came to Paul and said, 'Tell me, are you a Roman [citizen]?'

He said, 'Yes.' The tribune replied, 'I acquired this citizenship for a considerable sum of money.' Paul said, 'I was born [a citizen].' So those who had been about to examine him stood back; and the tribune was alarmed that he had had him bound.

This is the second time that we have heard the story of Paul's encounter with Jesus. This time, however, it is given a highly dramatic setting. Paul is allowed to tell the story himself, as an angry crowd presses round him. The interaction is on two levels. At one level, he is speaking Aramaic to fellow-Jews and explaining why he has taken the road that he has followed. Like the Paul we know from his letters (see, for example, Philippians 3:4-6), he is not afraid to list his qualifications. We may notice that in this version he emphasises Ananias's orthodoxy rather more than the narrator had in Chapter 9, when the event was first reported, and that Paul is made to talk of returning to Jerusalem and praying in the Temple.

At another level, Paul's interaction is with the Roman authorities, with whom Luke's readers will have been more in sympathy than with what they would have regarded as a fanatical mob. So he talks Greek to the tribune, and makes the centurion jump with the revelation that he is a Roman citizen. Now begins the final thread in the narrative, the one that will lead him to Rome, the 'end of the earth'.

Why does Luke give this second account of Paul's meeting with Jesus?

Paul before the Sanhedrin

22[30]–23[5] The next day, wanting to get at the facts of the Jewish accusation against him, he released [Paul], and ordered the high priests and the entire Sanhedrin into his presence. He brought Paul down and stood him [before] them.

Paul looked intently at the Sanhedrin and said, 'Brothers, I have conducted my life with a clear conscience before God, down to this very day.'

The High Priest Ananias ordered the bystanders to strike him on the mouth. Then Paul said to him, 'God is going to strike you, you whitened wall: do you sit in judgement in accordance with the Torah, and [then], contrary to the Torah, order me to be hit?' The bystanders said, 'Do you revile God's High Priest?' Paul said, 'Brothers, I had no idea that it was a High Priest. You see, it is written, "You shall not speak badly of a leader of your people."'

This is a very odd incident; Paul can hardly have been in ignorance of Ananias's identity. Perhaps the point is simply that high priests should not behave in that way; but the Exodus citation does not sit well with that interpretation. Perhaps Paul is the leader who is being 'spoken of badly'.

Is Luke here deliberately echoing the story of Jesus?

The Lord is in charge: to Rome!

6-11 Now Paul was aware that one part consisted of Sadducees, and the other part consisted of Pharisees, and so he cried out in the Sanhedrin, 'Brethren, I am a Pharisee and a son of Pharisees; and I am on trial about the hope for the resurrection of the dead.' When he said this, there arose a difference of opinion between the Pharisees and the Sadducees, and the meeting was divided. For Sadducees say that there is no resurrection, no angels, and no spirits, while Pharisees acknowledge the whole lot. There was a great clamour, and some of the scribes who were on the Pharisee side rose up and argued, 'We find no evil in this man; perhaps a spirit or an angel has spoken to him?' As the temperature of the discussion increased, the tribune was fearful that Paul might be torn in pieces by them, and ordered the troops to go down and seize him, and carry him out of their midst and into the barracks. The next night, the Lord stood over him and said, 'Have courage; as you bore witness to me in Jerusalem, so you must also do in Rome.'

> *Whatever happens, God is in charge, and the 'end of the earth' comes nearer, even though at present the witnessing is only in Jerusalem.*
>
> *What Paul says of himself in this speech is not unlike his boast in Philippians 3:5, 'a Hebrew of Hebrew stock, a Pharisee as far as the Torah is concerned'.*

The plot against Paul

12-35 When day came, the Jews called together a secret meeting. They bound themselves under a curse, that they would fast from food and drink until they had killed Paul. More than forty of them had entered into this conspiracy. They went to the High Priest and the elders and said, 'We have put ourselves under an oath to taste nothing until we have killed Paul. So now you people, along with the Sanhedrin, [must] make it clear to the tribune that he is to bring Paul down to you, because you are going to decide his case more precisely. Before he gets anywhere near, we'll be ready to do away with him.'

The son of Paul's sister heard about the ambush, and came and got into the barracks and reported to Paul. Paul summoned one of the centurions and said, 'Take this young man to the tribune, for he has something to report to him.' So he took him, and led him to the tribune and says, 'The prisoner Paul summoned me, and asked me to bring this young man to you, because he has something to say to you.' The tribune took him by the hand, and going aside with him in private, asked, 'What is it that you have to report to me?' He told him, 'The Jews have agreed to ask you to take Paul down to the Sanhedrin tomorrow, because it is going to decide his case more precisely. But don't do what they say – more than forty of them are going to ambush him. They have bound themselves by an oath not to eat or drink until they have done away with him – and now they're waiting for a promise from you.'

So the tribune let the young man go, and said, 'Don't tell anyone that you've revealed this to me.' He summoned two of the centurions and said, 'Prepare two hundred soldiers, to travel to Caesarea, and seventy cavalry and two hundred lightly armed troops, any time after the third watch of the night.' [He told them] to produce animals to give Paul a mount and bring him safely to Felix the procurator. He wrote a letter, and this was its content:

> Claudius Lysias to the Most Excellent Procurator Felix, Greetings.
>
> I came upon this man when the Jews had arrested him, and he was on the point of being killed by them. I rescued him when I discovered that

> he was a Roman citizen. I wanted to know what they were accusing him of, and so I took him down to their sanhedrin. I discovered that he was indicted on some questions of their Torah; but there was no charge [against him] that deserved death or imprisonment. Then I got information that there was going to be a plot against him, and I immediately sent him to you. And I have also ordered his accusers to put their case against him in your presence.

So the soldiers took Paul, in accordance with their orders, and brought him by night to Antipatris. The next day they let the cavalry go on with him, while they returned to barracks. The cavalry entered Caesarea, gave the letter to the procurator, and handed over Paul as well. He read the letter, and asked what province he was from. When he discovered that Paul was from Cilicia, he said, 'I shall give you a hearing when your accusers arrive.' He ordered him to be kept in Herod's praetorium.

There is a touch of James Bond about the story now, narrow escapes, and the battlelines clearly drawn: Paul's (mortal) enemies are his Jewish opponents, and it is Romans, aided by informers from his kinsfolk, who come to his rescue, in, it must be said, absurdly large quantities. The escort provided would look extravagant if they were protecting the Emperor! We notice (not for the first time) that Paul is very much in charge, giving orders to a passing centurion about what do to with his nephew. It is, no doubt, a tribute to Roman military discipline that these orders are faithfully carried out.

The story of the projected 'ambush' is told three times, like the stories of Paul's and Peter's conversions, so Luke obviously regards it as being of some importance.

Interestingly, the tribune's letter to Felix has the right 'feel' about it; and if it was not the actual letter, it was certainly the kind of thing that such an officer might have written to his political boss.

There is an echo here of Luke's version of Jesus' passion when the procurator finds out what province of the empire Paul comes from, and in consequence decides to postpone his hearing; Pilate did something of the same at Luke 23:6-12.

What accounts for the violence of the opposition to Paul?

The case against Paul – who is stuck in prison for two years!

24 [1-27] Five days later, the High Priest Ananias came down with some elders, and a barrister [called] Tertullus. They informed the procurator of [the charges] against Paul. Paul was summoned, and Tertullus began the speech for the prosecution: 'Most Excellent Felix, thanks to you we have experienced great peace; many improvements have come about for this nation, thanks to your foresight, as everywhere in every way we acknowledge with great gratitude. However, not to delay you any further, I beg you to listen briefly to us, with your [customary] graciousness. The fact is, we find this man to be a pest; he causes dissension among all the Jews

throughout the world, and is a ringleader of the sect of the Nazarenes. He tried to desecrate the Temple, and we arrested him. You can interrogate him yourself about all these things and ascertain the grounds of our accusations.'

The Jews also joined in the accusation, and alleged that it was so.

When the procurator gave him the nod to speak, Paul responded, 'I know that for many years you have been judge for this nation; and so I cheerfully make my defence. You can ascertain that it is no more than twelve days since I came up to Jerusalem, with the intention of worshipping [there]. And they did not find me in the Temple disputing with anyone, or collecting a crowd; nor [was there anything of that sort] in the synagogues or anywhere in the city. And they cannot prove any of the accusations that they now level against me. However, I [will] admit this [much] to you: it is in accordance with this Way, which they call a "sect", that I worship our ancestral God. I believe everything that is written according to the Torah and in the prophets. My hope is in God, and these people themselves entertain the same hope, that there will be a resurrection of the just and the unjust alike. Therefore I do my best to have a clear conscience towards God and towards human beings in every respect. After several years I arrived, to provide alms and offerings to my nation. In the middle of this they found me in the Temple, after I had been purified. There was no crowd, and no uproar; but there were some Jews from Asia, and [it is they] who should appear before you and make accusations, if they had anything against me. Or let these people themselves say what crime they discovered when I was up before the Sanhedrin. Or was it this single expression that I uttered when I stood among them, that "I am on trial before you today on the issue of the resurrection of the dead"?'

Felix adjourned them, being well informed on the subject of the Way. He said, 'When Tribune Lysias comes down, I shall decide your case.' He instructed the centurion that [Paul] was to be kept in custody, and that he was to have some freedom; the centurion was not to prevent his own people from looking after him.

Some days later, Felix arrived with his wife Drusilla, who was Jewish. Felix sent for Paul, and listened to him on the subject of faith in Messiah Jesus. As he talked about righteousness and self-control and the judgement to come, Felix became alarmed, and responded, 'For the time being, go. If I get a chance, I shall send for you.' At the same time he hoped that Paul would give him money. For that reason he sent for him quite frequently, and chatted with him. When two years were up, Felix got Porcius Festus as his successor; and wanting to do the Jews a favour, Felix left Paul in custody.

We are perhaps to make a contrast here, between the odious (and entirely probable) sycophancy of the barrister Tertullus, and Paul's honesty and integrity. Once again, Luke puts the blame on Paul's Jewish opponents, though Felix ('a mere freedman', they might have muttered, dismissively, since Felix was a former slave, who had been set free by the Emperor Claudius) does not escape unscathed; he wants money, and for political reasons is happy to leave Paul in prison for two years, though he knows that he does not deserve it.

The appearance before Porcius Festus, and before Herod Agrippa and Bernice

25 1-27 Three days after Festus had taken up his governorship, he went up to Jerusalem from Caesarea, and the high priests and leading Jews brought up the case against Paul, and begged him, asking for a favour (against Paul), to send for him to Jerusalem. They were going to set an ambush and kill him on the way. So Festus replied that Paul was in custody in Caesarea, while he himself was on the point of departing shortly. He said, 'So the influential people among you should come down with [me]; and if there is anything wrong about the fellow, let them accuse him.'

He spent no more than eight or ten days among them, and went back to Caesarea. The next day he was in session at the tribunal, and ordered Paul to be brought. When he arrived, the Jews who had come down from Jerusalem stood around him. They brought several serious charges [against him], which they were unable to substantiate, while Paul in his own defence said, 'I have not sinned against the Law of the Jews, nor against the Temple, nor against Caesar, in any respect.'

However, Festus, wishing to curry favour with the Jews, replied to Paul, 'Do you want to go up to Jerusalem, to be judged in my court on these matters?' Paul said, 'I am standing at Caesar's tribunal, and that is where I must be tried. I have done no wrong to the Jews, as you yourself know perfectly well. So if I am in the wrong, and have done something worthy of capital punishment, I am not trying to talk my way out of a death sentence. If, however, there is nothing in what they accuse me of, no one can throw me to them as a gift. I appeal to Caesar.'

Then Festus, having talked with his Council, replied, 'You have appealed to Caesar; to Caesar you shall go.'

Some days went by, and King Agrippa and Bernice arrived in Caesarea. When they had spent a number of days there, Festus brought up Paul's case. He said, 'There is a man who was left behind as a prisoner by Felix. When I arrived in Jerusalem, the high priests and the elders of the Jews told me about him, asking for a verdict against him. I told them that it is not [the] Roman custom to give a man over, with no questions asked, until the accused has been faced with his accusers and has had an opportunity for a defence against the indictment. So they came here; I made no delay, but immediately went into session, and had the man brought. They stood round him, but brought no charge of the crimes that I had been imagining, just certain questions about their own religion, and about one Jesus, a dead man, whom Paul alleged was alive. I was at a loss over the investigation of these things, and said [that] if he wanted he was to go to Jerusalem and there be tried on these matters. But when Paul appealed to be kept in custody, for Augustus's decision, I ordered him to be imprisoned until I should send him to Caesar.'

Agrippa said to Festus, 'I should like to hear the fellow.' 'Tomorrow,' he said, 'you shall hear him.'

So the next day, Agrippa and Bernice came in full state, and entered the auditorium, along with tribunes and with the most prominent men of the city. At Festus's command, Paul was brought [in]. Festus said, 'King Agrippa, and all you men who are here with us, you see this man. The whole crowd of the Jews appealed to me, both in Jerusalem and here, shouting that he ought not to live any longer. I realised that he had done nothing that was worthy of death; but when he appealed to Augustus, I decided to send him. I have nothing definite to write to the sovereign about him, so I produce him before you all, and especially you, King Agrippa, so that after a hearing, I may have something to put on paper. For it seems absurd to me to send a prisoner and not communicate the charges against him.'

The reader notices the similarities with Luke's account of Jesus' passion: a baying crowd of Jewish leaders is looking to kill someone who does not deserve it, and we have a weak and self-serving Roman official (we already know that Festus's speech to Agrippa is self-exculpating mendacity). And all the time, as throughout this book, the Holy Spirit is at work. Rome is now the destination (so there can be no question of a return to Jerusalem), the 'end of the earth' foreshadowed in the very first chapter of the work. It is no accident, therefore, that when Festus says, 'to Caesar you shall go', he uses Luke's favourite 'journeying' word.

This Agrippa is Herod Agrippa II, son of the one whom we earlier heard about, when he died in that unfortunate way (12:20-23), and therefore great-grandson of Herod the Great.

Why do you think Luke spends so much time on this story?

Paul's defence before Herod Agrippa: third account of his meeting with Jesus

26 1-32 Agrippa said to Paul, 'You have permission to speak about yourself.' Then Paul stretched out his hand and made his defence.

'With regard to all the matters of which I am accused by the Jews, King Agrippa, I think myself lucky that I am going to make my defence before you today, especially since you are an expert in all the customs and issues among Jews. So I implore you to listen patiently.

'All the Jews know [about] my way of life that I have followed since my youth, from the very beginning, amongst my people and in Jerusalem; for they know me from time past from the beginning, if they are willing to give evidence; because I lived according to the strictest school of our religion, as a Pharisee. And now I stand trial on the hope of the promise that came to our ancestors from God, the hope which our twelve tribes hope to attain to, as they persevere in their worship day and night: this is the hope for which I am accused, Your Majesty. Why do you people regard it as incredible that God raises the dead?

'Now I myself thought it incumbent on me to do lots of things in opposition to the name of Jesus the Nazarene. That is what I did in Jerusalem; and I locked many of the saints in prison; I had authority from the high priests – and I cast my vote against them when they were killed. In all the synagogues I punished them frequently – I tried to force them to speak against God; my fury knew no bounds, and I persecuted them even in cities outside this land [of Israel].

'In the middle of all this, I was journeying to Damascus, with authority and full power from the high priests. And about noon, Your Majesty, I saw a light from heaven shining, round me and those who journeyed with me, brighter than the sun. All of us fell to the ground, and I heard a voice speaking to me in Aramaic: "Saoul, Saoul, why are you persecuting me? It is hard for you to kick against the goad." I said, "Who are you, Lord?" And the Lord said, "I am Jesus, whom you are persecuting. Now – up you get, and stand on your feet. This is why I have appeared to you, to appoint you a servant and witness of what you have seen, and how I shall appear to you. I have rescued you from the people of Israel, and from the Gentiles, to whom I send you to open their eyes, to turn them from darkness to light, and from the power of Satan to God, so that they may receive forgiveness of sins, and a place among those who are made holy by faith in me."

'This being the case, King Agrippa, I did not disobey this heavenly vision, but, first to those in Damascus, then in Jerusalem, and the whole region of Judaea I preached that they should repent and turn to God, by doing deeds appropriate for repentance. Because of this, some Jews arrested me in the temple and tried to murder me. So I have had help from God, down to the present day, and stand giving witness to small and great; I say nothing other than what the prophets and Moses said was destined to happen, that the Messiah was liable to suffer, that as the first to rise from the dead he would proclaim light, both to Israel and to the Gentiles.'

When he had made this speech for the defence, Festus said in a loud voice, 'You're mad, Paul: [too] much education is turning you to madness.' Paul said, 'I'm not mad, Most Excellent Festus; no – I am uttering words of sober truth. The king, before whom I speak fearlessly, knows about these things – for I cannot persuade myself that any of this has escaped his attention. For this was not done in a corner. King Agrippa, do you believe the prophets? I know that you do.' Agrippa said to Paul, 'Soon you [will] persuade me to become a Christian!' Paul said, 'Would to God that sooner or later, not only you, but also all those who hear me today will become as I am, apart from these chains.'

The king arose, as did the procurator and Bernice, and all those who sat with them. As they withdrew, they started speaking to each other, saying, 'This man is doing nothing that deserves death or imprisonment.' Agrippa said to Festus, 'This fellow could have been freed if he had not appealed to Caesar.'

This is a highly dramatic, and quite personal, confrontation. It contains the third account of Paul's encounter with Jesus. It also establishes for the reader Paul's complete innocence of the charges, while at the same time setting him irrevocably on the final journey to Rome. There is a personal 'electricity' between Paul and King Agrippa, which takes us rather by surprise, both at the beginning, where he refers to Agrippa's knowledge of Judaism, and at the end, where Agrippa does not join in Festus's abuse of Paul, but seems almost on the verge of succumbing to his eloquence. There is a real passion in Paul's final remarks, which sounds very much like the Paul whom we know from his letters.

Are we now meant to feel a bit sorry that Paul is having to go to Rome?

The excitements of the journey to Rome; landfall at Malta

27 1-44 When it was decided that we should sail to Italy, they handed over Paul and some other prisoners to a centurion called Julius, of the Augustan cohort. We boarded a boat that belonged to Adramyttium, whose sailing-plan included various places down the coast of Asia, and set off. Aristarchus was with us, a Macedonian from Thessalonica. The next day we called at Sidon. Julius dealt kindly with Paul, and allowed him to go to his friends and get some attention from them. From there we put out to sea and sailed under the lee of Cyprus because the winds were contrary; we sailed across the open sea along Cilicia and Pamphylia, and came down to Myra in Lycia. There the centurion found an Alexandrian vessel that was sailing to Italy, and he put us on board. For some days we sailed slowly, and barely made it to Cnidos. Since the wind was against us, we sailed under the lee of Crete, off Salmone. We barely coasted past it, and came to a place called 'Lovely Harbours'; the city of Lasaea was nearby.

A considerable time had elapsed, and sailing was already dangerous, because the Day of Atonement had come and gone. Paul therefore gave them some advice: 'Men – I see that the journey is going to involve damage, and much loss, not just of the cargo and the vessel, but also of our own lives.' The centurion, however, followed the advice of the steersman and the captain, rather than what Paul said. Since the harbour was not suitable for wintering in, the majority decided to sail from there, to see if they could get to Phoenix for the winter. Phoenix is a harbour in Crete that faces the south-west and north-west winds.

When a moderate south wind began to blow, they thought they had secured their objective. So they sailed along closer to Crete. Quite soon, though, the hurricane called Euraquilo tore down on Crete. It seized the boat, which could not sail into the teeth of the gale; so we gave in, and were carried before it. We ran under the lee of an island called C[l]auda, and were only just able to get the ship's dinghy under control. They used cables and undergirded the ship. Now they were afraid of running aground on the Syrtis, so they lowered the floating anchor, and simply drifted. The next day, because we were being violently battered by storms, they jettisoned [the cargo]. The day after that, they threw the tackle overboard with their own hands. For several more days we saw neither sun nor stars, and a violent storm raged. From now on, all hope of being rescued was gradually abandoned. No one was eating very much at the time, and Paul stood up among them and said, 'You should have followed my advice not to sail from Crete, and spared [yourselves] this damage and loss. Now I recommend you to keep up your courage. For none of your lives will be lost; all you will lose is the boat. This very night, you see, a messenger of the God to whom I belong, the God I worship, stood by me. The messenger said, "Do not be afraid, Paul. It is ***inevitable*** that you will stand before Caesar; and behold! God has granted you as a gift [the lives of] all those who are sailing with you."

'So be of good spirits, men. For I trust God: it will be just as it was uttered to me. We shall certainly run aground on some small island.'

When the fourteenth night arrived, and we were still drifting around in the Adriatic, about the middle of the night, the sailors suspected that land was close by. They took soundings, and found twenty fathoms; after they had sailed a short distance further they took soundings again, and found fifteen fathoms. Fearful that we would run aground on some rocky areas, they let down four anchors from the stern, and prayed for daybreak to come. Then the sailors tried to escape from the boat; they let the ship's dinghy down into the sea, pretending that they were going to lay out anchors from the prow. So Paul told the centurion and the soldiers, 'If these people don't stay on board, you can't be saved.' So the soldiers cut the dinghy's ropes, and let it drift away.

Until just before daybreak, Paul kept encouraging all of them to take food, saying, 'Today is the fourteenth day that you have been waiting, and still you are hungry and taking nothing. So I am encouraging you to take food. This is required for your preservation – for none of you will lose a hair of your heads.'

Saying this, he took bread and gave thanks to God before all of them, broke it, and began to eat. They all cheered up, and took some food. (In all we were 276 souls on the boat.) When they had eaten their fill, they lightened the ship by throwing the wheat-grain into the sea.

When day broke, they did not recognise the land, but they noticed a bay with a good beach, and they planned to run the vessel on to [this] beach, if they could. They slipped the anchors all round, and let them fall into the sea. At the same time they loosened the couplings that held the rudders, hoisted the foresail to the wind, and steered for the beach. They struck a reef, and ran the ship aground. The prow was stuck fast and remained immovable, while the force of the waves was breaking up the stern.

The soldiers decided to kill the prisoners; otherwise someone might swim off and escape. However, the centurion wanted to save Paul, and stopped them from doing what they intended. He ordered those who could swim to lead the way and jump overboard, then get to land; the rest were to go, some on planks, and some on bits and pieces of wreckage from the ship. So it was that everyone got safely to land.

This part of the fourth 'we' passage is a breathless adventure story. For Luke's purposes, three themes come usefully together here: there is the excitement, which he maintains with considerable skill, the first person narrative giving us the feeling that we are actually there. Second, there is the character of Paul. Notice his steadfast courage, and his certainty about what is going to happen ('the journey is going to involve damage . . . You should have followed my advice . . . If [the sailors] don't stay on board, you can't be saved'). Like Jesus, in Luke 5:1-11, Paul's supernatural knowledge defeats the expertise of professionals. He is only a prisoner; but it is he who is giving the orders round here (and it sounds, we note, just like the Paul whom we know from his letters!). Third, as the boat drifts helplessly in this Mediterranean storm, the reader, while wondering how they are going to get out of it, is nevertheless confident that they will do so. The reason is that again and again we have been told that Paul will get to Rome, the 'end of the earth'. Notice

*Paul's divinely inspired confidence that it is '**inevitable**' that he will stand before Caesar. For Luke, the Holy Spirit is in charge, and the Spirit cannot be thwarted by anything, whether accident or human malice. It is a bit like the storms in Homer: we always know that Odysseus will get home to Ithaca.*

Acts is supposed to be the 'Gospel of the Holy Spirit'; could you see the Spirit at work in the preceding section?

Excitement in Malta: Paul and a snake

28 1-10 When we had got safely through, we found out that the island was called Malta. The natives (they were not Greek-speakers) showed unusual kindness. They lit a fire, and welcomed all of us, because of the rain that had come on, and because of the cold.

As Paul was gathering a heap of brushwood and putting it on the fire, a viper, driven out by the heat, came out and fastened on his hand. When the natives saw the snake hanging from his hand, they said to each other, 'This man is definitely a murderer; he was rescued from the sea, but justice has not permitted him to survive.' Paul shook the snake off into the fire, and suffered no harm. They waited for him to swell up, or suddenly fall down dead; but they looked and waited for a long time, and nothing untoward happened, so they changed their minds and said he was a god.

In the neighbourhood of that place, there was a property belonging to the chief official of the island, a man named Publius. He welcomed us, and for three days entertained us very kindly as his guests. Now Publius's father was sick, suffering from fever and dysentery. Paul went to him, prayed, and laid his hands on him and healed him. When this happened, everyone else on the island who had diseases approached [him] and were cured. They showed us great honour, and when we were going away they gave us all that we needed.

As the story moves to its end, the adventures are still not over. We see Paul through the eyes of the Maltese, first as a murderer, then as a god; and we know that neither is the case. Luke allows a touch of comedy here, perhaps even a patrician sneer, to enter into his portrayal of them. As always, it is the figure of Paul that catches the eye. Vipers have no terror for him; the sick are cured, just as effortlessly as Jesus used to cure them (see Luke 4:38, 39 for a parallel to Publius's father). And there is absolutely no sign at all that he is a prisoner.

Finally the story reaches Rome

11-14 After three months, we set sail in a boat that had wintered on the island. It was Alexandrian, and had Castor and Pollux as its figurehead. We put in at Syracuse, and stayed [there] for three days. We cast off from there and reached Rhegium. A day later, the south wind came up, and on the second day we came to Puteoli. There we found some fellow-Christians; they begged us to stay for a week. And so we came to Rome.

So the journey is over; but for Luke the journey is never over, because the Holy Spirit is running it. The narrative has still a way to go; but at least the seasickness and the attendant storms are behind us, and we are among Christians for the first time since Paul left James's house, back in Chapter 21.

Paul's discussions with the Jewish community in Rome

15-28 The brethren from Rome had heard all about us, and they came out to meet us, as far as Forum Appii and Tres Tabernae. Paul saw them, and gave thanks to God, and took courage.

When we entered Rome, Paul was permitted to live on his own, with the soldier who was guarding him.

After three days, he called together the most prominent among the Jewish community. When they gathered, he said to them, 'Brethren, although I for my part have done nothing against the people [of Israel], or against our ancestral customs, I was handed over [by those in Jerusalem] as a prisoner, and put in the hands of the Romans. They examined me, and wanted to set me free, because there was no capital offence in me. But because the Jews opposed this, I was compelled to appeal to Caesar, not that I had any accusation to make against my nation. For this reason, I requested you to [come and] see me and talk to me, because it is for the sake of the hope of Israel that I am wearing this chain.' They said to him, 'We have not received any letters about you from Judaea; nor has any of the brethren come and reported or spoken anything evil about you. We desire to hear from you what you think. For what we know about this sect [of yours] is that it is contradicted everywhere.' They agreed a date with him, and came to him in his lodgings, in large numbers. He expounded to them and bore witness to the kingdom of God. He tried to persuade them about Jesus from the Torah of Moses, and from the prophets. Some believed his words; but others refused to trust him. They were at variance with each other, and they broke up. Paul uttered a single remark: 'The Holy Spirit spoke accurately to ***your*** ancestors, saying:

"Go to this people and say:
Hearing you will hear and not understand.
Seeing you will see, and not look.
For the heart of this people has grown gross.
With their ears they hear with difficulty,
and they have shut their eyes,
lest they should see with their eyes
and understand with their hearts,
and turn back and I should heal them."

'So let it be known to you that it is to the ***Gentiles*** that this saving power of God has been sent. ***They*** will listen.'

This is an important moment. The reader has completed the journey to the 'end of the earth', and Paul follows the familiar pattern, of speaking first to his fellow-Jews. In this case they do not precisely reject the message, but are divided about it, and are given the quotation from Isaiah 6: 9, 10 to meditate upon, which Matthew has already used in his Gospel (Matthew 13:14) in a similar way. In this setting it seems a bit harsh, but from Luke's point of view the gospel has now arrived at its destiny, and that means, as Paul indicates in his final flourish, that it, the 'saving power', demands to be heard instantly. It is worth pointing out that the word that I have translated as 'saving power' appears elsewhere in the whole of Luke-Acts only at Luke 2:30 (where Simeon uses it in reference to Jesus) and 3:6 (where Isaiah is quoted, to explain the significance of John the Baptist). It is this opening of the 'saving power' to the wider world that engages Luke's attention, not the rejection of Judaism.

The point for Luke is, as always, nothing else than the work of the Holy Spirit. That is why the Isaiah quotation is referred specifically to the Spirit; that is why Paul needs the courage that he gains from the brethren who came out from Rome to meet him. The Spirit is free, and, although we hear of a soldier guarding him, so is Paul; he is free, for example, to summon the Jewish leaders, and address them with authority. We notice, too, how Paul has grown in independence and fearlessness in the course of the narrative. That is what the Holy Spirit does for a disciple.

How is the Holy Spirit at work here?

Journey's end

30, 31 He remained for two whole years at his own expense, and received all those who journeyed to him. He proclaimed the kingdom of God to them, and taught everything about the Lord Jesus Christ, in all freedom, and without hindrance.

This is a remarkable ending to the two-volume work. It ends, at 'the end of the earth', and an apostle (not one of the original Twelve) is witnessing to Jesus; Luke's final two phrases insist that nothing is preventing – nothing can prevent – the preaching. There is not a hint here of Paul's eventual martyrdom, which Christian tradition remembers, and of which presumably Luke's readers were well aware. The gospel's journey has ended, and instead, would-be disciples now journey to Paul. Luke does not encourage us to contemplate the fact, but Paul has at this stage been a prisoner for something over four years. Nevertheless, he has 'made it'.

The gospel's journey, one of 'fire and mighty wind', never ends. The Western world is for the moment apparently indifferent to the promptings of the Spirit, but there are many places in the world where the wind and fire receive an enthusiastic welcome.

Are you open to the Spirit's invitation?

Map

Palestine of the New Testament
Herod's Fortress
Caesarea Philippi (Paneas)
Tyre
SYRO-PHOENICIA
Trachonitis
Lake Huleh
Cadas
Gaulanitis
Batanea
GALILEE
Gischala
Ptolemais (Akko)
Chorazin
Bethsaida-Julias
Capernaum
Gennesaret
Dion
Magdala
Sea of Galilee
Gergesa
Mt Carmel
Tiberias
Abila
Asochis
Cana
Sepphoris
Nazareth
R. Yarmuk
Mt Tabor
Dora
Plain of Esdraelon
Nain
Crocodilon
THE GREAT SEA
Caesarea Maritima
DECAPOLIS
Pella
SAMARIA
Aenon
R. Jordan
Plain of Sharon
Sebaste (Samaria)
Gerasa
Mt Ebal
Sychar
R. Jabbok
Mt Gerizim
PERAEA
Antipatris
Jaffa
Gadara
Arimathaea
Philadelphia
Lydda
Ephraim
Jamnia
Jericho
Betharamphtha
Emmaus
Jerusalem
Ein-Kerem
Bethpage
Azotus
Bethany
Qumran
JUDAEA
Bethlehem
Ashkelon
Marisa
Bethsura
Gaza
Hebron
Dead Sea
NABATAEAN KINGDOM
En-gedi
R. Arnon
IDUMAEA
Masada